DATE DUE

Insanity as

Redemption in

Contemporary

American Fiction

Insanity as Redemption in Contemporary American Fiction

INMATES RUNNING THE

University Press of Florida

Gainesville
Tallahassee
Tampa
Boca Raton
Pensacola
Orlando
Miami
Jacksonville

ASYLUM

Barbara Tepa Lupack

Copyright 1995 by the Board of Regents
of the State of Florida
Printed in the United States of America
on acid-free paper
All rights reserved
99 98 97 96 95 94 6 5 4 3 2 1
Library of Congress Cataloging-in-
Publication Data
Lupack, Barbara Tepa, 1951–
Insanity as redemption in contemporary
American fiction: inmates running the
asylum / Barbara Tepa Lupack.
p.   cm.
Includes bibliographical references
(p.   ) and index.
ISBN 0-8130-1331-3
1. American fiction—20th century—
History and criticism.   2. Literature and
mental illness—United States—
History—20th century.   3. Psychiatric
hospital patients in literature.
4. Mentally ill in literature.
5. Redemption in literature.   I. Title.
PS374.M46L86   1995
813'.5409353—dc20   94-29265
The University Press of Florida is the
scholarly publishing agency for the State
University System of Florida, comprised
of Florida A & M University, Florida
Atlantic University, Florida
International University, Florida State
University, University of Central
Florida, University of Florida,
University of North Florida, University
of South Florida, and University of
West Florida.
University Press of Florida
15 Northwest 15th Street
Gainesville, FL 32611

To my mother, Jane H. Tepa,

and in memory of my father, George W. Tepa,

for sharing with me their sense of humor,

their love of knowledge, and their experience of life

And to my husband, Al,

for that, and for everything else

[The asylum was] not so much an
effort to free the insane from the
horrors of rat-infested cells as a
drive to bring madness under the
rigid and unbending control of
reason. . . . Through the asylum the
society would conquer madness by
undermining it into conformity.

Michel Foucault,

Madness and Civilization

Much Madness is divinest Sense—
To a discerning Eye—
Much Sense—the starkest Madness—
'Tis the Majority
In this, as All prevail—
Assent—and you are sane—
Demur—you're straightway dangerous—
And handled with a Chain—

Emily Dickinson

CONTENTS

Acknowledgments xi

Introduction 1

Chapter 1. Inmates Running the Asylum:
The Individual Versus the Institution   **7**

Chapter 2. Seeking a Sane Asylum: *Catch-22*   **19**

Chapter 3. Hail to the Chief:
One Flew Over the Cuckoo's Nest   **63**

Chapter 4. Pilgrim's Regress:
Slaughterhouse-Five   **99**

Chapter 5. Happening by Chance:
Being There   **135**

Chapter 6. When Dark Gods Prey:
Sophie's Choice   **155**

Notes 203
Selected Bibliography 227
Index 237

ACKNOWLEDGMENTS

I gratefully acknowledge the assistance of the National Endowment for the Humanities, for a grant which allowed me research opportunities I might not otherwise have enjoyed; the Fulbright Program, for allowing me to teach and to conduct research for this and an earlier manuscript abroad; and the State University of New York (ESC) Foundation, for a professional reassignment which gave me time to begin the writing. The Rush Rhees Library of the University of Rochester provided me with valuable services and materials.

I extend my thanks to the editors of the journals *The Polish Review*, *The New Orleans Review*, *The Connecticut Review*, and *Anglica Wratislaviensia*, and an anthology of essays, *Dionysus in Literature* (Popular Press), for publishing early versions of portions of *Insanity as Redemption in Contemporary American Fiction*.

For their encouragement and assistance, I would also like to thank Walda Metcalf, Deidre Bryan, and Heather Blasdell of the University Press of Florida.

INTRODUCTION

"O! matter and

impertinency mix'd;

Reason in madness."

King Lear

Madness has been a familiar motif in literature for centuries, from the myths and legends underlying the works of Homer, the Bible, and ancient Greek tragedy to the novels and poems of the present day. As Marilyn Yalom writes, "The greatest of writers—Aeschylus, Sophocles, Shakespeare, Dostoevsky, Nietzsche, Kafka—and their somewhat less celebrated brothers—E. T. A. Hoffmann, Gérard de Nerval, Rimbaud, Trakl, Lautréamont, Artaud, Salinger, Roethke— have explored that underworld where unconscious processes run amuck and created characters who often express profound human truths that lie beyond the threshold of reason."[1]

The contemporary American novelist, however, uses the familiar motif of madness in an unfamiliar way: not just to convey the result of an unnerving, disquieting, even infuriating reality, but also to comment on its hypocrisies. Symbolizing modern man's alienation from the goals of a mechanized society which deemphasizes human- istic—and humane—values, madness seems, especially in fiction, to be an effective method of challenging the social order. Out of step with the absurd world around them, "mad" protagonists typically withdraw from society as they struggle to internalize issues of family, culture, and history and ultimately return (though some- what circuitously) to effect some kind of social amelioration,[2] a process that is a variation of the monomythic pattern of departure- initiation-return described by Joseph Campbell.

Yet the withdrawal is not always voluntary: for presuming to challenge the Establishment, the protagonist is frequently relegated to the asylum or to some similar rehabilitative agency (for example, to the educational network of WESCAC in John Barth's *Giles Goat-Boy;* the prison ward of Walker Percy's *Lancelot;* or the military hospital of William Wharton's *Birdy,* Joseph Heller's *Catch-22,* and Kurt Vonnegut's *Slaughterhouse-Five*). Those agencies are themselves a kind of Catch-22, for instead of rehabilitating the hero, they further strip him or her of all identity and individuality, ironically at one time the very measures of sanity and health. But the contemporary protagonist often learns to turn the asylum, or its counterpart, into a kind of "temple of consciousness"[3] and to make a rebellion against its unnatural and totalitarian order a metaphor for the larger rebellion against oppressive social institutions (for example, religion, government, big business, the military), the protagonist's original and ultimate adversaries.

The current study focuses on five significant, representative experimental novels—*Catch-22* (1961), *One Flew Over the Cuckoo's Nest* (1962), *Slaughterhouse-Five* (1969), *Being There* (1970), and *Sophie's Choice* (1979)—that explore precisely the illogic (and, at times, the outright insanity) of contemporary existence. Each portrays a protagonist who is mad or is considered by others to be mad—a protagonist who, however, possesses or reveals a special insight into the dangers of the institution's demand for social, political, and cultural conformity. That insight usually compels him or her to respond to the collective threat that the institution poses. Sometimes the protagonists are successful: Yossarian escapes Pianosa as he heads for Italy and, ultimately, an even more neutral zone; Bromden breaks out of the hospital and returns to the natural world; and Billy Pilgrim survives, even triumphs over, daily life by time-traveling to the better world of Tralfamadore. Sometimes the protagonists are less successful and pay for their resistance with their lives: Sophie and Nathan, unable to live with the truth, choose to die in a mutual suicide pact; McMurphy is lobotomized and then mercifully smothered (though not before he passes his strength on to the other men on the psychiatric hospital ward). And sometimes their success or failure is ironic and ambiguous: Chance, for instance, may escape the blur of celebrity to return to the tranquility of the garden, or he may stay caught in the social whorl he neither understands nor enjoys. (In either case, Chance's simplemindedness makes him blissfully unaware of how troubled his society must be if he can be perceived as its "only chance.") And, while Stingo loses Sophie, he achieves fame with his novel, which resurrects and redeems him as much as it does her.

Though each of the novels offers a somewhat different perspective on the plight of the individual against the forces of the organized institution that, as Raymond Olderman observes, "in the name of reason, patriotism, and righteousness has seized control over man's life"[4] and constitutes the one real haunting terror of modern life, the protagonists all share common bonds. As minorities themselves, they often represent those powerless to speak for themselves. Yossarian, for example, is set apart from his companions not only by his cultural differences as an Assyrian but also by his continuing resistance to Colonel Cathcart's demand for increased numbers of missions. Chief Bromden, a half-breed who suffers from the government's takeover of his tribal lands and the tyranny of his white mother (and later of Nurse Ratched, who assumes his mother's despotic role in the ward), stands for Native Americans as well as for all disenfranchised people. Unlike Chief, who withdraws into voluntary mutism before regaining his voice, Chance is truly mentally deficient and thus represents a very real minority and one radically different from the mainstream. Yet, ironically, he is seen as part of the majority—in fact, as the voice of the majority—and even as a member of the elite. Like Chance, Billy Pilgrim, with his prosperous medical practice, picture-book home, two children (a boy and a girl), and devoted wife, seems to live the great American success story. But disillusioned by the emptiness of his life, Billy takes it upon himself to spread the happy truth he learns from the Tralfamadorians. And Sophie, a Polish-Catholic concentration camp survivor, finds herself, like Stingo, the recently transplanted Southerner, virtually alone in Brooklyn's "Kingdom of the Jews"—though, as she eventually discovers, her Catholic Poland, Stingo's Protestant South, and Nathan's Jewish Brooklyn all harbor hidden shames and breed similar guilts.

In the face of the asylum, the narcissistic media, the big-business-fueled military machine, the Nazi bureaucracy, and the other institutions that prohibit reclamation of individual identity, the protagonists nevertheless seek confirmation of their authenticity. After the Air Force's Catch-22 prevents Yossarian from being grounded, he simply decides not to fly again. Refusing to be sacrificed for the capitalistic ventures and the self-aggrandizing schemes of his superiors, he alone opposes both the incomprehensible protocol of war and Milo's capitalism. (The entrepreneurial Milo believes that what is good for the Syndicate is good for the individual, rather than advocating the principle's reverse.) Billy and Chance are victims of the myth of the American dream; both glimpse its dark underside. Chance, sucked into the vacuum of celebrity, gains a new social

3

identity as Mr. Chauncey Gardiner. But the image of him that the media create only distances him from his real identity, as a simple gardener—an identity he tries to reclaim, especially at the end of the novel. Billy, similarly trapped by the erroneous impression others have of his success and by his explosively nuclear family, breaks free only by escaping to another dimension. And, as McMurphy and Bromden resist the matriarchal monopoly of Big Nurse's ward, Sophie battles more paternalistic evils, from gender stereotyping to Nazi brutality, to retain some sense of her self.

All of the protagonists dwell, moreover, in a wasteland of sorts: the sterile ward of *Cuckoo's Nest*, which prohibits laughter and encourages dull, monotonous routine; the corrupt base operation and the ravaged Eternal City in *Catch-22*; the bombed-out city of Dresden and the plastic suburban life in *Slaughterhouse-Five*; the business-driven, media-run government, which plays to audiences of hollow and hollow-headed men in *Being There*; and the Nazi death camps of *Sophie's Choice*, whose sickly, bald, emaciated inmates are caught in a living death. Against these blighted backdrops and landscapes of nightmare, the protagonists, all Adamic prototypes or new-age messiahs, offer some hope. McMurphy, the Grail Knight, restores manhood to the wastelanders of the ward and gives voice to the mute Chief even as he deprives Nurse Ratched, the agent of the Combine, of hers in the final pages of the novel. Billy, Tralfamadore's first man, creates a new Paradise with his Eve, Montana Wildhack. Yossarian too seeks a new life: sharing the chaplain's newfound secular faith in miracles, he sails away from war-torn Italy for the new Eden of Sweden. Sophie, who lives through hell in Auschwitz, finds "rebirth" and almost heavenly bliss at first with her "savior" and "deliverer," Nathan; after the lovers' death, Stingo awakens from a night of Poe-esque dreaming to the "bless[ed] resurrection" symbolized by "Morning: excellent and fair."[5] And even Chance urges a return to the garden. (Unlike his alter ego Chauncey Gardiner, who offers his admirers little more than a reflection of their own shallowness, Chance can restore the wasteland in the most literal of ways, by working the barren soil.)

And most of the protagonists have been touched by war, a symbol for the even larger, ongoing violence in the contemporary world as well as for the destructive technologies that seek to make humanity obsolescent. McMurphy and Bromden, like Billy Pilgrim and Yossarian, are war veterans (McMurphy of the Korean Conflict and the others of World War II); Sophie and Nathan are both victims of the Holocaust; and Chance—though not directly affected by wartime events—is a type of his creator, a displaced man (as Kosinski himself was displaced by the events of the early 1940s in his native Poland).

The five novels, interrelated in their themes and approaches, are by no means isolated in their criticism of the American Establishment; nor is their only value in the controversial or countercultural attitudes they seem to espouse. Each, in fact, is sophisticated and complex, with deep roots in American political reality and in contemporary American literary tradition (discussed more fully in chapter 1).

Underscoring the struggle of the individual against the repressive, impersonal, technological, dehumanizing forces of contemporary society, these novels suggest that insanity may be one of the few sane alternatives available in a mad world. The restoration of a real order in modern society, they imply, will occur not by blind obedience to totalitarian systems but as a result of challenges to the bureaucratic institution—in other words, by inmates running the asylum.

CHAPTER 1

Amid the seeming

confusion of our

mysterious world,

individuals are so nicely

adjusted to a system, and

systems to one another

and to a whole, that, by

stepping aside for a

moment, a man exposes

himself to a fearful risk

of losing his place

forever.

Nathaniel Hawthorne,

"Wakefield"

Inmates Running the Asylum:

I shudder when I consider

the possibility that

squads of young people

are struggling to fit in. . . .

Look at the craziness.

Look at the fear. See the

sickness. Into this you

want to fit?

Gwendolyn Brooks,

Commencement Address

Trinity College,

May, 1990

The Individual Versus the Institution

A L T H O U G H Americans had managed to stay largely uninvolved in World War I, which was fought many miles from their country's shores, the war's end brought them an affluence and an expanded sense of their own identities. World War II, however, neither allowed for such detachment nor afforded any similar compensation in its aftermath. The attack by the Japanese on Pearl Harbor in 1941 not only precipitated a sharp redirection of American national development but also implicated Americans in the mounting disorders of the modern world and forced them to enter the historical mainstream. The resulting "sense of engagement with a bloodied modern history, perplexing, terrifying, and apocalyptic," as Malcolm Bradbury termed it, marked the end of American innocence; and that sense of involvement with the often violent historical process became "part of the new spirit that emerged, over the years of war and uneasy peace, in American fiction."[1]

The atomic bomb that American forces exploded over Nagasaki and Hiroshima came to symbolize the gross and frightening discrepancy between human technical capacities and human wisdom,[2] a horrible gap as formidable as the totalitarian adversary the bomb was supposed to quell; and the bomb's fallout, both physical and spiritual, ushered in a nuclear age of fear, anxiety, and distrust. Elation about the Allied victory over Hitler and Hirohito was diminished by the grim awareness that this new technological evil, released from its Pandora's box, could never again be contained. The same science that had fostered the development of a host of medical and labor-saving breakthroughs had apparently shifted its collective focus from improving life to systematizing death, and contemporary man could not help but feel betrayed. Kurt Vonnegut spoke for his generation when he said at Bennington College in 1970 that "I thought scientists were going to find out exactly how everything worked, and then make it work better. I fully expected that by the time I was twenty-one, some scientist, maybe my brother [a physicist who worked for General Electric], would have taken a color photograph of God Almighty and sold it to *Popular Mechanics* magazine. Scientific truth was going to make us *so* happy and comfortable. What actually happened when I was twenty-one was that we dropped scientific truth on Hiroshima."[3] In the classic behaviorist tract *Walden Two* (1948), B. F. Skinner's character Frazier, founder and chief Behavioral Manager at Walden Two, agreed that postwar society was indeed a mess, typified by the fact that "millions of young people . . . were . . . choosing places in a social and economic structure in which they had no faith."[4]

The discovery of the concentration camps and the realization of the atrocities that had been committed there only added to a growing sense of disconnection. Beyond logic and imagination, the total dehumanization of individuals by the SS machine paralleled the inhumane technology that created the war and became itself a symbol of the plight of modern man overwhelmed by totalitarian forces. Not surprisingly, in fiction the Jew—a modern victim compelled by history into existential self-definition, a definition that was not solely religious, political, or ethnic—evolved into one of the types of the modern age. Leslie Fiedler called that type "the metropolitan at home, though expert in the indignities, rather than the amenities, of urban life."[5] Malcolm Bradbury added that the Jew was also "alienated, victimized, dislocated, materially satisfied but spiritually damaged, conformist yet anomic, rational but anarchic."[6] The Jewish writer, from Bellow and Roth to Heller and Kosinski, increasingly emerged as the appropriate spokesperson for articulating the disaffiliation and dislocation of personal identity caused by the system into which the Jew did not quite fit. (In an almost parallel development, the Black too soon became an image of the existential and displaced hero, the "dark other in American culture."[7] From Richard Wright to James Baldwin and beyond, Black fiction expressed the individual's need to withdraw from a history that silenced or made invisible those out of the mainstream, and that was beyond their capacity to master or control. Yet it simultaneously tempered that urge to withdraw with a desire to reattach to a society in which that misfit's role had value beyond mere victimization. Ralph Ellison's *Invisible Man* [1952] evoked the alienation not just of the Black when he asked, "Who knows but that, on the lower frequencies, I speak for you?"]8

Politically, the change from a hot war to a cold one further intensified paranoia and changed the American character. By the '50s, a new enemy, the Red Menace, seemed to be lurking everywhere, ready to subvert American culture, and threatening to eradicate democracy by turning America into one more satellite of its godless, totalitarian Soviet empire. With the Soviets' exploding of the A-bomb and the fall of mainland China, the threat became even more immediate. Enlisting the aid of big brothers like J. Edgar Hoover, the politically manipulative, agitative Senator Joseph Mc-Carthy determined to prove that the enemy was infiltrating our society; taking it upon himself (with a monomaniacal zeal that recalled Hitler's) to purge the nation of its growing cancer, Mc-Carthy succeeded in bullying his opponents and branding them as un-American, or, worse yet, as Communists.

Alan Trachtenberg writes that the cold war state of mind, complete with its McCarthy-inspired witch hunts and paranoid hysteria, settled so deeply into the intellectual life of the nation that "fundamental criticism of American society, especially from radical perspectives, virtually disappeared from public life in the 1950s, a time described by some critics as an 'age of conformity.' "[9] Socialism became associated with Soviet Russia and Stalin; national liberation movements were linked with internationalism communism and subversion; and domestic dissent from foreign policy and from the values of big business was deemed proof of disloyalty. Deviation from the national consensus, either in political views or personal styles, was considered by many an unpatriotic and thus near-criminal act, as demonstrated by the power-wielding and opinion-shaping House Un-American Activities Committee.

In the resulting homogenization of American culture and thought, which some social scientists referred to as a "massification" of lifestyles, the measure of normalcy became the white, middle-class, suburban society of more or less contented consumers who suffered, if at all, from the spiritual malaise of too much consumption.[10] Middle-class modernization was evident in the myriad of household appliances designed to make the American housewife's job easier, in the popular all-electric homes and suburban tracts like Levittown, and, of course, in the availability and accessibility of the new medium of television, which broadcast international events directly into American living rooms. John Updike described well the mood of the country in his short story, "When Everyone Was Pregnant":

"Guiltlessness. Our fat Fifties cars, how we loved them, revved them: no thought of pollution. Exhaust smoke, cigarette smoke, factory smoke, all romantic. Romance of consumption at its height. Shopping for baby food in the gaudy trash of supermarkets. Purchasing power: young, newly powerful, born to consume. To procreate greedily. A smug conviction that the world was doomed. Beyond the sparkling horizon, an absolute enemy. Above us, bombs whose flash would fill the scene like a cup to overflowing."[11] Concomitant with such growth in consumerism was the increase in and growth of the organization—industry and government, especially the military, whose expansion was encouraged by Krushchev's cold war assaults on the American Way.

The '60s, particularly the mid and late 60s, brought a dramatic reversal of the absolute conformity of the earlier decade. Questions arose about the social order, and the presumption of consensus and homogeneity was shattered. In fact, as Robert F. Kiernan observed, "The besieged-garrison mentality of the 1950s was supplanted by the prevailing sense that the enemies were within the gates—not because they had breached the walls, but because they were born citizens."[12] John F. Kennedy won the 1960 presidential election on his promise for change and on his vision of a "New Frontier" in American life grounded in historical purpose and cultural sympathy. Even after his reign over the American Camelot was abruptly terminated by his assassination, some of his vision of that new society (for example, the Voting Rights Act) came to fruition during his successor's term. Violence, however, remained a metaphor for the time, as demonstrated by the assassination not only of John in 1963 but also of Robert Kennedy in 1968, of Black leaders Malcolm X in 1965 and Martin Luther King Jr. in 1968—and by the subsequent assassinations of or assassination attempts on prominent figures, from John Lennon (1980) and Presidents Gerald Ford (1975) and Ronald Reagan (1981) to Pope John Paul II (1981).

Even more than the loss of John F. Kennedy, the Vietnam War—the first "living room war" regularly beamed into American households and the most unpopular war America had ever fought (as well as the only war it ever lost)—violated the national innocence and haunted the national conscience in a way that World War II ("the good war") and the Korean War of the early '50s did not. The media's careful scrutiny of government conduct and misconduct (a scrutiny noticeably absent at other times, as later, during the Reagan years) resulted in popular dissatisfaction with both the undeclared war and the powerful politician behind it, President Johnson, who subsequently declined to run in the 1968 election.

Protests became more frequent. Campus antiwar demonstrations constituted only one of the many countercultural movements, which also included the women's rights movement and the rising Black and other urban protests for social justice. The challenges to the power of the American Establishment paralleled the emergence of dissident voices in Eastern Europe after the death of Stalin (beginning with the violent demonstrations in East Germany, Poland, and especially Hungary in the 1950s and culminating in the "Prague Spring" in Czechoslovakia in 1968) and the radical youth movements in other parts of the world (particularly in Germany and France, which led to the momentous student protests in Paris, and in Turkey and Japan, where student movements contributed to the toppling of regimes).[13] Other significant historical events, such as the Watergate scandal which resulted in Richard Nixon's resignation from the presidency in 1974, contributed further to the undercurrent of doubt, instability, and anxiety, and to an erosion of national confidence. Institutions such as government, the military, educational administration, and even organized religion seemed to have grown too big, too impersonal, and too menacing. Rather than serving the purpose for which they were intended, many of those institutions had metamorphosed into collectives that ignored the individual interest and celebrated instead the somewhat amorphous, at times narrowly defined, "greater organizational good."

Feeling the encroachments of mass society and the fear of the bureaucracy and the resulting personal anonymity that big organizations create, many Americans ironically began to take refuge in pursuits that negated their individual identities as much as the institutions they feared. Jerzy Kosinski observed, for instance, that innumerable Americans, especially youngsters and senior citizens, sought out other "collectives" like television and rock music, in which the medium became the message. Supplanting more durable role models with movie stars and musical personalities from Sinatra and Elvis to the Beatles and beyond, they hoped to escape the real world with more pleasant fantasies.

As far back as 1950, in *The Lonely Crowd*, David Riesman (with Nathan Glazer and Reuel Denney) anticipated the phenomenon that Kosinski and others described. Riesman contended that, due to the changing American character, Americans found themselves in a newly paradoxical situation: as part of a crowd of isolated, disconnected persons. Though possibilities for autonomy were abundant, most people became anxious if uncertain conformists and looked to advertising, mass media, mass political parties, and so on to fill the vacuums in their lives.[14] In *White Collar* (1951), C. Wright Mills painted a similar picture. The new postwar social man, he wrote, was like a cheerful robot with "no firm roots, no sure loyalties to sustain his life and give it a center." Subsequently, with no set of beliefs as in the old days, Americans as individuals "do not know where to go. . . . They hesitate, confused and vacillating in their opinions, unfocused to discontinuous in their actions . . . . They are a chorus, too afraid to grumble, too hysterical in their applause." He called them "rearguarders."[15]

Noted British anti-Freudian psychoanalyst R. D. Laing offered an even more radical view of social repression and societal transformation, one that was especially appealing·to writers and social thinkers of the '60s and '70s. Influential in shaping the deep current of contemporary dissatisfaction with external authority, his works (*The Politics of Experience* [1967] and *The Divided Self* [1969]) proposed that the distinction between conformity and nonconformity, sanity and insanity, madness and insight, was not always very clear. Laing conceived of madness as a struggle for liberation from false attitudes and values, an encounter with primary feelings and impulses that constitutes a possibility for the emergence of the "true self" hidden from the false outer being, whose chief function is adjustment to the demands of society and the family (as its offshoot). "True sanity," he wrote in *The Politics of Experience*, "entails in one way or another the dissolution of . . . that false self completely adjusted to our alienated social reality."[16] Insanity, Laing concluded, might very well be a state of health in a mad world.

Laing's ideas found their parallel in many novels. Even the notion that society itself resembles a madhouse, as Trachtenberg observed, has had a durable career in modern fiction. J. D. Salinger's rebel-hero Holden Caulfield's quest in *The Catcher in the Rye* ended in an insane asylum and, as Raymond Olderman contended, "signaled the end of American quests for the pure Utopia."[17] Subsequent novels, particularly those of the '60s, began their protagonist's journey of discovery where Holden left off—sometimes right in the actual asylum (as in Günter Grass's *The Tin Drum*, which influenced many

American writers, or Walker Percy's *Lancelot*), or in some comparable collective (as in John Barth's *Giles Goat-Boy*). Joseph Heller's
Catch-22, for instance, depicted a system of organized and absolute
illogic which applied not only to World War II but to contemporary
America as well. Ken Kesey's *One Flew Over the Cuckoo's Nest*,
according to Malcolm Bradbury, "saw American power as authority
ruling and containing a madhouse,"[18] while in Kurt Vonnegut's
Slaughterhouse-Five the explosive truth of the Dresden firebombing
is uttered only in the veteran's hospital, where Billy is being treated
for his mental and physical illnesses. The brain-damaged Chance in
Being There, fearing institutionalization by the Old Man if he does
not behave properly, soon finds himself in a world much crazier than
any asylum. And, in *Sophie's Choice*, the precise, efficient technology of the SS belies perhaps the greatest organized insanity of the
twentieth century and finds its parallel in the schizophrenic Nathan
Landau's postwar brutalizing of Sophie. As many other writers did,
Heller, Kesey, Vonnegut, Kosinski, and Styron expressed their doubt
about finding reason or meaning in a rational historical process; in
fact, they made history a landscape of lunacy and pain, a mirror of
psychic inner disorder. The very images in their fiction were disquieting. Bradbury accurately characterized them as "images of pattern,
power, process, and system, of the struggle of animate against
inanimate, of diminished self against increased force."[19]

To convey fully this tension, an experimental fiction emerged in
the 1960s and 1970s, one that was fabular (to use Robert Scholes'
term) and fantastic, surreal and absurd. Self-reflexive, it evidenced a
fascination with the springs of creativity and narrative, with the
tactics of fantasy and grotesquerie, with the wicked delight of black
humor (which Bruce Jay Friedman, who popularized the term,
described as "one-foot in the asylum kind of fiction")[20]—all evidently shaped by the need to react artistically against the horror and
grossness of the real historical world.

The experimental novelists, after all, were challenged in their
fiction to reconcile the history of single individuals with the larger,
often opposing, processes of an increasingly impersonal and technological society. Unlike their predecessors who faced different social,
political, cultural, and aesthetic concerns, these experimental novelists frequently had to shape the shapeless, define the undefinable,
legitimize the bizarre, and clarify the paradoxical. As Philip Roth

noted in "Writing American Fiction" (1961), contemporary American writers had their "hands full in trying to understand, and then describe, and then make *credible*, much of the American reality. It stupefies, it sickens, it infuriates, and finally it is even a kind of embarrassment to one's own meager imagination. The actuality is continually outdoing our talents, and the culture tosses up figures almost daily that are the envy of any novelist."[21] He concurred with Friedman's observation that the line between fact and fiction and between fantasy and reality was not only fine but fading.

The heroes of the experimental novel of the '60s and '70s reflect the plight of the novelist as well as of the later postwar generation: materially content but spiritually bereft, alienated from self and society, overwhelmed by the forces of an Establishment in which they have little faith or hope, these protagonists are indeed captive to a system that seems less than sane. Correctly perceiving that all relations are power relations, they in effect lack any power to relate to others or to their environment.

Moreover, unlike the earlier modernist hero, who was shaped by the humanist ethos—political, anthropological, and psychoanalytic—described so well by Irving Howe in the title essay of *Literary Modernism* (1967), the heroes of the postwar experimental American novel are shaped by the concern with the functioning and behavior that spawned and accelerated the growth of ego psychology in the late '40s, '50s, and '60s, and is characteristic of an age of increasing scientific sophistication.[22] Though they search for meaning (Ihab Hassan calls it "adaptation," Marcus Klein "accommodation") which will change their condition, their sense of self is often shattered, their personalities fragmented, and "the stabilizing forces of memory and attachment displaced by a sense of personal crisis that may be distinct to a culture in which the consolidation of economic power and estrangement from political process throw the individual back upon himself." Unable to accommodate themselves either to their society or to their historical realities, they become further estranged and disconnected, even from themselves. (Styron's Sophie, for instance, on her last day in Höss's employ at Auschwitz, cries aloud, "*I don't know what I am!*") The resulting jigsaw puzzle of values, mores, and personality, notes Josephine Hendin, forces these protagonists to "take refuge from the whole picture in its parts," which they, like the schizophrenic wise men in R. D. Laing's psychology, may self-consciously be refusing to connect.[23] Donald Barthelme advised to "only trust the fragments," but the protagonists find it hard to trust at all.

The heroes of the novel of the '40s and '50s (for example, Styron's Cass Kinsolving, Bellow's Henderson, even Ellison's Invisible Man) journeyed symbolically inward and ultimately returned to face life with a new understanding of themselves and their society. The protagonists of the novel of the '60s and '70s find the withdrawal aspect of the journey easy: Yossarian runs away to Rome; Bromden falls into a silent, fog-filled world; Billy time-trips. But reintegration is far more difficult for them, especially as their alternative realities become more real than the sociohistorical ones. Their quest for self-awareness, unlike their predecessors', is not linear in progression. Rather it is circular, like Yossarian's bombing runs to targets that have no military or strategic value in *Catch-22*; and oftentimes it starts as escape or flight. Bromden, for example, trapped in the cuckoo's nest since the end of World War II, merely stands mutely and pushes his broom in small circles along the ward floor as "the fog" of the Combine envelops him. Chance, in *Being There*, begins his story in the Old Man's garden; in the final chapter, exactly seven days later, he finds himself in a garden again, this time in the home of his new host and benefactor. The location has changed, though only slightly, but Chance's comprehension of his situation has not. Sophie, in *Sophie's Choice*, escapes the horrors of wartime Poland only to relive many of the same atrocities at the hands of her lover in postwar Brooklyn. And Billy Pilgrim seems to repeat his tragic circumstances as he travels backward and forward in time.

These patterns of circularity and convolution rather than of more traditional clarity and moral growth are common to other contemporary novels as well. In Pynchon's *V.*, for instance, while even Stencil's dreams compose endless flights of V-forms, a priest descends into the sewers to preach to rats. In an atmosphere even more bestial and equally bereft of faith, the child narrator of Kosinski's *The Painted Bird* gains no moral perspective from his odyssey; instead, forsaking the spiritual consciousness he once possessed, he learns to master the evil practices of his environment. Throughout the war, he sought only a peaceful place to hide so that he could stop roaming; at the war's end, he despises the thought of rejoining his family. In fact, he prefers to keep roaming, especially at night, because "the war continued at night."[24] The new world of Barth's

The Sot-Weed Factor is merely an extension of the old world Eben hoped to leave behind. And the journey—a retreat from his mother's lunacy—that Ignatius J. Reilly takes in *A Confederacy of Dunces* propels him into the arms of the equally loony girlfriend he had earlier tried to avoid. He merely trades one brand of absurdity for another.

But even relationships involving sex or love, particularly marriages, devolve into contests of power that reinforce traditional social values and thus provide few helpful referents by which the protagonists can define their own identities. Sexual encounters in the fiction from the '40s into the '60s were often fraught with meaning and symbolism (usually Freudian), and even in such comic treatments as Malamud's *The Assistant* or *A New Life* they were handled with a reasonable amount of realism: Holden Caulfield is shocked and disillusioned to discover that the girl he had idolized is a tramp and that the teacher he admired is a homosexual; *Rabbit, Run*'s progressive Sister Mim, with her ideas about detachment and cool sex, anticipates the free love movement and sexual liberation of the later '60s; and Mailer's *The Deer Park* and *An American Dream* offer fairly realistic pictures of sexual schizophrenia. But with the movement away from conventional realism and toward absurdism in the '60s and '70s, even sexual relations become confusing and bizarre. The innocent Billy Bibbit's first sexual experience occurs in the Seclusion Room of his psychiatric hospital ward; his partner is Candy, a drunken whore McMurphy has smuggled in through the window to celebrate his victory over Nurse Ratched. Fellow inmate Sefert has an epileptic seizure during intercourse with Candy's friend, who proclaims the experience to be her greatest sex ever. EE in *Being There* has similar accolades for Chance after he tells her he likes to watch and she misinterprets his words to mean that he wants her to masturbate in his view. And Billy Pilgrim's best sex is literally out of this world—the ultimate hard-core and science fiction fantasy with porn star Montana Wildhack on Tralfamadore. Sophie's liberal sexuality, on the other hand, is an attempt "to beat back death,"[25] while Stingo's sex life with Leslie is almost entirely lingual: as she admits to Stingo, after therapy she can say "fuck" but she still can't engage in the act. (He in turn suffers a swollen tongue as a result of the abortive lovemaking.) And Yossarian, trying to fill the void in his army existence, falls immediately in love with every woman he encounters, from the maid in the lime green panties who cleans the officers' quarters to General Scheisskopf's wife.

It is easy to see how, in a world as devoid of meaning as the one that all of these fictional characters inhabit—a world modeled closely on the real modern world—madness is both a legitimate response and an effective challenge to the superficial sanity of the social order and the historical process. If, as Dr. Lester A. Gelb observes, there is no "psychopathology more serious than . . . [the contemporary social] epidemic of dehumanization . . . by racism, violence, and war,"[26] only the person out of step with society has an appropriate vantage point from which to view its failings; only the person who fails to obey the institutions that mandate certain behaviors can appreciate their rigidity and the consequences of nonconformity. And only those who are victims of the system can bring about real reforms in it. Only the inmates can run the asylum—and, as much of the best experimental fiction of recent years suggests, only the inmates should.

CHAPTER 2

"But, sir, it's the truth,
sir! I swear it's the
truth."
  "I don't see how that
matters one way or the
other," the officer
answered
nonchalantly . . . .
  It was almost no trick
at all, he saw, to turn
vice into virtue and
slander into truth,
impotence into
abstinence, arrogance
into humility, plunder
into philanthropy,
thieving into honor,
blasphemy into wisdom,
brutality into patriotism,
and sadism into justice.
Anybody could do it; it
required no brains at all.
It merely required no
character.
  Catch-22

Seeking a Sane Asylum: *Catch-22*

I N an interview with Ken Barnard, Joseph Heller said one has "to be nuts or have a potential for being nuts to become a pilot."[1] He certainly should know: in 1942, as a nineteen-year-old, Heller enlisted in the Army Air Corps, and, in 1944, upon the completion of his cadet training, was sent to Corsica, where he served as a wing bombardier and completed sixty combat missions before being honorably discharged.

He flew more than twenty missions before seeing a plane shot down and men forced to bail out. "Till then," he reflected, "it was a lark. Even when the missions were dangerous, I was too stupid to realize it. It was like a movie to me."[2] Then, on his thirty-seventh mission—his second to Avignon—he discovered how passionately he wanted to become an *ex*-flyer; during that flight, the copilot went "a little berserk" and grabbed the controls away from the pilot. Stuck in the nose of the aircraft, not knowing what had happened, Heller thought that the plane had lost a wing and was going to crash. He had just observed the plane ahead of his blow an engine and watched as it fell, with no parachutes coming out. "Then suddenly after we dropped our bombs," he said, "our plane started to go straight down and I was pinned to the top of the cabin. The co-pilot had thought we were climbing too steeply and would stall. He grabbed the controls to shove us back down. We went down and I thought I was dying. Then the plane straightened out and flew through flak and my earphones were pulled out. I didn't know my headset was out. You know, when you press the button to talk, you hear a click, but I pressed it and heard nothing, so I thought I was already dead. For a while the rest of the crew couldn't hear me, and when I did plug in I heard this guy—the co-pilot—hysterical on the intercom yelling, 'The bombardier doesn't answer. Help him! Help him! Go help the bombardier.' And I said, 'I'm the bombardier; I'm

OK,' and he said, 'Go help the gunner.' "[3] The gunner was shot through the leg.

This experience, which Heller says he "added to . . . [by having the gunner] shot in the middle,"[4] becomes the central event in *Catch-22* (1961), Heller's blockbuster first novel, published just a few months before Ken Kesey's *One Flew Over the Cuckoo's Nest*. In it, Heller exposes the abject madness of the military-economic complex,[5] a dehumanizing institution that negates individuality and celebrates instead the organized chaos of its own bureaucracy, and lampoons the culture that allows and even encourages the military-economic complex's growth. Heller also aims his satire at those traditions that produced the culture, at the other institutions (such as religion and education) that capitalize on them, and at the people who adjust to or thrive within the system[6] by sacrificing their own principles. Although initial reviews were mixed, *Catch-22* is now recognized as "a triumph . . . a classic of our era"; "an apocalyptic masterpiece"; and a work "so wildly original, brutally gruesome, vulgarly, bitterly, savagely funny . . . . It will not be forgotten by those who can take it."[7]

As Kesey (*One Flew Over the Cuckoo's Nest*), Vonnegut (*Slaughterhouse-Five*), Kosinski (*Being There*), and Styron (*Sophie's Choice*) did, Heller drew deeply on his personal experiences and used them as the basis for *Catch-22*, especially in his depiction of Yossarian, the protagonist who struggles with the regimented bureaucracy so hostile to his values. Not only did Heller serve in the Mediterranean during the later years of World War II; like Yossarian, he was part of a squadron that lost a plane over Ferrara and soon came to the "startling realization—*Good God! They're trying to kill me, too!*";[8] ate better than he had ever eaten before; borrowed automobiles from the motorpool to slip out drinking with his friends; and enjoyed, as frequently as possible, the varied pleasures that Rome had to offer. As an officer, Heller—like Yossarian—had access to a large, centrally located apartment in Rome which was staffed by maids and leased by the squadron for the men's recreation and entertainment. And, again like Yossarian, he was decorated for his wartime service.[9] Despite some differences in their reactions to and experiences in the military, it is clear that Heller, who characterized himself as "a terrible coward" and proclaimed that "I'm just like Yossarian," combined "much of [his] own views . . . and [his] own personality"[10] with his memories of combat in order to transform some of his World War II adventures into the fictionalized misadventures of the men on Pianosa.

Heller's distaste for and fear of flight became so intense following the Avignon mission that, once the war ended, he took a ship home and refused to fly for fifteen years afterward.[11] (It wasn't until he spent twenty-four hours on a train from Miami to New York that he changed his mind: "I decided I'd rather be dead."[12]) And it was sixteen years after the end of World War II that he finally completed and published *Catch-22*. Heller had begun working on it in 1953, the same year he gave up college teaching for a career in advertising in New York.[13] At the time, he already had a number of short stories in print, fiction that had appeared in *Story*, *Atlantic Monthly*, and *Esquire* between 1945 and 1948, while he was still an undergraduate at New York University. But those stories, in his judgment, were too imitative, especially of Hemingway (whose fiction, based on his boyhood and his war experiences, had brought him a similar early literary success), and he was anxious to undertake the great comic satire that had been gestating for so many years.

Working by day as an advertising executive in *McCall's* Promotions Department, Heller plotted and wrote *Catch-22* at night.[14] As his charts and graphs reveal, constructing the novel "almost meticulously, and with a meticulous concern to give the appearance of a formless novel,"[15] was not easy; he had, by his own estimate, between forty and sixty characters to track in intersecting scenarios almost too numerous to count. But the continuing struggles of the combat pilots not with their foreign enemies but with their own military bureaucracy provided fertile literary ground (so fertile, in fact, that he was able to tap it in other black-humorous ways: years later, Heller wrote the pilot for what eventually became the comedy series, *McHale's Navy*).[16]

With *Catch-22*, Heller was striving not so much to produce a war novel, ripe with realistic and naturalistic details; in fact, he regarded war fiction as an inherently limited form.[17] Rather, he tried to depict—and distort—the ridiculous systems of twisted thinking that any entrenched officialdom can hatch. (Ironically, it is only ensuing events which have transformed the symbolic novel he thought he was writing into a realistic novel.[18]) Saying repeatedly that the book's comic irreverence does not reflect his attitude toward the war ("For everybody after Pearl Harbor, it was a war we wanted to fight—a war we knew had to be won"),[19] Heller reserves his unqualified condemnation not for war itself but for the absurd and meaningless patterns of behavior that sprang from American military-economic involvement. He targets for special criticism the business-minded military bureaucrats. Jockeying for power while riding the backs of lower-ranking officers and enlisted men, they institutionalize their illogic by way of the mutable Catch-22 and allow it, "in the name of reason, patriotism, and rightness," to seize control of the men's lives. Like the other organized institutions of the sixties (particularly Kesey's Combine, Barth's WESCAC computer, Toole's dunce-filled Confederacy), the bureaucracy those aspiring colonels and generals serve in *Catch-22* has, according to Raymond Olderman, "usurped our right to face chaos and to discover our own order and our own humanity—for the institution has provided a surer death of the spirit in the guise of a rational order . . . [than the chaos that permeated the novel of the fifties and] always signified the breakdown of the human spirit in the face of an orderless world."[20]

Despite Heller's claim that it was "a peacetime book" not really about World War II,[21] his novel was almost immediately categorized as a war novel because of its subject matter. Though it is true that in *Catch-22*, as in much good war fiction, the protagonist goes to war, loses his innocence while trying to comprehend the madness of battle, discovers the violence and cruelty of death, and makes his separate peace,[22] Heller's novel, which ends in the desertion of the hero, is obviously not typical. Nor is the casting of every senior officer as a maniacal sadist or blundering oaf or of every character who shows any zeal for his responsibilities as a dupe; such casting debunks conventional and heroic notions of war, especially those fought for a just cause.[23] For these reasons, Nelson Algren, in an early review, found Heller's novel different from and clearly superior to more traditional World War II fiction. "*The Naked and the Dead* and *From Here to Eternity* are lost within it," he wrote; and to compare a work like *The Good Soldier Schweik* favorably with *Catch-22* "would be an injustice, because this novel is not merely the best American novel to come out of World War II; it is the best American novel that has come out of anywhere in years."[24]

Moreover, while virtually all of the episodes of *Catch-22* are set during wartime, the war itself plays a relatively small part. Technically, in fact, the novel is no more about war than *Animal Farm* is about agriculture.[25] Heller uses the war primarily as an objective correlative,[26] to provide the community against which Yossarian can operate. The military establishment becomes an entire society, neatly self-contained and absolute, with human vagaries eliminated and human impulses subordinated to a pattern of mechanical efficiency and profit, as well as a microcosm for the larger American society and a symbol for all other organizations.[27] The juxtapositions of the arrogance and illogic of military and civilian behavior further confirm the parallels between service life and daily life. Major Major's father, for example, "a long-limbed farmer, a God-fearing, freedom-loving, law-abiding rugged individualist who held that federal aid to anyone but farmers was creeping socialism," specialized in alfalfa, "and he made a good thing out of not growing any. . . . The more alfalfa he did not grow, the more money the government gave him, and he spent every penny he didn't earn on new land to increase the amount of alfalfa he did not produce" (85). He justified his questionable dealings by arguing that he was merely fulfilling divine will: God, he felt, gave farmers two strong hands "so that we could take as much as we could grab with both of them" (86). Such capitalistic enterprise is raised to new levels by the military officers, particularly Colonel Cathcart, who pursues his own greedy bent by relying on his colleague's advice: "Colonel Korn was the lawyer, and if Colonel Korn assured him that fraud, extortion, currency manipulation, embezzlement, income tax evasion and black-market speculations were legal, Colonel Cathcart was in no position to disagree with him" (216). And Colonel Cargill, "a self-made man who owed his lack of success to nobody," becomes General Peckem's troubleshooter by virtue of his achievements in civilian life. Before the war, he "was so awful a marketing executive that his services were much sought after by firms eager to establish losses for tax purposes" (28).

Also distancing *Catch-22* from the conventional war novel is its lack of any ideological debate about the conflict between Germany and the United States or about definitions of patriotism. Heller deliberately set *Catch-22* in the final months of the war, during which the action is winding down, the Allied Forces are in control, and Hitler is no longer a significant threat to Europe. The missions required of the flyers have no military or strategic importance except in the corollary battles for self-aggrandizement through promotion, money, and fame among the administrators, each of whom wants to come out of the war with a profit. Inversely, the danger to Yossarian from his own superiors intensifies as the war in Europe draws to a close. Yossarian, notes Heller, was able to say in the end of the book "that the war against Germany is just about over and the country's not in danger anymore, but he is. It's essentially a conflict between people—American officers and their own government. They are the antagonists of *Catch-22*—much more so than the Germans and Hitler, who are scarcely mentioned."[28] Indeed, realizes Yossarian, the enemy is "anybody who's going to get you killed, no matter *which* side he's on" (127).

Heller further distances the novel's events from World War II by making them "contemporaneous" with "the Korean War and the Cold War"[29] and with the civilian situation in the United States in the 1950s, the period in which he was writing, "when we did have such things as loyalty oaths to say when we were at war in Korea and MacArthur did seem to be wanting to provoke a war against China, when Dulles was taking us to the brink of war against Russia every other week and it seemed inevitable that we were going to plunge right into another major war." Heller was also surprised by the factionalism, the antagonism, the "moral enmity between groups" which, while so prevalent today, was to him a new phenomenon, especially for a nation supposedly in the process of healing itself. "I chose the war," he wrote, "as a setting because it seemed to me we were at war. . . . [The period of the mid to late fifties] was the start of the civil rights movement, for example. There were whites who wanted to kill every black . . . [and then] there was the same type of antagonism developing between Joseph McCarthy—and Nixon and his committee—and people who, well, it then was called the Communist conspiracy."[30] So Heller said he "deliberately seeded the book with anachronisms like loyalty oaths, helicopters, IBM machines and agricultural subsidies to create the feeling of American society from the McCarthy period on,"[31] since American society and the principles that govern it are ultimately as antagonistic to him and other modern men as the generals and colonels of Pianosa are to Yossarian.

The essence of the military's hypocrisy and bureaucratic illogic is contained in "Catch-22," the phrase for the pandemic paradox of evil[32] from which the novel takes its name. Catch-22 is the unwritten loophole in every written law,[33] the rider attached to every code of the rights of men that gives those in authority the power to revoke those rights at will. Because its ellipsism defeats perception and ultimately frustrates all sense by rendering absurd an otherwise coherent universe, Catch-22 defies solution and ends in paradox, like the question posed of Appleby, "How can he see he's got flies in his eyes if he's got flies in his eyes?" (47). (The same concept of paradox extends to the novel as a whole, since the very notion of a comic war novel is itself a paradox.)

In the book, Catch-22 has many clauses, the most memorable of which concerns Yossarian's tentmate, the dwarfish Orr, who has managed to crash his plane every time he flies a mission. Doc Daneeka, the squadron's medical officer, agrees with Yossarian that Orr is crazy and should be grounded. "All he had to do was ask," Daneeka explains:

> and as soon as he did, he would no longer be crazy and would have to fly more missions. Orr would be crazy to fly more missions and sane if he didn't, but if he was sane he had to fly them. If he flew them he was crazy and didn't have to; but if he didn't want to he was sane and had to. Yossarian was moved very deeply by the absolute simplicity of this clause of Catch-22 and let out a respectful whistle.
>
> "That's some catch, that Catch-22," he observed.
>
> "It's the best there is," Doc Daneeka agreed. (47)

Like Orr, Yossarian wants out; justifiably paranoid that people are trying to kill him, he is a bombardier who wants the bombing to stop, a flyer whose primary mission now is to avoid flying further missions. But Colonel Cathcart, whose courage in volunteering others for dangerous duty is boundless, keeps raising the number Yossarian must complete in order to be sent home. Twenty-seventh Air Force Headquarters requires only forty; yet Cathcart, who represents all corrupt, avaricious administrators, has declared his belief that his men are at least ten missions better than the average, and "any who did not share this confidence he had placed in them could get the hell out" (59). The only way they could get the hell out, though, was by flying the extra ten missions.

Yossarian, with forty-eight missions behind him, contends that he has met Headquarters' requirements and should be sent home. When he makes his case to ex-P.F.C. Wintergreen, the mail clerk who is quietly and almost singlehandedly running the war, Wintergreen assumes he must be crazy and reminds him of Catch-22, which "says you've always got to do what your commanding officer tells you to." Back at the squadron, Daneeka reiterates Wintergreen's reminder: "Even if the colonel were disobeying the Twenty-seventh Air Force order by making you fly more missions, you'd still have to fly them, or you'd be guilty of disobeying an order of his. And then the Twenty-seventh Air Force Headquarters would really jump on you" (60).

Thinking his only recourse is to ask for a grounding slip, Yossarian appeals to Daneeka, who insists the matter is beyond his control: even if he approved grounding, "there's a catch"—Catch-22, which stipulates that Group must approve his action—"and Group isn't going to. They'll put you right back on combat status" (179). (Of course, the far greater, but unstated, Catch-22 in this instance is that while Group must approve all actions, ex-P.F.C. Wintergreen actually makes all the crucial strategic decisions.) Yossarian, who realizes the insanity inherent in a principle so evil that it mocks justice and victimizes the innocent,[34] is insane enough himself to continue challenging it. Yet he is sufficiently sane to know that trying to use reason against Catch-22 is futile and that, as Jean Kennard observed, the only way out is "simply to rebel, in Camus' sense, to take a stand, to say 'no.' "[35]

His rebellion begins in the hospital, the one place that offers relative safety and security yet which itself is a microcosm of a world where "everything is a few notches out of kilter," as symbolized by Yossarian's temperature always being two degrees above normal and Doc Daneeka's always being two degrees below.[36] In order to escape the pernicious disease of mortality looming beyond its doors, Yossarian retreats to the hospital each time the number of missions is raised. After all, "there were usually not nearly as many sick people inside the hospital as Yossarian saw outside the hospital, and there were generally fewer people inside the hospital who were seriously sick. There was a much lower death rate" inside than out, and "a much healthier death rate," since few people died unnecessarily (170). And, most importantly, there was none of that "crude ostentation" about dying that was so common elsewhere on the base—no people blowing up in mid-air, like Kraft or the dead man in Yossarian's tent, no people freezing to death in the blazing summertime, like Snowden.

Yet even in the hospital, Yossarian feels the presence of the omnipresent catch. "All the officer patients in the ward were forced to censor letters written by all the enlisted-men patients" (8), and Catch-22 required that each censored letter bear the censoring officer's name. Despite the fact that in such instances the "humanly obvious categories of life and death," as Tony Tanner calls them, are utterly confused and inverted with "a pseudo-reality of forms, papers, rules and regulations,"[37] Yossarian turns the mandate into a game for his own amusement and an exercise of his own power over the system. On one occasion, it was "Death to all modifiers"; the next it was war on articles; another time it was a more "dynamic intralinear tension" that necessitated the blacking out of all words *but* articles. Having exhausted the creative possibilities in the handling of the actual letters, he attacks the envelopes, blacking out and thus obliterating whole homes, streets, even towns. Most letters, however, he doesn't read at all, and it is those he signs with his own name. (Like Major Major, who is in his office only when he is out, Yossarian signs that he has censored a letter only when he has failed to censor any part of it.) On the ones he does read, he signs "Washington Irving," and, when that gets boring, "Irving Washington," a witty nod both to the inversion of values within the bureaucracy and to the new fiction his selective censoring creates. But his unorthodox approach constitutes an unfamiliar break from the norm and produces a ripple of anxiety among the higher-ups, who dispatch a series of C. I. D. investigators to uncover the conspiracy. Like dangerously powerful Keystone Kops unable to let "hell enough alone,"[38] the C. I. D. men remain oblivious to the insanity of the system's larger conspiracy and, hot on each other's trails, turn up only enough information to implicate the most innocent bystander, Chaplain Tappman. Although the chaplain is wrongly accused as a result of the game, Yossarian nevertheless succeeds in further convoluting the convoluted system. By tampering with the flow of paper on which the system depends, he causes it to run in circles, like a dog chasing its own tail.

Yossarian's hospital stays mark the beginning of his increasingly dramatic acts of insubordination: he initiates these self-hospitalizations first as a way of avoiding calisthenics at the base in Colorado and later in response to the injustice of the growing number of flights ordered by Cathcart. Unable to surmount the protean Catch-22 but unwilling to be broken by it, he returns to the hospital to be healed and to develop strategies, often as mad as the system that oppresses him, for circumventing its illogic. The end of the novel brings him back again to the hospital, and it is there that the chaplain reveals to him the news that leads to his greatest and most liberating act of insubordination yet.

Catch-22 also has an impact on others in Yossarian's squadron. When Captain Black is angered by Major Major's promotion to major and appointment as commander, he implements his Glorious Loyalty Oath Crusade to prove that his nemesis is a Communist. Black insists that everyone in the squadron "voluntarily" sign loyalty oaths—except, of course, Major Major, who will not be allowed to sign one "even if he wants to." Loyalty oaths, more of the pseudo-real forms to which Tony Tanner referred, soon become necessary for the most routine functions: enlisted men and officers on combat duty have to sign in order to get map cases from the intelligence tent, to receive flak suits and parachutes from the parachute tent, to be allowed rides to the airfield in one of the motor vehicle officer's trucks, to collect pay from the finance officer, to obtain PX supplies, and to have their hair cut by the Italian barbers. When other officers follow Black's urging and introduce loyalty oaths of their own, he goes them one better, initiating the recitation of the pledge of allegiance and the singing of the national anthem. The helpless combat soldiers, caught in the middle, quickly discover that they are just pawns in the officers' games and that the administrators appointed to serve them instead seek to dominate them. Bullied and harassed all day by one loyalty-professing superior after another, each alleging more loyalty than the one before, the men voice their objections. But their only recourse is to complain to their unsympathetic superiors, who are responsible for the oaths in the first place—another frustrating Catch-22. Black (in an eerie echo of the Bush administration as much as of Senator McCarthy) responds that "people who were loyal would not mind signing all the loyalty oaths they had to. To anyone who questioned the effectiveness of the loyalty oaths, he replied that people who really did owe allegiance to their country would be proud to pledge it as often as he forced them to" (117). When Milo Minderbinder, entrepreneur extraordinaire, by nature opposed to any innovation that disrupts his comfortably profitable routine, questions the captain's judgment, Black again dredges up Catch-22, the blanket principle that covers any absurd situation:

National defense is *everybody's* job . . . . And this whole program is voluntary, Milo—don't forget that. The men don't *have* to sign Piltchard and Wren's loyalty oath if they don't want to. But we need you to starve them to death if they don't. It's just like Catch-22. Don't you get it? You're not against Catch-22, are you? (118)

Before Milo has an opportunity to spew any of his perversely patriotic clichés in response, the loyalty oath crisis is resolved by the man of few words, Major —— de Coverly. When the catch prevents him from being fed, the Major, who is so formidable that no one dares ask him his first name, grunts "Gimme eat . . . Give *everybody* eat" (120). Hardly an eloquent pronouncement, it nevertheless is as simple and as effective as Yossarian's refusal to fly. (But the Major disappears—or is "disappeared"—soon afterwards: his is part of a pattern of disappearances that usually involve those who in some way get too close to the secrets of the system.)

Even the well-connected Wintergreen feels the pinch of Catch-22 so familiar to Yossarian. A regular AWOL from the base in Colorado, Wintergreen establishes for himself a routine almost as comfortable as Milo's: he manages to get caught, court-martialed and busted, and sentenced to dig holes six feet deep, wide, and long as punishment ("not such a bad assignment in wartime"). Imagining himself to be an American hero who makes a valuable and unique contribution to the war effort by his lassitude, he accepts his Sisyphean role "with all the uncomplaining dedication of a true patriot." His effort, however, is not unique at all; it is typical of the pointless, repetitive actions that most of the characters wittingly or unwittingly perform.

In another of the novel's many paradoxes, Wintergreen understands that the work isn't steady and he stands to lose it each time he goes over the hill, yet he has to keep going over the hill to maintain the work. But "I can't even keep doing that," he remarks sadly. "There's a catch, Catch-22. The next time I go over the hill, it will mean the stockade . . . or wind[ing] up overseas" (108). Wintergreen cannot fathom such a gross misappropriation of talent, since he has been doing his duty digging his holes more faithfully than the men in combat have been doing theirs, and he sees no reason why Catch-22 should send him abroad to do their jobs, too. Indeed, he is soon transferred to Headquarters, where useless skills such as his are consistently rewarded by rapid promotion. There, he assumes the role of mail clerk, which allows him to run the war by regulating the flow of the top brass's correspondence. Precisely because of his clerical role as purveyor of messages,[39] in no time he dictates the war's protocol—discarding correspondence from General Peckem, for example, because he feels it is "too prolix" (27), and giving the competing General Dreedle a higher status as a result—and becomes the most powerful man around. In the novel, after all, the hand with the readiest access to the flow of paper controls the system. Paper is the war's most powerful weapon, as Yossarian demonstrates by simply moving the bombing line on the map. By serving as the prime means of transmitting the messages which give the military administration its raison d'être, paper, as a substance, takes on connotations of death and even becomes fatal, as the M & M shares that replace morphine in the medical kits and parachutes in the flight packs attest.[40]

The six-foot holes Wintergreen leaves behind in Colorado are a bitter foreshadowing of his new assignment at Headquarters, through which he continues to dig others' graves. Superficially comical and seemingly insignificant in terms of the military hierarchy, Wintergreen is really an immensely dangerous character whose selfishness, business acumen, and political savvy make his acquaintance with Cathcart and his eventual alliance with Milo unsurprising.

But perhaps the most far-reaching application of Catch-22 occurs when Yossarian, shadowed by Nately's whore (another universal principle that reminds Yossarian that he will always be unjustly beset—and will probably always deserve it),[41] goes AWOL himself and returns to Rome, only to find the former whorehouse in ruins, like much of the rest of the city. "Soldiers with the hard white hats and clubs" (M.P.s) chased the women away, explains the old crone who is the house's sole remaining resident. When Yossarian wonders what reason the soldiers had, she responds that there was no reason, only "Catch-22. Catch-22 says they have a right to do anything we can't stop them from doing" (416). Her knowledge of Catch-22 and her tacit acceptance of it so unnerves Yossarian that he sets out on a journey through the streets of Rome, much like Bloom's journey through the underworld of Dublin, and in an almost Joycean epiphany finally realizes the secret behind the ubiquitous regulation. Catch-22 was not an actual legal document; it "did not exist, he was positive of that, but it made no difference.

What did matter was that everyone thought it existed, and that was much worse, for there was no object or text to ridicule or refute, to accuse, criticize, attack, amend, hate, revile, spit at, rip to shreds, trample upon or burn up" (418). Protean to the point of perversity, Catch-22 cannot be defeated logically, as Yossarian discovers when he returns to Pianosa and is offered a deal whose substance reduplicates the moral degeneration he witnessed in Rome.

The implicit and familiar catch defines not only the philosophy of the novel but also its structure. Although at times *Catch-22* seems little more than a "succession of scenes following and sometimes interrupting each other like a jumbled series of playlets," related only in that they take place within the purview of Yossarian,[42] its organization is actually as repetitive and self-perpetuating as Catch-22 itself. The circularity of the plot[43] is mirrored in the reflexiveness of the dialogue and the imagery, both of which are set against a background that Vance Ramsey describes as "something like an asylum for the criminally insane,"[44] with its pervasive atmosphere of fear and anxiety, or what Milton R. Bass calls a "weirdness . . . that makes you feel trapped in a mental institution after the caretakers have left for the day."[45]

To find some kind of logical frame for *Catch-22*'s illogic, Heller looked to the Theater of the Absurd, where time and the orderly arrangement of events are not visualized as a logical, continuous flow from past to present to future; rather, echoing the discordance inherent in the reality of the human condition, everything is in the present tense, because modern man no longer views or relates in a concrete way to life in a sequential manner. Using absurdist drama as a model, Heller set up structural patterns of images and scenes that are arranged nonsequentially and that take on meaning in the novel only after being brought together and seen in proper relationship to each other and from the proper perspective. In short, as Howard J. Stark described it, "*Catch-22* does not explain, analyze, or argue situations or causes; it effectively presents the absurdity of modern life through the careful juxtaposing of seemingly incongruous scenes and images" which recur throughout.[46] Yet it is precisely by fracturing the continuity of his narrative that Heller paradoxically forces the reader to examine the nature of its connections—in his words, "to *experience* the book rather than simply to read it." David Seed suggests that the unpredictability caused by such fracturing guarantees the reader's interest or insecurity. "And if we

32

begin to suspect that we are victims of a practical joke," Seed wonders, "aren't we essentially repeating the characters' suspicions of a joking and indifferent God?"[47]

Heller felt he had to give *Catch-22* a structure "that would reflect and complement the contents of the book itself" and derive from "our present atmosphere . . . of disorganization, of absurdity."[48] The creation of a literary déjà vu, without reference to its scientific or clinical aspects, allowed him to do just that. Using déjà vu as a structural device, he was able to merge the welter of digressions, flashbacks, and anecdotes in the construction of his narrative as he contrived thematic patterns so that the reader has the experience of seeing things twice—or even more often—the way many of the characters do.[49] As a kind of literary echolalia similar to Billy Pilgrim's "disease" in *Slaughterhouse-Five,* déjà vu establishes a sense of timelessness, that the same things do happen and will happen again. Subsequently, the reader, who feels the "subtle, recurring confusion between illusion and reality" (209) created by the deliberate recurrences, is pulled further into the action in order to distinguish between the two.

To that end, the novel is replete with repeating images, from the names of the officers (Yo-Yo, the nickname the young pilots give Yossarian; Major Major, whose name in full is actually Major Major Major Major; General P. P. Peckem) to the nature of their roles (continuous circular bombing flights; redundant pointless activity; repeated flights from human contact). The redundancies are indeed numerous. Chief White Halfoat—whose plight, so typical of exploited, dispossessed Native Americans like Bromden in *Cuckoo's Nest,* becomes one of the targets for Heller's social satire—always has to keep moving, because wherever he or his family settles, even on the base in Colorado, the discovery of oil follows. A young lieutenant is ultimately left to suffer convulsions on the streets of Rome after his colleagues, who impotently attempt to relieve his distress, throw him up and down like a rag doll. ("Why don't you lift him up and put him on the hood of that car?" asks one. "Why don't you lift him up off the hood of that car and lay him down on the ground?" answers another [422].) Nurse Cramer, with no real life of her own to relieve the stress and tedium of Pianosa, at a distance silently imitates all of Nurse Duckett's movements on the beach. After stripping them of their identities by throwing their uniforms out of the apartment windows, Dunbar provokes the officers in

Rome by echoing their conversations. ("Stop it!" yells one officer. "Stop it," replies Dunbar. "That's what I said." "That's what I said." "Are you deliberately repeating everything I say?" "Are you deliberately repeating everything I say?" "I'll thrash you." "I'll thrash *you*" [363].) Cathcart, whose problems with Yossarian are multiplying, suspects that the actual number of "Yossarians" in his outfit is increasing; he believes that only two, possibly three, people named Yossarian could cause him so much trouble. Dobbs, made crazy by the rising number of missions required of him, repeatedly enlists Yossarian's help in assassinating Cathcart; Yossarian, in turn, later solicits Dobbs's assistance for the same purpose. General Dreedle has a similar penchant for violent resolution: he deals with each crisis or challenge to his command by ordering that the offender be taken out and shot, and each time must be gently reminded that such measures, while tempting, are not feasible. Yossarian, proving that men in love are just as anguished and ridiculous as men in war,[50] finds himself falling for virtually every woman around him— Dreedle's nurse, the maid in the lime-colored panties, the bald-headed prostitute, Mrs. Scheisskopf, Nately's whore. Gus and Wes, Heller's memorably insipid pair of docs, are indeed a paradox: the twin idiots have a standard prescription for all ills—painting their patients' gums and toes gentian violet and dispensing laxatives. And at one point virtually everyone is forging Washington Irving's name to official documents or purporting to be T. S. Eliot by phone.

In a system that has no place for individual or meaningful gestures, repetitive actions and empty rituals abound. There are the interminable parades introduced by Scheisskopf (who, as his name implies, is the shithead in charge), followed by the endless correspondence announcing their cancellation; Peckem's barrage of memos concerning the placement of the combat forces under his division of Special Services ("If dropping bombs on the enemy isn't a special service, I wonder what in the world is" [331]); Major Major's signatures on a proliferation of useless official documents; the multiplicity of reports for any incident ("they can prepare as many official reports as they want and choose whichever ones they need on any given occasion. Didn't you know that?" [452]); Cathcart's unholy and unsuccessful quests for the cover of the *Saturday Evening Post*; the constant attacks on Yossarian, after Nately's death, by Nately's whore, who lurks menacingly around every corner.

Even the novel's title reflects the reflexiveness and repetitiveness so integral to the plot. Although Heller's original title was *Catch-18* (changed only because popular author Leon Uris was coming out with his novel, *Mila-18*, prior to *Catch-22*, and Heller's publisher worried that the two like-sounding titles might be confusing to potential buyers, who would probably gravitate to the better-known writer), the number twenty-two is far more relevant. Since so many events occur twice, Heller writes that "the two 2's struck me as being very appropriate to the novel."[51]

The dying soldier in the hospital, a victim of the anonymity of the system and a symbol of the constancy of death and suffering, sees everything twice—a condition Yossarian soon duplicates. In need of a new disease that will allow him to extend his hospitalization at his stateside post, Yossarian observes the soldier with great humility and admiration before assuming his unusual brand of double vision. "The walls! The walls!" cries the soldier. "Move back the walls!" Yossarian, knowing he is in the presence of a master of the con, repeats, "The walls! The walls! Move back the walls!" To determine the extent of Yossarian's illness, the doctors insist that Yossarian report how many fingers they are holding up. To each of their tests, Yossarian responds, "Two." One of the doctors says jubilantly that Yossarian is right: "He *does* see everything twice." Only after his talented roommate dies does Yossarian decide to stop emulating him, and he announces, "I see everything once!" His recovery is confirmed by a similar finger-counting test; this time Yossarian reports each time that he sees only one finger, thus leading his doctors to conclude that now "He does see everything once! We made him all better" (186–87). The experience of seeing things twice recurs when he arrives on Pianosa and encounters a bureaucracy even less logical than that of the hospital and base in Colorado.

Chaplain Tappman, writes Heller, also "thinks that everything that happens has happened once before."[52] After meeting Yossarian for the first time, he senses that he already knows him, that Yossarian is somehow related to the mystical apparition he beheld at Snowden's funeral. (Ironically, though the chaplain is unaware of it, Yossarian *is* the apparition he beheld at Snowden's funeral.) Tappman's belief that he has "experienced the identical situation before in some prior time or existence" causes him to endeavor "to trap and nourish the impression in order to predict, and perhaps even control, what incident would occur next, but the afflatus melted away unproductively, as he had known beforehand it would" (209). Yet his feeling of déjà vu is not inaccurate, because all of the things he thinks he has experienced have in fact happened before.

Milo Minderbinder, Yossarian's nemesis, also sees twice—twice the profit, that is. Milo, typically involved with both sides in any negotiation, doublebills for his services: he charges both the Americans and the Germans, for example, for demolishing the same highway bridge at Orvieto (realizing "a fantastic profit from both halves of his project for doing nothing more than signing his name twice" [261]). Milo's double-deals are legendary: he buys and sells cork that goes to New York, shoes for Toulouse, ham to Siam, nails from Wales, tangerines for New Orleans, and any other commodities that he can mark up for resale, including the entire crop of Egyptian cotton. He even makes money buying eggs at seven cents apiece and selling them for five cents to his own kitchen in Pianosa. When Yossarian wonders how Milo can claim to make a profit by selling at a loss, he explains that he buys the eggs for one cent in Sicily and sells them for four and a quarter cents each to his Syndicate in Malta, which in turn resells them at seven cents to Milo; thus, the Syndicate makes six cents per seven-cent egg. After Milo's own kitchen purchases the eggs at five cents, the final profit is still four cents. But Milo compounds that profit through good public relations, so the payoff is again doubled: he mollifies the enlisted men who advance his cartel by feeding them the best food they have ever eaten while he earns the admiration of the administration for being able to acquire the hard-to-find eggs at two cents below the market price. His superiors, allied to Milo by their greed and selfishness as well as by their other common appetites, urge him to continue his efficient operation and even underwrite his costs by providing manpower and planes. Those planes, originally named for "such laudable ideals as Courage, Might, Justice, Truth, Liberty, Love, Honor, and Patriotism" (259), have since been painted over by Milo's mechanics and stenciled with the M & M logo. Ignobly, they bear advertising for the day's specials.

Since the majority of men in the squadron are victims of Milo and the other profiteers who outrank them, their frequently repetitive, perfunctory motions suggest both their powerlessness and, by implication, the powerlessness of all human actions. Hungry Joe, for example, torn between "furgling" women or photographing them, uses his pretense of being a photographer for *Life* magazine as a kind of foreplay for his would-be seductions. But "the pictures never came out, and Hungry Joe never got in. [And] the odd thing was that in civilian life Hungry Joe really had been a photographer for *Life* magazine" (54). He is unlucky in other ways as well; although he has completed all of the required missions and is waiting to be sent home, he doesn't make it out before Cathcart raises the number of flights and so must keep on flying. Understandably convinced that *something* is going to get him, he compiles lists of fatal diseases, arranged in alphabetical order for easy reference. Paradoxically, though, he seems at peace only while in combat. At the squadron between missions, his screaming nightmares keep almost everyone awake: he dreams that tentmate Huple's cat is sleeping on his face, suffocating him; and when he wakes up, he finds Huple's cat asleep on his face. After Hungry Joe challenges the cat to a fight—Heller cannot resist punning on both "catfight" and "face-off"—the cat runs away and Joe is declared the winner; he goes to bed victorious, only to dream again that the cat is sleeping on his face and suffocating him. When Joe dies (the last of Yossarian's flight pals to go), the cause of his death is neither combat nor a fatal disease: as the chaplain tells Yossarian, "He died in his sleep while having a dream. They found a cat on his face" (445). Like Halfoat's, Hungry Joe's death is a self-fulfilling prophecy.

Nowhere, however, is the men's powerlessness better conveyed than in the "trial" scenes of Clevinger and Tappman, which foreshadow Yossarian's final confrontation with Cathcart and Korn. Clevinger is a good, solid, intelligent man whom Yossarian considers to be a dope: "one of those people with lots of intelligence and no brains" (70). Indeed, as David Seed observes, he "knows Aristotle but is incapable of 'reading' Scheisskopf's words."[53] Against Yossarian's advice, Clevinger takes his democratic rights literally and responds to Scheisskopf's rhetorical question about morale. The men don't want to march in parades every Sunday, he tells the then-lieutenant, and they prefer to elect their own officers from the ranks. Scheisskopf, who is so obsessed with his parades that he even considers implanting nickel alloys in his men's thighbones to force them to march straighter, follows some of Clevinger's recommendations, and his squadron wins the parade pennants for several consecutive weeks. But Scheisskopf soon brings Clevinger up on charges for conspiring to advocate the overthrow of the cadet officer he has appointed and for a host of other heinous offenses, including "breaking ranks while in formation, felonious assault, indiscriminate behavior, mopery, high treason, provoking, being a smart guy, listening to classical music, and so on" (77). The trial, with Scheisskopf serving as judge, prosecutor, and defense attorney, is a complete travesty.

But Clevinger's real crime is that he supports and believes in the system. Yossarian had warned him before his appearance at the Action Board that he hasn't got a chance because "they hate Jews." Even after Clevinger protested that he wasn't a Jew, Yossarian promised, "It will make no difference. They're after everybody" (83). And in the end, "Clevinger was guilty, of course, or he would not have been accused, and since the only way to prove it was to find him guilty" (82), it was the Board's patriotic duty to do so.

Tappman's situation is similar to Clevinger's, and his trial equally Kafkaesque.

> "Everything's going to be all right, Chaplain," the major said encouragingly. "You've got nothing to be afraid of if you're not guilty. What are you so afraid of? You're not guilty, are you?"
> "Sure he's guilty," said the colonel. "Guilty as hell."
> "Guilty of what?" implored the chaplain, feeling more and more bewildered and not knowing which of the men to appeal to for mercy. The third officer wore no insignia and lurked in silence off to the side. "What did I do?"
> "That's just what we're going to find out," answered the colonel
> . . . . (389)

The chaplain is finally charged with "being Washington Irving and taking capricious and unlicensed liberties in censoring the letters of officers and enlisted men"; like Clevinger, he is found guilty because "if they're his crimes and infractions, he must have committed them" (395). Tappman's inability to prove his innocence against the absurd claims fills him with indignation and moral outrage, and instead of feeling betrayed—as Clevinger did—by the system he supported, he attempts to confront Korn and even decides to take his concerns to the General. But his new bravado is completely undercut when Korn informs him that Dreedle is no longer in charge; Peckem is. As Korn gloatingly reminds Tappman, who feels more ineffectual than ever, the chaplain has no influence with Peckem at all, whereas Cathcart is Peckem's good buddy—and, by extension,

38

so is Korn.[54] So Tappman seems to have no redress; the conspiracy of the institution has triumphed yet again.

Evident not only in the trial scenes, the bureaucratic doublespeak, as convoluted as the Möbius strip with which John Barth opens his *Lost in the Funhouse*, obfuscates all logic, underscores the men's frustration, and highlights their impotence in mounting any effective challenge to the ludicrous principles that define the system. Essential to the smooth dysfunctioning of the military machine (whose operation dictates, for example, that firemen must leave the burning hospital to be present on the airfield in case a fire *might* occur there), doublespeak is the superior officers' favorite tool. Without its verbal voodoo, which magically justifies the most outrageous conduct, they are as vulnerable to attack as their uniformless colleagues in the Rome apartment were. The duplicitous Cathcart, for example, afraid of the kind of straight talk that might force him into taking any real moral position, explains the possible change of commanding officers to Tappman in the following way: "it looks like General Dreedle is finally on the way out and that General Peckem is slated to replace him. Frankly, I'm not going to be sorry to see that happen. General Peckem is a very good man, and I think we'll all be much better off under him. On the other hand, it might never take place, and we'd still remain under General Dreedle. Frankly, I wouldn't be sorry to see that happen either, because General Dreedle is another very good man, and I think we'll all be much better off under him too" (198). Cathcart's imprecision in logic as well as language leads him on another occasion to order Tappman to socialize nightly with the men and then to punish him for spending so much time at the Officers' Club.

"Is that a chaplain I see over there?" [asks Dreedle.] "That's really a fine thing when a man of God begins hanging around a place like this with a bunch of dirty drunks and gamblers."

Colonel Cathcart compressed his lips primly and started to rise. "I couldn't agree with you more, sir," he assented briskly in a tone of ostentatious disapproval. "I just don't know what's happening to the clergy these days."

"They're getting better, that's what's happening to them," General Dreedle growled emphatically. (291)

. . . .

"That's a fine thing," General Dreedle growled at the bar, gripping his empty shot glass in his burly hand. "That's really a fine thing, when a man of God begins hanging around a place like this with a bunch of dirty drunks and gamblers."

Colonel Cathcart sighed with relief. "Yes, sir," he exclaimed proudly. "It certainly is a fine thing."

"Then why the hell don't you do something about it?"

"Sir?" Colonel Cathcart inquired, blinking.

"Do you think it does you credit to have your chaplain hanging around here every night? He's in here every goddam time I come."

"You're right, sir, absolutely right," Colonel Cathcart responded. "It does me no credit at all. And I *am* going to do something about it, this very minute."

"Aren't you the one who ordered him to come here?"

"No, sir, that was Colonel Korn. I intend to punish him severely, too." (292)

On another occasion, when the newly arrived Colonel Scheiss-kopf assumes, with a look of dim comprehension, that his responsibility is to capture the "enemy Dreedle," Peckem, with a benign laugh, instead of clarifying the matter only muddies it further: "No," he says, "Dreedle's on our side, and Dreedle *is* the enemy" (332). Peckem also agrees to allow Scheisskopf to send out memos about his beloved parades, "As long as you don't schedule any." Peckem soon concedes that scheduling parades and then calling them off is "a wonderful idea," and on further reflection he conceives an even better idea: "just send out weekly announcements *postponing* the parades," he tells Scheisskopf. "Don't even bother to schedule them. That would be infinitely more disconcerting" (333) because it implies that the administrators *could* schedule a parade if they chose to. As David Seed notes, "this detachment of official documents from any observable reality reflects the general fate of language at the hands of the administration, whose inventions become more and more blatant matters of expediency."[55]

Group Headquarters engages in a similar military mumbo jumbo when it becomes alarmed that the soldiers who attend the scheduled education sessions might actually participate, "for there was no telling what people might find out once they were free to ask whatever questions they wanted to" (36). So Headquarters adopts Colonel Korn's rule, that the only people allowed to ask questions are those who never do. The infernal doublespeak manifests itself again with the middle-aged military big shots holding Nately's whore. They will not release her until she says uncle, which she immediately does; but her reply is unsatisfactory because, as they tell her, "We can't really make you say uncle unless you don't want to say uncle. Don't you see? Don't say uncle when I tell you to say uncle. Okay? Say uncle" (361).

Since most actions in *Catch-22* are redundant and language avoids precision, it is not surprising that even time does not provide a meaningful referent. John Wain observes that life, for the bomber pilots, simply "does not flow in a regular, unfolding ribbon, experience following on from experience, as it does in even the most tumultuous life in peace-time"; it "teeters round and round in a continual stalemate."[56] Past incidents recur so often that they form part of an ongoing present, while the future offers nothing more than a repetition of situations already experienced, such as flying, waiting, escaping to Rome for rest and relaxation. Therefore, in his narrative, Heller largely dispenses with the artificial order of clocks and calendars, as Vonnegut breaks with the traditional notion of clock time to present Billy Pilgrim's story through a series of flashbacks and flashforwards in *Slaughterhouse-Five*.

Yossarian, like many other antiheroes of modern fiction from Leopold Bloom to Moses Herzog,[57] exists in a world dominated by psychological time. His "clock" is internal, and his "time" is made tangible only through his individual consciousness and memory.[58] So, instead of by months, Yossarian measures his service by numbers of missions and hospital stays and by remembrances of dead friends: the greater the number of missions required, the more frequent his hospital stays and the higher the number of deaths of his flyer-colleagues. Linear chronology, associated with official versions of reality, is thus effectively discredited,[59] and actual time structure, or "chronological time," according to Heller, "becomes immaterial" since most of the novel's events (Snowden's death, the mission to Bologna, Milo's bombing of his squadron) "have already taken place."[60]

Dunbar explicitly addresses the issue of the relativity of time in one of his conversations with Yossarian. "You're inches away from death every time you go on a mission," he says. "How much older can you be at your age?" (40). He is indeed correct. All of the other combat officers are in the same race with time, specifically, to be sent home before the number of missions is raised. Most lose. When the elderly pimp asks Nately his age, he responds, "I'll be twenty in January." The old man replies, "If you live" (253). And, in fact, Nately dies, paying with his life for his impetuousness in love and combat.

In *Slaughterhouse-Five*, all of Billy's actions either anticipate or look back to the fateful night he spent in the Dresden slaughter-house and to the subsequent execution of the innocent school-teacher, Edgar Derby; in *One Flew Over the Cuckoo's Nest*, Chief finally escapes his hallucinatory world and regains control of his life by recalling those incidents in his childhood and adolescence that caused him to feel ostracized and propelled him into "the fog" in the first place; Chance recalls past events in terms of whether there was television then or not; and in *Sophie's Choice*, Sophie gradually shares with Stingo the remembrance of the chilling choice she has long repressed. Similarly, one particular recollection is pivotal to Yossarian's burgeoning awareness of his self and to the novel's cyclic structure: Snowden's losing his guts, quite literally, over Avignon, at the same moment that Yossarian, more metaphorically, loses his. The loosely autobiographical incident occurs at some point—possibly several months—before the novel begins. Yet like Von-negut, Kesey, and Styron, Heller does not describe the incident for the reader all at once; instead he reveals it by degrees, allowing it to emerge slowly and to deepen with each recollection or retelling.

Moreover, like Joyce in *Ulysses*, Heller uses the simple device of releasing information first and later providing the context that makes that information comprehensible.[61] Therefore, the reader never learns things as a whole but in disjointed fragments and, like Yossarian, senses that he has "experienced the identical situation before" because it parallels other situations or is thematically related to them.[62] The first mention of Snowden comes in the fourth chapter, when Yossarian interrupts Captain Black's education ses-sion to ask, "Where are the Snowdens of yesteryear?" The haunting question seems important primarily because it upsets the session and precipitates the imposition of Korn's gag rule on questions at subsequent sessions; all we discover about Snowden is that he is dead, "killed over Avignon when Dobbs went crazy in mid-air and seized the controls away from Huple" (35–36).

The incident is mentioned again in the next chapter. The mission to Avignon is described passingly as a "mess," a "pitiful time." Plastered helplessly to the ceiling after his plane dives, Yossarian restores his headset and hears Dobbs's pathetic cry to "help the bombardier." Yossarian answers that *he* is the bombardier and he is all right. Dobbs begs, "Then help him, help him." Meanwhile, Heller adds almost casually, "Snowden lay dying in back" (51–52), and the whole affair is forgotten.

More than fifteen chapters elapse before Heller picks it up again to describe the effect of Snowden's death on Yossarian, who is now standing naked in formation to receive a medal for another mission, a botched flight during which he had to make two bombing passes before hitting his target. Captain Wren tells an amused General Dreedle, who assumes that Yossarian's uniform is not back from the laundry yet, the reason for the nudity: "A man was killed in his plane over Avignon last week and bled all over him. He swears he's never going to wear a uniform again" (223). The following chapter further clarifies Yossarian's odd behavior and explains his aversion to his clothing. Apparently, "Yossarian lost his nerve . . . because Snowden lost his guts, and Snowden lost his guts because the pilot was Huple, who was only fifteen years old, and their co-pilot was Dobbs, who was even worse" (230). Regaining his composure after the near-fatal dive, Yossarian heard not only Dobbs's pleas for help but also Snowden's feeble whisper, "I'm cold." He also saw Snowden "freezing to death in a yellow splash of sunlight" (231). But the chapter quickly shifts from Snowden's pain to Dobbs's anger at Cathcart for raising the number of missions and his plans to assassinate him, with Yossarian's help.

Each subsequent time the incident over Avignon is recalled, progressively more small but horrifying details emerge: Yossarian, says Daneeka, stepped down from the plane "naked, in a state of utter shock, with Snowden smeared abundantly all over his bare heels and toes, knees, arms and fingers" (267); during the flight, Yossarian had attempted to treat Snowden's "yawning, raw, melon-shaped hole as big as a football in the outside of his thigh," and though it caused Yossarian to moan in shock and sympathy and even to vomit, it turned out to be the wrong wound (341); Kid Sampson's legs, standing upright for a few seconds after the horrible accident on the beach, remind Yossarian of Snowden's freezing to death in the heat of the plane, "holding his eternal, immutable," but as yet undefined "secret concealed inside his quilted, armor-plate flak suit" as Yossarian ministers to his injured leg (355); and, while trying unsuccessfully to console Nately's whore after telling her of

Nately's death, Yossarian recalls his inadequate response—"There, there. There, there" (405)—to Snowden's complaints about the cold despite the warmth of the day and the heat of the plane.

Only in the penultimate chapter is the scene fully rendered and the significance of Snowden's death finally revealed. "Bathed in icy sweat," acutely aware of his own mortality, Yossarian thinks of his dead pal. He remembers Snowden's injuries, both the obvious one, which he had spent so long sterilizing and bandaging, and the hidden, fatal one (which Vance Ramsey suggests is "mortality itself"[63]), caused by a three-inch piece of flak that blasted through— and out—Snowden's ribs, but that Yossarian discovered too late; remembers Snowden's liver, lungs, kidneys, ribs, stomach, even the stewed tomatoes Snowden had eaten that day for lunch, slithering out all over him; remembers Snowden's secret, now revealed, that "Man was matter . . . . The spirit gone, man is garbage . . . . Ripeness was all" (445–50);[64] and remembers Snowden's warning. Suddenly all of the fragments coalesce; Yossarian's abhorrence of flying, his paranoiac fear of hidden danger, his refusal to wear a uniform which he associates with his official role as an agent of destruction and death, his walking backwards while carrying a loaded gun so no one can sneak up on him from behind—all make perfect sense. His "insane" behavior, in fact, seems quite rational, given the trauma he has experienced, and confirms Dr. Stubb's diagnosis: "That crazy bastard may be the only sane one left" (114).

Other important events in the novel are revealed in a similar, progressive, incremental manner, which gives them freshness and immediacy and prevents them from seeming distant in time. Heller, who stated that his main models for disrupting a time scheme were *Absalom, Absalom!* and *The Sound and the Fury,* characterized the method as Faulknerian—"tell[ing] a large narrative largely in terms of fragments and slow feeding of interrupted episodes"[65]—and used it to describe not only Chaplain Tappman's mystical apparition ("the most extraordinary event that had ever befallen him, an event perhaps marvelous, perhaps pathological—the vision of the naked man in the tree" [279]) but also Clevinger's ill-fated mission, in which Clevinger simply vanishes behind a cloud; McWatt's danger-ous habit of buzzing people on the ground, which results in the gruesome death of Kid Sampson, McWatt's suicide, and Doc Daneeka's untimely demise; and Orr's encounter with the prostitute, who beats him over the head with her shoe, and his escape to Sweden.

In the novel's circular pattern of events, as the institution diminishes the characters' individuality and erodes their sense of identity, the players sometimes become interchangeable. Dunbar and Yossarian switch places with each other in the hospital and even briefly assume the identities of other patients by usurping their beds. The game, however, proves costly to Yossarian. He finally convinces the doctors that he is crazy, but the release orders are issued to A. Fortiori, whose bed Yossarian has borrowed, and not to Yossarian. As Howard J. Stark demonstrates, the involvement of Lieutenant Fortiori at this point in the narrative is significant in that *a fortiori* is a term used in logic "to denote an argument to the effect that because one ascertained fact exists, therefore another, which is included in it, or analogous to it, and which is less improbable, unusual, or surprising, must also exist." Because Yossarian was in Fortiori's bed, he is Fortiori. Yossarian is crazy; therefore Fortiori is sent home.[66] Thus, in its logical simplicity, *a fortiori* becomes another way of defining Catch-22.

The interchangeability of the characters is evident again after the death of Giuseppe, the soldier who saw everything twice. When Yossarian, who is persuaded to pose as the dead man, objects that Giuseppe's parents "didn't come to see me . . . . They came to see their [dying] son," he is told that "they'll have to take what they can get. As far as we're concerned, one dying boy is just as good as any other, or just as bad. To a scientist, all dying boys are equal" (187). Regrettably, James McDonald notes, "this is the official attitude: those in charge view all human beings as 'dying boys,' statistics, means to an end," pawns used to wage their "constant battle for position and glory."[67]

Since the boys are all equal (and all dying), the administration accepts their dispensability without any responsibility or emotion. As Korn explains to Tappman, it doesn't really matter whether the casualties are experienced or new pilots. The men are merely cannon fodder; their individual lives are of no significance.[68] They are there to follow orders and to serve the self-interests of their superiors. Cathcart even tells Yossarian after Ferrara, "I don't give a damn about the men or the airplane. It's just that it looks so lousy on the report" (142). And he later endangers many lives when he orders a bombing run over a small, undefended village. The mission's ostensible purpose is to create a roadblock but in reality it simply satisfies Cathcart's desire for a good aerial photo of a tight bombing pattern—a phrase he himself admits means nothing—to show his superiors. (The aerial photo is a further example of the lethal dimension paper assumes and of the precedence of official documents over human life.) One man's death is as inevitable and as unremarkable to Cathcart as the next—or as the one before. The all-purpose form letter of sympathy he commissions demonstrates his complete and callous indifference to the welfare of those under his command:

> Dear Mrs., Mr., Miss, or Mr. and Mrs.: Words cannot express the deep personal grief I experienced when your husband, son, father or brother was killed, wounded, or reported missing in action. (289)

The squadron, in fact, is strewn with casualties who are equally faceless and irrelevant in the eyes of their superiors. There is Mudd, for instance, the soldier whose name symbolizes his rude and common treatment.[69] A replacement pilot who was sent immediately into action upon his arrival at Pianosa, he was blown to bits over Orvieto only two hours later. Because "he had never officially gotten into the squadron, he could never officially be gotten out" (111) and is considered technically alive. Yossarian, already obsessed with death and stunned by the military's inefficiency, wants Mudd's things, which he refers to collectively as "the dead man," removed from his tent. But because there is no provision for handling the belongings of a man who never officially arrived, Mudd's things stay put—at least until the young officers, newly assigned to the tent and unfamiliar with the bureaucracy, simply pitch them out. No one in the squadron can recall what Mudd looked like; but Yossarian, who never saw him, knows exactly who he was: "the unknown soldier who had never had a chance, for that was the only thing anyone ever did know about all the unknown soldiers—they never had a chance. They had to be dead" (112).

The converse of the situation with Mudd, a dead man who is considered alive by the bureaucracy, is reflected in the plight of Doc Daneeka, a live man who is pronounced dead. As a formality, Doc—who hates flying but wants to continue collecting his flight pay—is included on the flight log each time McWatt pilots a mission. But when McWatt crashes into the face of a mountain and Daneeka, who is not on board, fails to parachute out of the plane, he is declared a casualty. His untimely demise leaves Sergeant Towser, who runs the squadron in Major Major's chronic absence, to contend with the additional paperwork, a task made more difficult by the fact that Daneeka remains underfoot; but even Doc's presence is insufficient to negate the official report. As Towser strikes Daneeka from the squadron personnel roster, he tries discreetly to avoid "any conversation with Doc Daneeka himself as he moved by the flight surgeon's sepulchral figure" (350). Since Daneeka has been certified as deceased, all of his colleagues terminate their contact with him, and the doctor has no choice but to act out the role in which he has been cast—he becomes a ghost of a man. When he shows up at Medical complaining of a chill, Gus and Wes assure him that the reason he feels so cold is that he's dead.

Like Clevinger and Dunbar, Doc is spurned in his time of need by the superiors he has always served well and is thrust into the never-never land of administrative death, unable to convince even his wife that he is still alive. After receiving Cathcart's form condolence, Mrs. Daneeka assumes the imploring letters being sent to her from her husband are a cruel trick. (Again, the official military document supersedes the reality of the situation.) So she does the reasonable thing: she takes the money from her widow's insurance, gets a beauty makeover, and runs. She is Doc's last hope, and once she too has disappeared without leaving a forwarding address, he fades away in the novel as he already has faded away in the eyes of the bureaucracy.

The ultimate in faceless inhumanity, however, is the recurring figure of the soldier in white. First seen in the hospital in the opening pages of the novel, he is a mountain of white gauze and bandages. The nurses, reminiscent of the staff on Big Nurse's ward, treat him with the utmost impersonal efficiency: they hook two jars up to him. The first drips liquid in, the other collects liquid as it drops out. When one is full, the jars are reversed. The process leaves the officers wondering why they can't hook the two jars up to each other and "eliminate the middleman" (174). (In the original form of this chapter, published separately as "Catch-18" but deleted in the novel, Heller makes the process even more explicit: the reversible drips, explains the Surgeon-Major, represent "a cycle. . . . Everything moves in cycles."[70]) Though the soldier in white never utters a word, the other patients resent "him malevolently for the nauseating truth of which he was a bright reminder" (172). That truth is the imminence of death, both his and their own, and the reality of their negative status and utter unimportance within the military system.[71]

When the soldier in white finally expires, thermometer still stuck in his mouth, he is removed. But soon he is back on the ward, and his reappearance is enough to make Dunbar crazy. Though rumors circulate that it is actually Mudd underneath those bandages, Dunbar stares into the soldier's open mouth hole, sees nothing, and insists that "There's no one inside" (374). Having guessed the secret of the system, Dunbar is thus "disappeared" (an action reminiscent of *1984*, another novel about the dehumanizing effect of a centralizing bureaucracy, which may have been an influence on Heller).[72] Dunbar's disappearance on the heels of the soldier in white's reappearance confirms the patients' belief in the infinite abilities of the agents of the system to manipulate life and death and to extend their reach everywhere, even into the relative safety of the hospital; and the inmates recognize they have a new terror with which to contend.

Like Dunbar, many others (Clevinger, Major ——— de Coverly, Orr, Daneeka, Daneeka's wife, and several of the Italian prostitutes) have also mysteriously disappeared or "been disappeared." Early on, fearing Chief Halfoat's threat to cut his throat from ear to ear, Captain Flume vanishes into the woods and resurfaces just before Halfoat dies of pneumonia. Halfoat's death, in fact, is partly brought on by Flume's reappearance, just as Dunbar's disappearance follows the return of the soldier in white on the ward. Major Major also drops out of sight, though under somewhat different circumstances. The victim of his father's joke in naming, as Mrs. Daneeka believed herself to be the victim of her phantom correspondent, Major Major is promoted to his current rank by a computer error yet remains a man without identity. (His name ironically reduplicates a word that is not a name and draws attention to the military rank he tries to evade.[73]) A total stranger, even to himself, he is abandoned by all of the people around him, some of whom resent his resemblance to Henry Fonda and some of whom suspect him of being Henry Fonda. He acquiesces to his loss of identity by assuming a literary mask (Washington Irving *et al.*) on official documents and then by voluntarily withdrawing from contact within the squadron, effectively "disappearing" himself by allowing visits in his office only when he is out. A basically moral man who cannot survive within the immoral climate of the military organization and who, like the chaplain, eventually finds pleasure in "sinning" by breaking the rules, Major Major acts in a way that reduces the official protocol to absurdity and parodies it by turning it upon itself.[74] Some of Heller's funniest scenes involve Major Major's shadowy figure in the woods fleeting past those whom he manages to avoid on the base.

Perhaps the most significant recurring image is not of an individual character but of the opposing ethics that define the real conflict and make the novel a contemporary morality play. The first ethic, associated with venal capitalism and false patriotism, epitomizes the competitive, business orientation of the military-economic complex and is exemplified by Colonel Cathcart and the other high-ranking officers who selfishly, often maliciously, run the machinery of war. They try to profit by others' losses and blatantly hope to advance their careers at the expense of their subordinates. Constance Denniston characterizes them as "aggressors" who prey on those who are sensitive to the brutalities in the world, who are maligned and helpless to do anything about their victimization, and who are not aggressive and therefore misfits in a world in which only power has value. "Yankee types who express their American know-how and individuality in a will to power," the profit-oriented officers succeed "in bullying those they cannot deceive."[75] The conflicting outlook, exemplified primarily by Yossarian, is far more humane. It is, according to Victor J. Milne, an "ethic of universal benevolence, which, as the symbolic importance of Sweden suggests, expresses itself economically in terms of socialism and politically in terms of non-repressive government."[76] The conflict between the two codes establishes the novel's moral, at times biblical, dimension.

Colonel Korn articulates the capitalistic ethic when he explains his and Cathcart's ambitions: "Everyone teaches us to aspire to higher things. A general is higher than a colonel, and a colonel is higher than a lieutenant colonel. So we're both aspiring" (435). Cathcart, obsessed with making the cover of the *Saturday Evening Post* because it would boost his career, is willing to try anything newsworthy or to engage in any questionable behavior. Not only does he keep volunteering his men for hazardous duty, thus becoming an anti-Christ who sends innocent young soldiers in cruciform war planes to their deaths to satisfy his own venality; he even enlists the assistance of the chaplain to help him achieve his goal. He tells Tappman to come up with an appropriate prayer to recite before the men embark on their missions: "Haven't you got anything humorous that stays away from waters and valleys and God? I'd like to keep away from the subject of religion altogether if we can" (197). Cathcart abandons the idea only after he discovers that enlisted men pray to the same god as officers do. For Cathcart, the notion of God is as convenient—and as dispensable—as Yossarian and the other flyers, the supply of whom seems inexhaustible.

Milo Minderbinder, another aspiring capitalist, is equally guilty. He justifies his unconscionable acts by saying he didn't start the war but is merely putting it on a "businesslike basis" (262) by making it more efficient and cost-effective. In a bittersweet parody of the American dream of success, he unilaterally commands M & M Enterprises, whose power rivals—and probably surpasses—the government's, and exercises his omnipotence by observing his own similarly unilateral code of immoral conduct. A prophet of profit, he becomes the New Age deity: "the corn god, the rain god and the rice god in backward regions where such crude gods were still worshiped by ignorant and superstitious people, and deep inside the jungles of Africa . . . large graven images of his mustached face could be found overlooking primitive stone altars red with human blood" (244). One in a long line of characters, fictional and real, who pervert theological principles for political gain, he also becomes Assistant Governor-General in Malta, knighted Major of the Royal Welsh Fusiliers, Vice-Shah of Oran, Caliph of Baghdad, Imām of Damascus, Sheik of Araby, and mayor of virtually every town and village in Italy in which he deals. But though he is revered by his trading partners and his superiors alike, both of whom benefit from his providence, Milo is really the embodiment of evil: the false god of a society whose only value is the bottom line, a sinister serpent who poisons innocence and good. As his name suggests, he achieves his success by binding minds and by shackling thought and decent human feelings. Curiously, though, Milo has a high regard for Yossarian because he cannot be bought: "anyone who would not steal from the country he loved would not steal from anybody" (64), Milo reasons. And he appreciates, as Cathcart does, the essential leadership role that Yossarian plays within the squadron: if Milo is to convert the other men to his thinking, he knows he must first have Yossarian on his side.

Provided there is an opportunity to make a sale or to negotiate a deal, Milo is willing to abandon all good will, as he does when he fails to secure the promised lodging for Yossarian in their travels and again when he deserts him during his search for the "kid" in Rome;

and in his monomaniacal pursuit of profit for his cartel, Milo is responsible for many of Pianosa's casualties. Despite his denial, he is indisputably, if indirectly, involved in the death of Mudd, who was killed while bombing the bridge at Orvieto, a mission Minderbinder initiated. Milo is also linked to Snowden's sufferings: when Yossarian reaches into the flight kit for morphine to relieve the gunner's pain, he finds that the morphine has been removed, leaving "no protection for Snowden against pain but the numbing shock of the gaping wound itself" (446). The Syrettes have been replaced by a note saying that what is good for M & M Enterprises is good for the country, a message that recalls Secretary of Defense Charles E. ("Engine Charlie") Wilson's famous remark about General Motors.[77] As David Seed points out, it is crucial that Milo speaks in slogans borrowed not only from Wilson but also from Ben Franklin (on the value of thrift), Calvin Coolidge ("the business of government is business"), and others; these self-promoting slogans identify Milo with a tradition of national enterprise,[78] which gives his greed currency.

And when the Syndicate falls on hard times because of Milo's impetuous desire to corner the world cotton market, he lands a lucrative contract with the Germans to destroy his own outfit. The Germans' promptness in paying their bills seals the deal for him, and he is able to disregard wholly the very real danger he creates for his own men. After an initial bombing and strafing of the base, he orders a second run to bring down the one supply shed still standing ("That will never do, Purvis," he tells a pilot in his fleet; "I've spoken to you about that kind of shoddy work before" [265]). The bombing is too much for even "the most phlegmatic observer" to stomach: high-ranking government officials are brought in to investigate; Congressmen denounce the atrocity and clamor for punishment; mothers with children in the service organize into militant groups and demand revenge. "Not one voice was raised in his defense"—until Milo opens his books to the public and discloses his tremendous profits. Naturally there is enough money on account to reimburse the government (which ultimately he doesn't do—"In a democracy, the government is the people," he reasons; "We're people, aren't we? So we might just as well keep the money and eliminate the middleman" [266]—the same curious premise advanced to eliminate the soldier in white) and to continue buying Egyptian cotton. The sweetest part of the arrangement, he points out, is that everybody, even Mudd, owns a share of the enterprise and therefore reaps a benefit.

The moral of the story is that Milo's operation is a story without a moral; and any act, no matter how heinous, can be forgiven so long as it results in a profit. Only Yossarian recognizes the sheer lunacy and irony of the situation—that the abused flyers who fight the real war are forgotten, while a noncombat mess-hall officer who bombs his own comrades is hailed as a hero for his effort. Both in his tired rhetoric about serving the best interests of his country and in his volunteering to fly additional missions (knowing that Cathcart will never let him do so), Milo represents the patriotic cant that usually accompanies American greed.[79]

By contrast to Cathcart and the other profiteering aggressors and villains, Yossarian, a man of principle, repudiates and challenges their selfish values. Personally he could not care less about being promoted, receiving medals, or becoming a hero: he simply wants to stay alive—or, as he puts it, "to live forever or die in the attempt" (30). His attitude, however, puts him outside the system. Yet, ironically, the further outside the system Yossarian goes, the greater are the conventional rewards he receives: he is awarded the Distinguished Flying Cross for his failed mission over Ferrara after Cathcart decides "to act boastfully about something we ought to be ashamed of. That's a trick that never seems to fail" (143); and he is promised another medal, a promotion, and elevation to national hero after he goes AWOL and refuses to fly anymore.

The position of outsider is a familiar one to Yossarian. Heller originally conceived of his protagonist as being "*out*side the culture in every way—ethnically as well as others"; for that reason he made him an Assyrian, "somebody who was almost a *new* man . . . somebody as a person who has a capability of ultimately divorcing himself completely from all emotional or psychological ties."[80] Thus, unlike even the most minor characters who have some personal history from which they draw in their relationships with others in the novel, Heller specifically withholds such information about Yossarian: there is no mention of his home, his parents, his schooling. Once, and only once, does Heller refer to Yossarian by his first name, John ("the name that call girls use to identify customers . . . so typically *nebbish*"), which, given Yossarian's penchant for falling in love with Italian prostitutes—and his occasional near-prostitution of his own values—is both comic and symbolic. Just as

52

Milos Forman in his film adaptation of *One Flew Over the Cuckoo's Nest* gave Big Nurse a first name, Mildred, to make her seem more vulnerable, Heller uses Yossarian's first name to keep him from becoming completely a symbol and to satisfy his own authorial whim: "There were certain instances in there where I could not avoid putting something in because it made me laugh."[81]

Yossarian, though, *is* a symbol—of moral protest and thoughtful defiance against the absurd injustice symbolized by Catch-22. His unusual surname and racial origin as well as his isolation suggest he is also an Adamic figure, like Chance in *Being There,* though more deliberate, much more conscious of his role and his effect on others. While for him Pianosa is hardly an idyllic surrounding, he is nonetheless a type of the first man, initially naive, later anxious to return to a state of innocence and even, at the end, to the new Eden of Sweden and the paradisaical munificence it offers.[82] "Where were you born?" asks a fat colonel; "On a battlefield," replies Yossarian. "No, no. In what state were you born?" he asks. "In a state of innocence," counters Yossarian (440). War has violated that innocence and created in him a deeper awareness of the violent death he already fears and of his complicity, however unintentional, in the deaths of others. His flight over Ferrara, for example, resulted in the death of Kraft (one of the characters in the novel, like Orr, who never appears except in memory) and his crew. And Yossarian believes that his inability to help the young gunner precipitated Snowden's death. Significantly, that fatal mission during which Yossarian loses his faith in man's immortality occurs over Avignon, "the city where Christianity suffered its grave doubts as two Popes struggled for power, in the manner of generals Dreedle and Peckem."[83]

Disgusted by the system's hypocrisy and feeling dirty (an externalizing of his guilt) after Snowden "spilled his secret," Yossarian sheds his clothing. The decision to go uniformless both asserts his individual existence and subverts military rank (literally and metaphorically), since without their uniforms all men are reduced to the same level of humanity.[84] His attempt to retrieve some of his lost "primal innocence" is first manifested at Snowden's funeral. He climbs a tree and, like a second Adam in his naked innocence,[85] at a distance observes the ceremony, which occurs on the third day after Snowden's death and marks the third day of Yossarian's nudity.[86] While sitting in what he calls "the tree of life and of knowledge of good and evil" (269), he is approached by Milo, the capitalistic

53

serpent, who reenacts with him—somewhat surrealistically—the biblical fall of man. Wearing sinister, dark garments, Milo "inches" up the tree, "hisses" at Yossarian, and offers in place of the fruit a piece of chocolate-covered Egyptian cotton. The larger symbolic meaning of the scene brings the opposing ethics into focus: Milo is really trying to tempt Yossarian into ceasing his resistance and submitting to further exploitation by the system; by surrendering, Yossarian would give Milo the tacit approval to take advantage of all the men in his mess halls (and by implication to exploit them in any way the institution or the Syndicate finds profitable). But the transubstantiation of cotton into candy is ultimately unsuccessful;[87] Yossarian refuses the cotton ball as fully as he rejects Milo's rationalizations about the deadly repercussions of his business schemes. He had earlier rejected Major Major's temptation to fly only milk runs and ultimately rejects Cathcart's even more costly bargain.

Yossarian soon experiences another loss of innocence—the death of his friend Nately ("newly born"),[88] the idealistic all-American boy. Like Snowden, whose name also implies his unviolated purity, Nately is the diametrical opposite of wicked Milo; and after his death Yossarian's strange behavior intensifies: he refuses to fly again and becomes to others a model of resistance. Yossarian's mission—the very word alluding to his high calling and his biblical, at times messianic, dimension[89]—to end additional missions is oddly heroic. Even Korn intuits his mythic stature. "Who does he think he is—Achilles?" (401), he asks, making an interesting analogy to the *Iliad* and the whole epic tradition.

Yossarian's innocence is further corrupted, and his faith severely tested, during and after his last journey to Rome. Walking through the devastated streets, he sees a world that has gone completely awry: the "Eternal City," the symbol of Western man's philosophic, moral, and artistic ideals (comparable to the Dresden of *Slaughterhouse-Five* before the fateful firebombing), is off balance, and "nothing warped seems bizarre anymore" (421), as grotesque visions of humanity pass through the shimmering, sulphurous, surrealistic atmosphere.[90] He observes suffering soldiers, despondent women, drunken men, poorly clad and sickly looking children; he sees a small boy cruelly knocked to the ground—all the images from Freudian nightmares.[91] There is even a man beating a dog, a sight that confirms that what was simply a dream for Raskolnikov is a fact for Yossarian.[92] A neon sign reads "TONY'S RESTAURANT. FINE FOOD AND DRINK. KEEP OUT." The entire night "was filled with horrors, and he thought he knew how Christ must have felt as he walked through the world, like a psychiatrist through a ward full of nuts, like a victim through a prison full of thieves" (424). (Heller's original title for the chapter, appropriately, was "Night of Horrors."[93]) And the farther Yossarian travels into the city, the more normal and logical the strident grotesqueness and insanity seem.[94]

On previous trips to Rome, Yossarian was interested only in himself, in escaping the lunacy of Pianosa by plunging into sexual liaisons which momentarily relieved his frustration over Cathcart's tyranny. But on this journey, which Heller described as "a surrealistic scene told in realistic details,"[95] he is also concerned with someone else, Nately's whore's kid sister, who is as much a victim of the system as he. Wholly rejecting Milo's profit orientation, Yossarian embraces more than ever its extreme and admits his culpability in creating some of the evils in the world and his responsibility to bring about change. It is not enough for him to dismiss societal wrongs by arguing, as Milo does, that he didn't start them. Yossarian realizes he must repudiate the original sin in order to return to grace: "Every victim," he explains, "was a culprit, every culprit a victim, and somebody had to stand up sometime to try to break the lousy chain of inherited habit that was imperiling them all" (414).

His descent into the underworld of the Roman streets is a solitary one. The diabolical Milo, who knows the territory well, at the last moment decides not to accompany Yossarian: apprised of another business opportunity, Milo chooses instead to deal in profitable black market tobacco. The police, either indifferent or involved in the conspiracy, turn out to be as unsupportive as Milo.[96] Even inanimate objects take on the disturbing characteristics of their surroundings: the ambulance becomes an engine of torture, not a vehicle of mercy, as it bypasses an ailing soldier to incarcerate a screaming civilian. The grating sound of a snow shovel is heard, but there is no snow on the ground to shovel, only a shower of teeth and blood. The familiar fountain that Yossarian uses as a landmark to guide him to the Officer's Club is dry when he tries to drink from it, a perfect symbol of the aridity and barrenness of the surrounding wasteland.[97]

Despite his resolve for positive action, Yossarian begins to feel as powerless as the denizens of the city, as unable as they to challenge the control of the "mobs with clubs." Confirming his fear that all may indeed be lost, he encounters Michaela's corpse on the pavement. One of the few women associated with the army who was *not* a whore, Michaela had been raped by Aarfy, held hostage, and finally killed and thrown from the officers' apartment window. For Yossarian, the demonic distortion that has corrupted the world culminates in the image of her maimed body,[98] and he is outraged by Aarfy's passivity over her brutal murder. Aarfy, whose surname and nickname suggest his bestial nature and lack of humanity, says simply that Michaela has no right to be lying in the street: "It's after curfew" (428).

Aarfy's cruelty is not without precedent: on another occasion, he had suggested to Nately and Yossarian that they keep their three whores "until after the curfew" and then push them out the window; and he brags about the time he and his fraternity brothers tricked "two dumb high-school girls from town into the fraternity house and made them put out for all the fellows," then trapped them in the house for ten hours and "smacked their faces a little" before throwing them out (246). Earlier Aarfy had observed Snowden's suffering over Avignon with a similar dispassion and showed neither concern nor empathy.

Yossarian's cries for justice seem answered when the military police arrive. But once again regulation proves more important than reality, a military form more significant than a corpse. "They arrested Yossarian for being in Rome without a pass. They apologized to Aarfy for intruding and led Yossarian away between them, gripping him under each arm with fingers as hard as steel manacles" (429). And (as Minna Doskow points out, as if to emphasize the metamorphosis of humane law into its demonic opposite), "the M.P.'s no longer retain even their superficial humanity; their flesh having turned to steel, they resemble unyielding machinery rather than men."[99] Yossarian learns in this climactic chapter that there is no justice in the world, that the good are victims in the hands of malicious forces, who are overpowering in their numbers.[100] And he finally understands Aarfy's double entendre that he "never paid for it" in his life.

It is no coincidence that, upon his return from Rome, Yossarian joins, albeit briefly, in the conspiracy of evil around him by accepting Cathcart's "odious deal," a temptation of greater substance than

Milo's. The only condition is that he must agree to be "pals" with Cathcart and Korn and to like them. While Yossarian realizes that *some* catch is inescapable, this one is particularly loathsome because it requires him to repudiate the values he has fought to preserve and to betray his loyalty to his dead friends—his *real* pals, Nately, Hungry Joe, McWatt, Dunbar, Clevinger and the other victimized flyers—of whom he is reminded by the phantom who appears and reappears, cryptically whispering that "We've got your pal" (442). At first Yossarian jumps at the chance to escape the absurdity of Pianosa, no matter how high the moral cost, and wrestles with the temptation. "Between me and every ideal I always find Scheisskopfs, Peckems, Korns and Cathcarts. And that," he says, "sort of changes the ideal" (454).

After he is stabbed by Nately's whore, who acts allegorically as a projection of his own conscience,[101] Yossarian decides to refuse the offer. Heller says that, by forcing him to associate his injury with Nately's death, Nately's whore "becomes a symbol of [his] guilt and responsibility for never intervening in the injustices he knows exist everywhere." Although Yossarian had done nothing directly to cause Nately's death, he also had "done nothing to prevent it."[102] Unlike the formerly apathetic prostitute who now devotes herself to avenging the wrong she believes Yossarian committed by allowing Nately to die, he has failed to change his behavior because he believes that nothing he does will have an impact on the system. Thus he is more guilty of prostitution than she. The flesh wound he receives at her hand is minor compared to his psychic wound, but it sends him back to the hospital to contemplate his options and plan his strategy.

Cathcart, never one to pass up an opportunity to capitalize on someone else's weakness or misfortune, uses the occasion of Yossarian's hospitalization to set him up further. He announces that Yossarian has saved him and Korn from a murderous Nazi assassin and proclaims him a hero. ("Can you imagine that for a sin?" Yossarian asks Tappman. "Saving Colonel Cathcart's life! That's one crime I don't want on my record" [444].) In his anguish, Yossarian relives Snowden's wounding and death (as he had earlier relived Nately's death) and remembers Snowden's secret about the importance of man's spirit in the face of his mortality, which strengthens his resolve. Even though capitulating to Cathcart would ensure the safety he has zealously pursued, he knows now that there are greater horrors than physical pain and death. To yield to the aggressors is to kill the spirit and deny the truth of Snowden's secret. Without protest against the forces that render human beings garbage, he would become nothing more than garbage, a corpse to be flung from a window or a faceless rotting mass to be buried anonymously.

"Goddammit," he tells Danby, "I've got friends who were killed in this war. I can't make a deal now" (456–57). At the same time, though, it seems there is no way he can avoid the deal, because by staying he must either continue to fly or face a court-martial on trumped-up charges that the other men would probably believe. And, either way, in the end he would again become the victim of the exploiters who would use him as an example to keep others in line.[103] Worse still, especially if he were to remain in the hospital, he would linger passively, like the lobotomized McMurphy in *Cuckoo's Nest*, as proof that the authorities of Catch-22 indeed have the right "to do anything we can't stop them from doing" (416).

Significantly, while in the hospital, Yossarian learns from the chaplain that Orr is alive and well and in Sweden. Victor J. Milne points out that Orr's escape, the redemptive and healing miracle Yossarian so desperately needs, has an obvious religious significance, "for seen in a theological context, his crash-landing in the Adriatic is a symbolic baptism and the sudden news of his safety gives the whole episode the quality of resurrection following death—a miraculous reversal of the seemingly irrevocable catastrophe."[104] It is a baptism foreshadowed by at least two other prominent events: Kid Sampson's blood raining down on all the bathers at the beach and Snowden's bloody guts spilling out over Yossarian above Avignon. Orr, the "freakish, likeable dwarf with . . . a thousand valuable skills that would keep him in a low income group all his life" and "an uncanny knowledge of wildlife" (321–22), proves by his miraculous rebirth that he is not the mere innocent everyone assumed him to be but an adaptable, inventive survivor. A doer rather than a contemplative, he personifies the qualities of intelligence and endurance that make possible the survival of humanity under the worst conditions of oppression and exploitation. Moreover, Milne notes, "While the chaplain engages in futile efforts to reason with Colonel Cathcart, while Yossarian carries on a futile and dangerous revolt, Orr quietly practices the skills that will ensure his survival. Only after Orr has acted can Yossarian grasp the possibility of escape that was and still is open to him, and then he realizes he must imitate Orr,"[105] whose very name suggests the alternative he provides. Yossarian tells Danby to "bring me apples, and chestnuts too" (459); it is not too late to heed the message Orr had been trying to teach him all along through his parables.

Making a separate peace, Yossarian, in the words of John W. Hunt, "bids his own farewell to arms with hope in his heart."[106] His decision to desert is more than defiance and certainly not cowardice; he has done his duty and flown more missions than anyone else in the squadron.[107] Flying additional missions would not be a service to his country in a just war, which by this point is waning; the real threat is no longer from Hitler but from Cathcart, Korn, Scheisskopf, Milo, and the other aggressors who perpetuate the absurdity for their own profit. Thus, concludes Milne, Yossarian "enacts Heller's ethical judgment that an individual has no right to submit to injustice when his action will help to maintain an unjust system for the desertion is a positive moral act calculated to discomfort the exploiters, whereas facing the court-martial would represent a paralysis of the will, a desire to maintain purity of conscience at the cost of inaction."[108] Choosing not simply to survive but to act morally by refusing a world that is immoral,[109] for the first time Yossarian demonstrates true courage as a hero. As if in celebration of Nately's aspirations and Snowden's ideals, he reverses Nately's axiom and decides to live on his feet rather than to die—or live—on his knees.[110] (And, as Heller says, his action also "saves" innumerable future Natelys and Snowdens.[111]) In embracing desertion, Yossarian commits to the only sane and moral choice for himself in a world of insane choices. "I'm not running *away* from my responsibilities. I'm running *to* them" (461), he tells Danby. And run he does—for his life.

He intends to start his redemptive mission by "saving the life" of Nately's whore's sister, an act whose morally responsible nature is underscored by Yossarian's allusion to a well-known biblical paradox: Cathcart's deal, he acknowledges, is not a way to save himself but a way to lose himself. Heller has already established Yossarian as a kind of Christ figure who suffers on behalf of others; is forced to undergo trials and temptations of the flesh and spirit; and is linked to crosses (plastered on the crosslike ceiling of his plane, awarded the Distinguished Flying Cross for his special mission). The selflessness he displays at the end, however, is his most outstanding redemptive act, and it gives strength to others. Though his society (like Chance's) may, as a whole, be too far gone to be saved, he not only finds salvation himself but also offers hope for Danby, who encourages and subsidizes his flight.

Yossarian's example of passionate defiance particularly emboldens Chaplain Tappman, who decides to stay and "persevere. I'll nag and badger Colonel Cathcart and Colonel Korn every time I see them. . . . I'll even pick on General Dreedle. . . . Then I'll pick on General Peckem, and even on General Scheisskopf" (461). The ostracized and utterly ineffectual chaplain,[112] by patiently accepting all the indignation cast upon him, had become no more than "a sincerely helpful man who was never able to help anyone" (280). His faith, shaken by the stream of meaningless deaths he observed, compounded by his inability to convince Cathcart to stop raising the number of missions, had made him question both his own role and the "wisdom and justice of an immortal, omnipotent, omniscient, humane, universal, anthropomorphic, English-speaking, Anglo-Saxon, pro-American God" (293). But through Yossarian's redemptive act, Tappman's faith is restored. While initially confused by Yossarian's avoidance of combat, he eventually follows him into the hospital with a disease of his own invention, "Wisconsin shingles" (372). (He had sinned, says Heller, and it was good; in fact, the chaplain felt positively marvelous.) The liberation the chaplain experiences through lying is the result of his learning to detach language from truth (something the military has long done[113]) and to "turn vice into virtue and slander into truth" through the "handy technique of protective rationalization" (372). The "miracle" he announces to Yossarian becomes as real to him as his mystical apparition was. "If Orr could row to Sweden" and Yossarian could emulate Orr's example, Tappman determines that he too "can triumph" (461) over his superiors.

It is precisely Yossarian's crazy challenge to the system by his defiance of Catch-22 that makes him so likeable and, paradoxically, so sane. Like McMurphy in *One Flew Over the Cuckoo's Nest*, he takes up a fight against an institution so large that he has no real chance to win because he realizes that the significance of the protest is in the effort, not necessarily the result. Just as McMurphy bloodies his hands trying to lift the control panel even though he knows he cannot succeed, Yossarian answers Danby's warning that he will never make it to Sweden with, "Hell, Danby, I know that. But at least I'll be trying" (462).

His final gesture is the most affecting because it most affects the system: he simply ceases to be a part of it.[114] In following his own convictions and not those of his superiors,[115] in celebrating life over the sterile bureaucracy, Yossarian brings a kind of salvation to those he leaves behind, as McMurphy brought salvation to the men on the ward. And, like McMurphy, he also confirms that, in a world of illusions, insanity is sometimes a mask for true sanity. Ultimately, Yossarian's brand of "insanity is contagious" (14)—as contagious as both the laughs and the truths in Heller's novel.

CHAPTER 3

But it's the truth even if it

didn't happen.

One Flew Over the

Cuckoo's Nest

In the shadow land the

hawks are just as

dangerous dreamed or

actual.

Seven Prayers by

Grandma Whittier

Hail to the Chief:

One Flew Over the Cuckoo's Nest

K E N K E S E Y has been described as a psychedelic outlaw and a madman, the "Dr. Strange" (one of his nicknames from the sixties) of American letters. An outstanding high school athlete and champion wrestler, he graduated from the University of Oregon and continued study on the West Coast, where he first discovered the bohemian life he still follows. In fact, over the years, like a handful of other prominent American authors (particularly Ernest Hemingway, F. Scott Fitzgerald, and Jerzy Kosinski), he has turned his life into a kind of fiction: traveling across the country with his band of Merry Pranksters (whose adventures were chronicled by Tom Wolfe in his own cult classic, *The Electric Kool-Aid Acid Test;* by fellow Prankster Ken Babbs in *On the Bus;* and by Kesey himself in *The Further Inquiry* [1990]); fraternizing with Timothy Leary and other philosophers of the hippie movement; fleeing to Mexico to avoid prosecution for marijuana possession; living communally with wife Faye (by whom he has three children) and others, including Mountain Girl, who bore his fourth child, Sunshine; and, of course, writing two major novels and other fiction.

While attending graduate school at Stanford University on a creative writing fellowship in the late fifties, Kesey met Vik Lovell, a graduate student in psychology. Lovell told him about experiments with "psychomimetic" drugs at the Veteran's Hospital in Menlo Park. Kesey soon volunteered to be a paid subject. He began taking Ditran, LSD, and other hallucinogens (especially peyote and mescaline) regularly, a practice he continued outside the hospital as well. When the original drug experiments ended, Kesey accepted a job as night attendant on the psychiatric ward at Menlo Park, again at Lovell's suggestion. The confluence of these stimuli—the drugs and the hospital environment—caused him to abandon the novel he was writing about San Francisco's North Beach, entitled *Zoo*,[1] and to undertake one about a topic much closer to him: the plight of

64

inmates on a psychiatric ward who defiantly assert their humanity in the face of overwhelming forces that dehumanize and destroy.[2] That novel, published in 1962 and dedicated to Lovell, "who told me dragons did not exist, then led me to their lairs," was *One Flew Over the Cuckoo's Nest,* and it became the credo for an entire generation of rebels.

Kesey himself recalls the events that prompted his best-known and sometimes controversial work. In an essay entitled "Who Flew Over What?" and published in *Kesey's Garage Sale* (1973), he writes:

> Finally only the grinning echos remain, the pencilled flesh rearing outta the past in authoritarian attitudes, like guides in a museum tour leading us back to nineteensixty or so . . . and me, a stoodunt, gets asked by my buddy, a sighcologiz, does I wanna go over to the local VA nuthouse, sign up for the government experiment, take some of these new mind-altering chemicals?
>
> Does I get paid? I wanna know.
>
> Twenty bucks a session, he says.
>
> All right, I say. Long as it's for the U S of A.
>
> . . . and me, a jock, never even been drunk but that one night in my frat house before my wedding and even then not too drunk—just a token toot for my brothers' benefit—going to the *nut house* to take *dope* under of course official auspices . . .
>
> "See anything yet?" asks the doctor.
>
> "Nope," I tell him, visions swirling indescribable between us.
>
> "How about auditory, any sounds?"
>
> "Not a thing." Just the room full of men outside my door (the experiment being conducted on an actual ward) clamoring their mutual misery, calling with every word and laugh and cough for help, for light, for God at least . . .
>
> Six hours later out of my room on the ward back in the doctor's office he gives me a check for twenty dollars, pulling on a smile like it was a surgical mask, and tells me come back again next Tuesday when "We'll try another one on you." "What was this one?"
>
> "It's called lysergic acid diethylamide twenty-five."
>
> I was there on the next Tuesday, and the next and the next. Six weeks later I'd bought my first ounce of grass. Six months later I had a job at that hospital as a psychiatric aide, and an issue of white uniforms, and a key that opened the doctor's office.[3]

After a few months in his new position, Kesey settled into a midnight-to-eight shift which gave him stretches of five to six hours, five days a week, during which he "had nothing to do but a little mopping and buffing, check the wards every forty-five minutes with a flashlight, be coherent to the night nurse stopping by on her hourly rounds, write my novel, and talk to the sleepless nuts."[4] With access to the various medicines, Kesey would often write under the influence of drugs.

During one of these sessions, he got the inspiration for Chief Bromden, the novel's narrator. Tom Wolfe, in *The Electric Kool-Aid Acid Test*, reports that "for some reason peyote does this . . . Kesey starts getting eyelid movies of faces . . . from out of nowhere. He knows nothing about Indians and has never met an Indian, but suddenly here is a full-blown Indian—Chief Broom—the solution, the whole mothering key, to the novel."[5]

Peyote was the inspiration for Chief, Kesey claimed, "because it was after choking down eight of the little cactus plants that I wrote the first three pages. These pages remained almost completely unchanged through the numerous rewrites the book went through, and from this first spring I drew all the passion and perception the narrator spoke with during the ten month's writing that followed."[6] Kesey attributed the fact that the narrator was an Indian[7] to the well-known association between peyote and certain tribes of the southwest. " 'The drug's reputation is bound to make one think of our red brothers,' was how I used to explain it to admiring fans"— though now even he admits the story seems a bit apocryphal.[8]

However Chief came to be, it is his first-person narration—highly subjective and often hallucinatory—that gives *Cuckoo's Nest* its metaphoric richness, its peculiar horror, and ultimately its emotional force. In fact, to render successfully and credibly Chief's schizophrenic point of view, Kesey felt he needed more than the initial, if fortuitous, hit of peyote and so he precipitated temporary mock-psychotic states in himself through the continued use of psychomimetic drugs and even arranged to be given electroshock therapy. The writing of the novel "on the ward and on drugs" was, according to him, a way of "double-checking my material so to speak,"[9] and the resulting account of Chief's condition, so grimly accurate, is an excellent portrait of contemporary man fragmented, debilitated, and emasculated by institutionalized technology (a familiar theme among contemporary writers, especially Vonnegut).

What makes *Cuckoo's Nest* so memorable is the way that the individual ultimately triumphs over the institution's anonymous horrors: the inmates learn to run the asylum and finally, like Bromden, they discover how to escape it completely and make themselves whole and potent again.

Few characters in fact or fiction could survive over two hundred electroshock therapy treatments (ESTs), but the hulking six-foot-eight, almost 300-pound Chief is a giant of a man. A former high school athlete and a combat veteran of World War II, he possesses enormous physical strength. In the dehumanized and dehumanizing environment of the Combine and Nurse Ratched's ward, however, he feels small, puny, and incapable of real action. Nicknamed Chief Broom, he is reduced to a topic of ridicule for the Black orderlies and regarded simply as an object, indistinguishable from the broom that he pushes. Virtually his only moving appendage, the broom symbolizes his impotence, both in American society and in the institution that serves as a microcosm of that society. Yet his metamorphosis from a man once so mighty that he speared salmon barehanded to a mere tool for the Nurse's staff has more than a sexual dimension; it also illustrates the central contrast in the book, of machine (or "inside," typified by the wheels and cogs of the Combine, whose agent is the Big Nurse Ratched and whose victims are the emasculated inmates) vs. nature (or "outside," typified by the world of natural sights and smells away from the Combine, a world that exists for the fog-enshrouded patients only in memory and recollection).

As Barry Leeds demonstrates in his excellent study of Kesey's work, even Chief's legal name, a kind of false identity imposed upon him by others, is a depreciation of his worth. His father, a once shrewd and powerful tribal chief whose Indian name Tee Ah Milla-toona meant "The-Pine-That-Stands-Tallest-on-the-Mountain," was so henpecked by the white woman who became his wife (and who represents the pressure brought upon Indians by white American society) that—in a reversal of marital customs in both Indian and white societies—he changed his name and adopted hers. This abandonment of his native heritage, compounded by the subsequent usurping of his land by the government, caused Tee Ah Millatoona to lose his identity entirely. The repercussions of this loss, which Kesey invests with great significance, are felt most strongly by their son, who also bears his mother's name of Bromden and not his father's Indian one. "At the heart of the twentieth-century problem of Bromden, his father, and their people," writes Leeds, is the separation from their cultural past. "The artificial identities of 'Mr. Bromden' and 'Chief Broom' imposed upon Bromden [the son] by the matriarchal and mechanistic elements of society diminish him enormously. The first robs him of his masculine pride and his racial identity, the second of his very humanity." For Kesey, the plight of the Indian, the "Vanishing American," represents, in a highly distilled form, that of all American individualists. Like Heller, who through the character of Chief White Halfoat in *Catch-22* portrayed the displacement of Indians, Kesey "forces us to abstract from this extreme case [of Bromden] the realization that our own identities as self-determining individuals have been considerably eroded and are further threatened by a computerized civilization,"[10] particularly by those repressive institutions that, because of the weight of their authority, prohibit meaningful action.

Bromden responds to the erosion of his identity by pretending to be a deaf mute. Initially unable—and later unwilling—to communicate with others, he progressively withdraws from society. But, as he notes, that society had already withdrawn from him: "it wasn't me that started acting deaf; it was people that first started acting like I was too dumb to hear or see or say anything at all."[11] Even as a young boy he felt his invisibility in a white man's world and learned that Indians are misfits, bereft of any real sense of self. He remembers how, when he was ten, the government agents who came to appropriate his tribe's lands dismissed him as an "overdone little Hiawatha" (180) and then overlooked him completely. Droning on in front of him about the squalor and primitivism of his family's adobe hut, the sole female agent in the group—"an old white-haired woman in an outfit so stiff and heavy it must be armor plate" (179) who bore a striking resemblance in appearance, tone, attitude, and mechanical demeanor to Ratched—didn't bother to listen when he spoke. Moreover, she prevented the other agents from attempting to negotiate with his father, the chief, because direct contact with Mrs. Bromden, a white woman more familiar with government and technology, would make "our job . . . a great deal easier" (182). Other incidents in the community and later in the service (when he watches a buddy at Anzio tied to a tree, screaming for help and water, but is unable to respond for fear "they'd of cut me in half" [122]; or when superiors—"anybody with more stripes" [178]—

ignored him and treated him as if he were too stupid to respond)
cause Bromden to question his own worth, and eventually he
assumes the cover of complete silence to avoid such painful engage-
ments altogether. This kind of self-induced mutism, shared by
characters as diverse as Oskar Matzerath in *The Tin Drum* (1962),
the nameless Boy in *The Painted Bird* (1965), and the violated
heroine, Anna, in *Lancelot* (1977), is, in contemporary literature, an
effective symbol for alienation. Within the asylum walls, however,
Chief is further alienated; he becomes just one more hopeless case
lost in the anonymity of the institution, and no one even tries
anymore to communicate with him.

Repeated visits to the asylum's "Shock Shop" have left Bromden
in a mental twilight zone that he calls "the fog," a decidedly
unnatural element which represents for him the perversion and
corruption by Big Nurse and the mechanistic Combine of all that is
natural. Serving throughout the novel as a barometer of his emotional and psychological state, the imaginary fog thickens and
dissipates according to the fluctuations of his mental and spiritual
health.[12] Although the fog exists only in Chief's muddled mind, the
"machine" that he thinks produces it has a basis in two very real,
very painful experiences: the tranquilizing but brain-benumbing
EST treatments ordered by Ratched, and the actual fog machine of
World War II, operated by military intelligence to hide what was
occurring on the airfield. "Whenever intelligence figured there
might be a bombing attack," recalls Chief, "or if the generals had
something secret they wanted to pull—out of sight, hid so good that
even the spies on the base couldn't see what went on—they fogged
the field" (116). (Ironically, Bromden is correct in suggesting that
the real fog is the larger institutional bureaucracy of the military,
as evidenced also in *Catch-22*, *Slaughterhouse-Five*, and *Sophie's
Choice*.)

Chief believes that the Combine's authority figures have installed
a similar machine in the walls of the ward to weaken and control
him—an instrument of deception which can distort his thinking and
contain him within the artificial order of the institution. Yet after a
while, Chief accedes to the fog's hypnotic thickness. "You had a
choice," he explains; "you could either strain and look at things that
appeared in front of you in the fog, painful as it might be, or you
could relax and lose yourself" (117). In his quiet desperation, he opts
for the latter.

But Chief's recovery is contingent upon his reentry into the world of the living, particularly the community of nature. For him, though, it is a long journey back: with the exception of the Chronics, he is the patient who is the most far gone and therefore the hardest to reach.[13] Only with the help of Randle Patrick (Mack) McMurphy, the new arrival in the asylum, is Chief able to begin sorting out what is real and what is not. As he learns to distinguish between fact and hallucinatory fantasy, he redevelops some of his manhood and asserts his new strength. Over Ratched's objection, he casts the crucial (but disqualified) vote to watch the World Series on television. Chief's vote not only breaks the 20–20 tie; it makes twenty-one, "a majority," significant here as the legal age of manhood and also the winning hand in blackjack.[14] He joins the other patients on the excursion away from the asylum, a male bonding ritual which builds his confidence and prepares him for his return to the natural world "outside"; and afterwards, at McMurphy's urging (in a special and secret bond between them), lifts the control panel in anticipation of his ultimate escape.

But as the fog diminishes, Chief finds that his new, unobfuscated vision is painful. It hurts, he says, "the way I was hurt by seeing things in the Army, in the war. The way I was hurt by seeing what happened to Papa and the tribe" (121). Without the security of the fog to separate him from his traumatic reality, he becomes more aware of the world and thus more vulnerable to the dangers inherent in it. Yet only by confronting the forces that initially caused him to lose his identity and propelled him into the fog—the petticoat tyranny of his mother, the bitterness of Anzio, the sadness at the loss of Columbia Gorge—can Chief successfully escape it. Bromden starts to use the negative experiences in constructive and instructive ways, to reorganize the sources of his own pain and paralysis so that each time he recalls key moments in his past, he retrieves a part of himself and becomes more conscious.[15] Every recollection of a painful memory marks a return to health, and only out of these fragments can he become whole again.

The further Chief moves out of the fog, the more the nature of his narrative changes. No longer tentative and fantasylike, his story becomes stronger, more lyrical. The paranoiac hallucinations about the cogs of the Combine machine that pervade the early parts of the novel give way to a clarity, even a poetry. Perhaps the best example of the change is in Chief's recounting of an earlier conversation with

McMurphy. Heading back to the ward after the fishing trip, they drove through the town in which McMurphy had lived as a boy. The sight of a rag hanging from a tree branch reminded Mack of his first sexual experience, which had occurred when he was ten and which established his reputation as a "dedicated lover." The memory of that experience prompted Mack to share the details with Chief, who was not at all surprised to learn that his new friend's sense of identity and mission had always been secure; after all, even in the asylum Mack maintained a strong sense of his individuality. On admission, he corrects Ratched's mispronunciation of his name and warns her never to call him "Mr. McMurry" again. Chief, on the other hand, has lost his identity and prefers the anonymity that his muteness and the Combine's fog provide. Yet his recollection and appreciation of Mack's story (a contemporary parallel to the naming scenes in heroic epics) demonstrates his growing recognition that identity is destiny; it is evident that Chief is beginning very consciously to prepare himself for the power that McMurphy will transfer to him. "I noticed vaguely that I was getting so's I could see some good in the life around me. McMurphy was teaching me. I was feeling better than I'd remembered feeling since I was a kid, when everything was good and the land was still singing kid's poetry to me" (216).

He records the conversation just that way—in a kind of kid's poetry, as the following section (quoted here with line divisions added to Kesey's text) of that passage indicates:

"Look over there, see
a dress?" He pointed out back.
"In the branch of that tree?
A rag, yellow and black?"
I was able to see
a thing like a flag,
flapping high in the branches over a shed.
"The first girl ever drug me to bed
wore that very same dress.
I was about ten and she was probably less,
and at the time a lay seemed like such a big deal
I asked her if didn't she think, *feel*,
we oughta *announce* it some way?
Like, say,
tell our folks, 'Mom,

Judy and me got engaged today.'
And I meant what I said,
I was that big a fool;
I thought if you made it, man, you were legally *wed*,
right there on the spot,
whether it was something you wanted or not,
and that there wasn't any breaking the rule.
But this little whore—
at the most eight or nine—
reached down and got her dress off the floor
and said it was mine,
said, 'You can hang this up someplace,
I'll go home in my drawers,
announce it that way—
they'll get the idea.'
Jesus, nine years old,"
he said, reached over and pinched Candy's nose,
"and knew a lot more than a good many pros."
She bit his hand, laughing,
and he studied the mark.
"So, anyhow, after she went home in her pants
I waited till dark
when I had the chance
to throw that damned dress out in the night—
but you feel that wind? Caught the dress like a kite
and whipped it around the house outa sight
and the next morning, by God, it was hung up in that tree
for the whole town,
was how I figured then, to turn out and see."
He sucked his hand, so woebegone
that Candy laughed and gave it a kiss.
"So my colors were flown, and from that day to this
it seemed I might as well live up to my name—
dedicated lover—and it's the God's truth:
that little nine-year-old kid out of my youth's
the one who's to blame."
The house drifted past.
He yawned and winked.
"Taught me to love,
bless her sweet ass." (217–18)

72

Various critics, beginning with Malcolm Cowley, who taught creative writing while Kesey was at Stanford, have commented on the primitive but remarkable poetry of Chief's words. M. Gilbert Porter, for instance, who discusses this aspect of the novel at length, notes that Chief displays rhyme on his way to reason; he has "both the special vision that characterizes the seer and the power of description that characterizes the sayer. His sentences are vivid with image, metaphor, simile, and analogy, rhythmical with meter, sometimes roughly harmonized with rhyme, and expansive with symbol. He also employs synecdoche as a central poetic element, and . . . not conscious of his poetic devices, [he] serves as Kesey's intimate functionary in the perception, articulation, and embodiment of the thematic progress from fragmentation to wholeness."[16] As Chief learns to articulate his memories and experiences, he begins to possess and master them.

This clarity of vision and poetry of expression is again apparent in the final EST scene. Ordered to undergo another treatment as punishment for coming to McMurphy's aid in the shower fight (a scene that suggests that McMurphy can't go it alone much longer), Chief vows not to get fogged in afterward. He forces himself to keep repeating McMurphy's words, "guts ball," and to recite very deliberately the chant his grandmother taught him: ". . . one flew east, one flew west, one flew over the cuckoo's nest." The poem—its rhyme scheme indicating control, its very recitation an ordering principle—helps him to resist his usual postshock chaos and oblivion. But the intensity of the treatment nevertheless addles his brain and distorts his perspective, so that as he awakens he believes himself to be trapped inside dice that are showing snake eyes, the throw that eliminates the shooter from competition.[17] Yet he quickly separates the illusion of the crap shoot from reality and recognizes that he is not inside the dice; instead, "the number one, the snake eye up there, the circle, the white *light* in the ceiling . . . is what I've been seeing . . . in this little square room." Having made this crucial but hitherto elusive distinction between fact and paranoid fantasy, Chief asserts his control over those random elements that had earlier controlled him and is able to put the "dice at rest" (241). More importantly, he finally affirms that he is a conscious player and not just a pawn. By working at coming out of the shock in a way he has never worked at it before, he knows "this time I had them beat" (241). Having learned from Mack the gambler that the only sure bet is on himself and on his own power as an individual against the power of the Combine, Chief masters his actions as well as his language.

Because Chief has been on the ward longer than any of the other inmates—longer than anyone else, except Big Nurse—he is familiar with all of Ratched's tactics as well as the adverse effects of her destructive therapies. He therefore serves not only as narrator of *One Flew Over the Cuckoo's Nest* but as its central intelligence, who provides a kind of implicit moral commentary on the happenings on the ward. Like Nick Carraway in *The Great Gatsby*, Ishmael in *Moby-Dick*, and Stingo in *Sophie's Choice*, he not only records the events but also interprets them. And like the narrator of "A Rose for Emily," whose sympathy for the heroine allows him to see her as an icon and a town monument and not as a pathological eccentric, his affectionate vision of McMurphy as deliverer rather than as profiteer defines the novel.[18]

Although years of conditioning have inured Chief to the deadly monotony of the asylum and taught him that "Whoever comes in the door is usually somebody disappointing" (14–15), McMurphy manages to surprise him. He doesn't simply slide along the wall, as new admissions generally do; instead he explodes on the scene, like the bombs of which Scanlon dreams. On the ward where all men are made to feel small, even McMurphy's voice "sounds big . . . . He talks a little the way Papa used to, voice loud and full of hell" (16).[19] When McMurphy, only minutes after his arrival, dismisses the orderlies who try to steer him to the shower and plants himself firmly in the day room, thumbs in his pockets, boots wide apart like some mythic cartoon character or cocky Western hero, Chief is convinced he is some magical giant fallen from the skies. And when McMurphy laughs out loud at the absurdity of the situation on the ward, Chief immediately recognizes that "this sounds real. . . . it's the first laugh I've heard in years" (16). It is so loud and so real that it registers on the machinery of the institution: "Dials twitch in the control panel at the sound of it." The unfamiliar sound stuns everyone; they look spooked and uneasy, "the way kids look in a schoolroom when one ornery kid is raising too much hell with the teacher out of the room and they're all scared the teacher might pop back in and take it into her head to make them all stay after" (22). Even the Acute inmates sense that this red-headed Irish brawler is "different from anybody been coming on this ward for the past ten years, different from anybody they ever met outside" (83).

McMurphy *is* different: his resonant voice and hearty laugh pierce the silent void and assail the asylum's order. Yet his very disruption of the mechanical routine is a restoration of normalcy. Like the Grail Knight who returns life to the wasteland, McMurphy's eccentric behavior generates some passion in an otherwise passionless environment. Unwilling merely to bear passive witness to the other inmates' lethargy, he fills the sterile ward with sounds long unheard—ribald jokes and songs, which echo in the halls and challenge the Combine's authority as they revive the patients' saltpetered spirits. His laughter is especially welcome because it is unlike the derisive and belittling noises the inmates are used to: the snickering orderlies, "mumbling . . . and humming hate and death and other hospital secrets" (10); the falsity of "Public Relation," leading his tours through "mother" Ratched's model ward; the tight-lipped pleasantries of the hypocritical Big Nurse and her surrogates.

McMurphy uses the recuperative power of laughter to turn even the worst situations to his advantage. When Ratched assigns him latrine duty, he responds graciously that every time he swabs a crapper, he will think of her. Then, instead of just cleaning the toilets, he writes scatological words on the inside rims since he knows that when she inspects them with her hand mirror she will find his hidden messages. When Big Nurse lectures him about the rules of the ward, he completely deflates her matriarchal authority with a question about her bra size and the distance between her nipples. And when her ward policy prohibits him from leaving the mess hall until exactly 7:30 A.M. even though he is finished eating his breakfast long before, he uses the extra time to make bets on whether he can shoot a pat of butter onto the face of the clock and make it stick. When he misses the clock altogether, he bets on how long it will take for the butter to trickle down to the floor.[20] The warmer the patients' reception of his jokes, the icier Ratched becomes. McMurphy's liberating laughter is, after all, a countertherapy to her own regimen of fear and silence,[21] and his success terrifies her because it radically undermines her authority.

He also uses it as a weapon to short-circuit Ratched's machine. When she approaches McMurphy, who is dressed only in his cap and a towel, "her smile's going out before her like a radiator grill . . . and every step hits the floor she blows up a size bigger" (87). When she asks him where his clothes are, he politely responds that they were stolen. Ratched is confused until she realizes that the "outfit was *supposed* to be picked up" and that McMurphy should be in his hospital "greens." As Ronald Wallace demonstrates, "McMurphy apologizes and obligingly begins to remove the towel, flustering the Nurse into commanding him to leave it on. McMurphy pretends confusion and redirects the Nurse's anger against the attendant, an extension of herself." After insisting that the attendant neglected to issue him a uniform, "McMurphy crowns his victory by casually removing the towel to reveal his black-with-white-whales under-shorts, ridiculing the Nurse's fear that he was naked underneath."[22] Thus he succeeds in turning Ratched's humorlessness against her, as Yossarian had defied military code by appearing in formation without his uniform.

Unused as they are to humor, the men don't laugh easily at first. The institution itself prohibits it; Chief says "the air is pressed in by the walls, too tight for laughing. There's something strange about a place where the men won't let themselves loose and laugh" (48). Billy "opens his mouth but can't say a thing" (92), and only after McMurphy ribs him about his sexual prowess (and physically gooses him in the process) does he finally blush and grin a little. Harding tries to laugh but makes merely a "mousy little squeak" (158). And Chief doesn't speak or laugh at all. When he finally utters his first words and attempts to laugh along with McMurphy, "it was a squawking sound, like a pullet trying to crow. It sounded more like crying than laughing" (185). Even for a performer as seasoned as McMurphy, the inmates prove to be a tough audience. He has to manipulate them, the way a carny operator—an image Kesey uses several times to describe McMurphy—works his crowd. "He's being the clown," says Chief, "working at getting some of the guys to laugh. It bothers him that the best they can do is grin weakly and snigger sometimes" (92).

McMurphy, though, persists. "He knows you have to laugh at the things that hurt you just to keep yourself in balance, just to keep the world from running you plumb crazy," observes Chief. "He knows there's a painful side . . . but he won't let the pain blot out the humor no more'n he'll let the humor blot out the pain" (212). And he realizes that once the men are able to laugh at themselves, they will be less likely to be hurt by the vitriolic remarks of Ratched and her staff.

In addition to giving them the gift of healing laughter, McMurphy touches the patients with a friendly hand that helps them to regain their potency. As soon as he is admitted, he makes a point of shaking hands with everyone. The human touching contrasts with the cold and sterile treatment they receive from Big Nurse; his is a warm, natural, spontaneous gesture, unlike her mechanical actions. Consequently McMurphy's big hand, symbolizing masculinity and power, becomes the answer to Ratched's momism and represents his power to save the inmates[23] from the deadly and emasculating monotony of her ward.

In fact, one of Bromden's first impressions of Mack is of his muscular hand, extended in greeting. For Bromden, who feels so weakened by the fog that he imagines himself stuck to his chair, McMurphy's hand—tattooed, scarred, and calloused—seems as "big as a dinner plate." A virtual road map of his travels up and down the West, it carries in its cracks the dirt of the land that McMurphy hoed and under its fingernails the carbon from the garages where he worked. But even more striking than the way it looks is how it feels to Bromden:

> I remember the fingers were thick and strong closing over mine, and
> my hand commenced to feel peculiar and went to swelling up out
> there on my stick of an arm, like he was transmitting his own blood
> into it. It rang with blood and power. It blowed up near as big as his.
> . . . (27)

Although Bromden introduces the motif of the hands with McMurphy's entrance, he also uses it to record faithfully the afflictions in the ward[24] and to show how different the inmates' weak hands are from McMurphy's huge ones. Harding, who is perhaps the most erudite and self-composed man in the unit, responds somewhat tentatively to McMurphy's outstretched paw. Harding's pretty hands betray an effeminacy that makes him the object of Big Nurse's thinly disguised contempt. His fingers are so "long and white and dainty" that they seem to be carved out of soap; sometimes they get loose and glide like "two white birds" (23) until he traps them again between his knees. Big George, the water freak, is more hesitant than Harding. Terrified of being touched by anyone, he shies back from McMurphy's "unsanitary" hand, a phobia that anticipates the confrontation between McMurphy and the orderlies in the shower, a fight that ultimately leads to Mack's demise. Ellis, more enfeebled than George and so frozen into numbness and inactivity that he cannot move the few steps to the latrine, imagines himself nailed to the asylum wall and is unable to respond in any way whatsoever.

McMurphy's raw energy invigorates all of them to some degree. Even the perpetually tired Pete Bancini comes to life briefly, his hand "pumping bigger and bigger." But Pete soon remembers that he was "born dead" while the others at least still "got chances"; and "his iron ball shrank back to a hand" which he holds cupped in front of him, as if offering something to the other patients. The sudden activity breaks his watch and cuts his arm, and thereafter he becomes "like an old clock that won't tell time but won't stop neither, with the hands bent out of shape and the face bare of numbers and the alarm bell rusted silent, an old, worthless clock that just keeps ticking and cuckooing without meaning nothing" (51–53). Though Bancini is one cuckoo who will never leave the nest, his frenetic, spasmodic movement (the result of too much tranquilizing and EST burnout) is a warning to Mack and a foreshadowing of his fate. The comparison of the spent Bancini to a broken clock is especially apt, since clocks are virtually useless on the ward; as Chief notes, all time is in Big Nurse's control. She sets the daily schedule, approves all of the activities, and even determines the length of the inmates' stays. That unchallenged power makes her hand the most terrifying of all. Unlike McMurphy's hand, which pumps blood and life, hers merely deadens and incapacitates. As with Taber, her hand "[locks] on his arm, paralyzes him all the way to the shoulder" (35).

Therefore, throughout the novel McMurphy uses his grip on the inmates, both literally and metaphorically, to counteract Ratched's debilitating influence and to transmit his strength. He strains, for example, to lift the control panel even though he knows he cannot succeed. The attempt leaves his hands bloody and bandaged—"His hands are froze into red claws, and he can't work the fingers," says Chief—but his effort has clear results. He tells them: "I tried, though . . . . Goddammit, I sure as hell did that much, now, didn't I?" (111). The impact of his futile but inspiring effort—a gesture comparable to Yossarian's escape by raft to the coast of Italy and beyond—is felt the next day, when Ratched takes a new vote on the World Series. The men follow his example and try too: all but the Chronics raise their hands to defy Big Nurse in support of McMurphy. For the first time they believe that passivity may not be the solution to their problem.

Having shown them that they can function as individuals within the asylum walls, McMurphy decides to prove to the inmates, most of whom are voluntary admissions, that they can manage outside the institution as well. With the help of his "aunt" Candy, a woman far sweeter in every regard than "mother" Ratched, he arranges a fishing excursion and cons Dr. Spivey into accompanying the group and legitimizing the experience for them. (The doctor, who feels overwhelmed by Ratched, is in almost as much need of a cure as the inmates are.) When they stop at a filling station, however, the attendant intimidates the doctor by trying to foist on him various needless items such as oil filters and sunglasses before he will pump their gas. McMurphy won't abide the cheap hustle: he stands up to the attendant—one con man to another—and literally puts his hands in the man's face and holds them there "a long time, waiting to see if the guy had anything else to say." The man immediately backs down; Mack's bravado restores the tenor of the trip and leaves the whole group feeling as "cocky as fighting roosters" (201–02).

At the dock, when they encounter another obstacle, McMurphy once again saves the day by commandeering a fishing boat and launching the expedition. But as the inmates start landing fish and calling for his assistance, he stands aside, refusing to help them out. Even after Candy's breast is bloodied by the reeling line and Chief's thumb is cut and everyone is unnerved and exhausted by the exertion of catching a big fish, he keeps watching and laughing but remains conspicuously detached. His uncharacteristic passivity is not a sign of callousness or indifference; nor is it the result of increasing physical weakness. Rather, it is a demonstration of real caring. McMurphy knows that mere example is not enough of an answer to the men's problems: he must empower them to act on their own behalf. By forcing them to use their own hands, to rely on their own resources and to feel responsible for each other, he allows them to reclaim their identity as independent functioning persons. Soon they are able to laugh loudly "at their own selves as well as at the rest of us" (212), and when they dock, even the locals who had belittled them must acknowledge their skill in capturing the biggest fish anyone has ever seen. The fishing trip, which serves as a kind of Pentecost for all aboard, not only shows the men that the way out of the institution is to return to the natural values of the world "outside"; it also encourages them to grow both individually and collectively. Their camaraderie sustains them back on the ward, where they celebrate their victory by standing up to Ratched. Ultimately, only their collective force defeats her forceful collective, which has—until late—steadily eroded their confidence and self-worth.

From the beginning, no one benefits more from Mack's friendly hand than Bromden. Whereas others have come to take Chief's hulking silence for granted, McMurphy pays attention to him and manages to bring him back from his self-imposed silence by offering him a stick of Juicy Fruit. (The black orderly had earlier removed Chief's stash of used gum from under his bed. Feigning muteness, Chief could not object; and being indigent, unlike most of the other inmates, he had no money to buy new gum.) Thus McMurphy's act of friendship—but even more of understanding—prompts Chief to utter "thank you," the first words he has spoken since coming to the asylum soon after the war. When McMurphy then unties Bromden's bed sheets and promises to make him big again, he helps to eliminate other restrictions that have bound Chief and kept him feeling small. The restoration of a part of Bromden's psychological manhood long repressed has an obvious sexual dimension as well; just by talking about the spectacular results Chief will see from Mack's special "body-building course," he helps Chief to experience his first erection in years. ("Look there, Chief. Haw. What'd I tell ya? You growed a half a foot already" [190].) And by signing Chief up for the fishing excursion and paying for his share, McMurphy gives him the courage he needs to defy the aides for the first time and to stand up for himself as a man. The next morning, "When they stuck a broom out for me to do their work up the hall," Chief says, "I turned around and walked back to the dorm, telling myself, The hell with that. A man goin' fishing with two whores from Portland don't have to take that crap" (191). His potency regained, Chief does not need the broom's dead wood to define him ever again.

Chief reciprocates when McMurphy's self-sacrifice renders him incapable of further struggle. Effectively reversing their roles, Chief assumes McMurphy's power and responsibility. To save Mack, now a symbolically castrated and literally lobotomized shell of a man, from further abuse, Chief smothers him. "I was only sure of one thing: he wouldn't have left something like that sit there in the day room with his name tacked on it for twenty or thirty years so the Big Nurse could use it as an example of what can happen if you buck the system. I was sure of that" (270). But even in his vegetal state McMurphy retains a tough grip on life. To suffocate him, Chief must climb up on his bed in an almost sexual posture (Leslie Fiedler calls it "a caricature of the act of love"[25]); he recalls lying "full length on top of [McMurphy]" and "scissor[ing] the kicking legs with mine while I mashed the pillow into the face. I lay there on top of the body for what seemed days. Until the thrashing stopped. Until it was still a while and had shuddered once and was still again. Then I rolled off" (270).

Though homosexual rape is frequently practiced by the orderlies, there is no suggestion of homosexuality in this scene (as at least one critic has implied); instead, Chief's suffocation of Mack is a remarkably moving consummation of a different kind of affection, of a deep and abiding friendship based on mutual respect. Chief, having espoused the values for which McMurphy so valiantly fought, must reclaim his ailing friend from his silent world, just as McMurphy had earlier freed Chief from his bed restraints and reclaimed him from muteness and the cold silence of the institution. In a gesture of compassion and heroism, Chief, whose quality of life McMurphy unselfishly restored, allows his friend to die with a comparable dignity. Ironically, by murdering Mack, he saves his own savior. Scanlon's "Is it finished?" serves as a reminder of the double sacrifice and especially of McMurphy's messianic function. The suffocation scene also parallels McMurphy's earlier attempted strangulation of Big Nurse, an act performed not out of self-interest but for the spiritual and psychological liberation of the other men.

But Chief's role in this drama is not complete with the benevolent murder. He reaches on the bed stand for McMurphy's familiar cap, which, like the mantle of a fallen leader or a magical amulet, is laden with meaning for him. As big a man as McMurphy is, Chief, however, is bigger—made bigger still by the energy McMurphy has pumped back into him—and the cap doesn't fit. The symbolism, though, is clear: to make good his escape, Chief cannot merely adopt another identity; he must define his own. Although he can look to McMurphy's values and example for guidance, he must go beyond them. McMurphy, after all, was beaten by the cold, efficient, mechanical system; Chief must turn the machine against itself, use the very instrument that runs the Combine to destroy it, employ the key McMurphy had shown him their very first week together on the ward.

In the tub room, Chief lifts the control panel, which represents the monolithic weight of the Combine, a machinery that seems to be invulnerable to the efforts of any single man to move it;[26] he heaves it through the screen and the window—the same escape route McMurphy had planned to use for his breakout—with a ripping crash. "Like a bright cold water baptizing the sleeping earth" (271), the glass shatters and a reborn Chief vaults to freedom, leaving behind him forever the fog and the Combine and Big Nurse's frozen smile. He runs toward the highway and heads west, to the Columbia Gorge and his tribal land, to reestablish his sense of self, because he has "been away a long time" (272). With his powerful hands, Mack shook the asylum; with his even stronger hands, Chief all but destroys it and everything for which it stands.

Barry Leeds suggests that Chief is able to surpass his own teacher in the capacity to survive in the asylum and in America and to maintain personal identity in spite of the Combine because he is a half-breed. This mixed heritage, which contributed to his alienation and identity problems, represents his ability to combine the strengths of the Indian (especially patience and cunning, or "caginess") and the white man. McMurphy, he argues, "because he fights the Combine head-on, dies; but Bromden, who learns to practice a fusion of evasive cunning and sheer courage, survives as the hope for the future."[27]

While Chief becomes McMurphy's second self and secret sharer, Harding also enjoys some of McMurphy's transferred force. Harding is an intellectual whose sexual dysfunction has led to his voluntary incarceration. When McMurphy first asks Harding why he permits himself to be berated and degraded in the group sessions by Nurse Ratched, McMurphy "laps his big hand" (54) over a wooden chair nearby, swings it around so the back faces Harding, and straddles it as if it were a tiny horse in an overtly masculine posture that suggests his raw sexuality and his mythic frontier Western quality. By contrast, Harding sits in a very submissive feminine posture with his "thin shoulders folded nearly together around himself, like green wings, and he's sitting very straight near the edge of his chair, with his hands trapped between his knees" (54), like the victim of the pecking party to which McMurphy alludes in his conversation. "Monster chicken" Ratched, McMurphy tells Harding, doesn't go for the patients' eyes but for their "everlovin' *balls*." She is one of the "people who try to make you weak so that they can get you to toe the line, to follow their rules, to live like they want you to. And the best way to do this, to get you to knuckle under, is to weaken you by gettin' you where it hurts the worst. . . . And that's what that old buzzard is doing, going for your vitals" (57).

As McMurphy explains his theory, Harding's hands begin to creep out from between his knees, "like white spiders from between two moss-covered tree limbs . . . toward the joining at the trunk" (57). His hands twitch and tremble, and for a moment he leans forward to grasp McMurphy's one hand in both of his. Only after this gesture of strength-taking from the brawny and vulgar Irishman who is not intimidated by Big Nurse is Harding able to concede for the first time that Ratched is a bitch, as McMurphy said, not the good woman he earlier contended she was.

But even McMurphy's bluster does not immediately embolden Harding or reverse the emasculation that has been occurring for years. Steadily and progressively, however, Harding begins to assert himself and to defy Ratched. Although worried that Big Nurse will cut off more than just his hand, he raises it to vote against her on the World Series. The defiance helps to restore his sense of manhood, which neither his wife Vera's visit nor her conversation about his limp-wristed friends (which Harding knows Ratched will use later in group therapy to taunt and demean him) can undo. On the fishing trip, which fortifies him further, he volunteers to do without a life jacket on board the boat, helps reel in a prize fish, and laughs loudly at himself, acknowledging that his mental illness has given him "an aspect of power, *power*" (202).[28]

By the end of the novel, Harding is confident enough to reaccept leadership of the unit. In fact, during the evening of debauchery that follows the trip, his calm cover-up about the noises emanating from the bathroom, where Turkle, Candy, and others are hiding, is plausible enough to placate the night nurse and save everyone's hide. Before being removed from the ward following Billy's death, McMurphy shakes Harding's hand one last time, symbolically transferring authority back to him: Harding, in what he believes will be Mack's brief absence, again becomes the head bull goose loony. While Ratched is recuperating in "Medical," he assumes Mc-Murphy's role and his voice: he addresses the men in phrases McMurphy used to use and deals cards, as Mack did, in the tub room, which they have reappropriated. Ironically, as Big Nurse has lost her voice, Harding has found his. A sign of his new potency is his readiness to return to life outside the ward with Vera.

Ellis too eventually draws some strength from Mack. As the group of "disciples" leaves for the fishing trip, "Ellis pulled his hands down off the nails in the wall and squeezed Billy Bibbit's hand and told him to be a fisher of men" (198). Billy becomes that—and a fisher of women, too—and for a while it seems that even he will be redeemed. Asserting his masculinity, Billy chooses (as Harding did) to go without a life jacket on the boat; then he imitates Mack's strong hands by drawing ink tattoos on his own; and finally he loses his virginity to McMurphy's girl.

While Billy Bibbit's name suggests the stuttering innocent Billy Budd[29] and the guileless victim Billy Pilgrim, McMurphy's name connotes movement. His initials, R. P. M., suggest "revolutions per minute," and McMurphy's "revolution" starts the moment that he appears on the ward. His rebellion demonstrates to the inmates that *anti*order is sanity, that true madness, what Raymond Olderman calls "the real dry root of the waste land," is not their alleged irrationality but the deadly order, system, and rationality of the institution.[30] When the rational is perverted, as on Ratched's ward, reason becomes madness, and the only solution lies in the disease. The society that tries to cure its misfits by standardizing and straitjacketing them only causes the illness it quarantines.[31]

Although at first McMurphy seems a rather unlikely hero, in fact he is a decorated war veteran who led an escape from a Chinese Communist prison camp. But, rather characteristically, soon after he won the Distinguished Service Cross for his bravery he was dishonorably discharged from the service for insubordination. (He manifests a similar insubordination on Ratched's ward, which is compared several times to a Communist camp.[32]) A vagrant and a self-styled psychopath—"They tell me a psychopath's a guy fights too much and fucks too much" (18), he announces proudly— McMurphy is not above feigning insanity to avoid hard labor, though he later learns from the symbolic lifeguard at the hospital that his commitment can far exceed the remaining few months of his sentence. Like Mark Twain's tall-tale frontier heroes, he bets on anything, starting with his own contest of wills with Big Nurse. Yet his gambling is not purely selfish, as Ratched wants the men to believe. He teaches the inmates to gamble on themselves: he shows them how to take chances, how to stack the deck in their favor, how to play out their hands, how to bluff—in short, how to win at survival, the only game which matters. And, like another frontier hero, Bret Harte's John Oakhurst, he knows when he is holding a losing hand (symbolized by the aces and eights, the traditional "dead man's hand," tattooed on his arm) but still stays in the game until the end, as any real sporting man would.

McMurphy is also vain and egotistical; he advertises his sexuality openly, not just in his conversations but also on his shorts (which provoke Ratched into uncharacteristically raising her voice). Adorned by white whales on a black satin background, his unusual underwear is a gift from an Oregon State coed, a lit major who presciently tells McMurphy he is a "symbol." The symbolic allusion is at least in part to Melville, since McMurphy is, as Terry Sherwood notes, "a representation of certain qualities shared by Moby Dick—natural vitality, strength, immortality, anti-social destructiveness." Moreover, the white whales, which bear devilish red eyes linked to Mack's red hair and volatile Irish nature, "emphasize his sexually intoned vitality"[33] and play on more colloquial connections with the title of Melville's famous novel.

But McMurphy's performance as a "dedicated lover" extends beyond his relationships with the coed, with Candy, and with his other women to the love of more enduring values like friendship and freedom. And it is for that kind of love, not sexual love, that he sacrifices himself by presenting the fearless face of the hero to inspire the inmates and hiding from them the exhausted face of the overextended man (the price he pays for such superhuman behavior) as he drives himself to existential heroism in the face of absurdity.[34] His genuine compassion for the residents of the ward grows until it becomes his sole purpose for being. Earlier, he had warned Harding about Big Nurse, "that old buzzard . . . going for your vitals" (57); and, ironically, so long as he protects his own vitals, McMurphy is reasonably immune to her attacks. When he signs on "for the whole game"—that is, when he stops protecting his own vitals and commits to protecting those of others—Ratched is finally able to get to him. She sets him up in the shower after the fishing trip: he buys into what he knows is a losing fight with the orderlies because he cannot allow George, who is unable to fend for himself, to be sacrificed as Cheswick was when he failed to come to his aid. That sense of both obligation and inevitability helps to explain why, at the end of the novel, given every chance to leave for a new life in Mexico or Canada with Candy, McMurphy chooses instead to stay with the men. And, while no saint (as Ratched points out when she sows seeds of doubt within the group), his self-sacrifice makes him their savior, an image reinforced by *Cuckoo's Nest*'s many religious elements: Scanlon's question, with its biblical resonances, when Chief smothers McMurphy; the numerous cross images (the self-crucified Ellis, nailed to the ward's wall; Pilbow's crucifix, prominently displayed on her neck chain; the position of crucifixion into which all EST patients are strapped; the description of the lead goose in the V-formation as "a black cross" [143]; McMurphy's service medal, the Distinguished Service Cross); Mack's taking his twelve disciples out into the world and teaching them to become fishers of their own manhood; his acceptance of the EST equipment as if it were a crown of thorns ("Anointest my head with conductant" [237]); and his betrayal by Billy after Ratched interrupts the idyll with Candy.

If McMurphy's R. P. M. suggests one kind of force, Big Nurse represents another. She is a mechanical marvel: precise, efficient, and robotlike; her cold sterility sharply contrasts with McMurphy's earthy sexuality and fertility. Ratched has "dry-ice eyes" (31); she "freezes" (88) people with her stare or blasts them with a "blizzard"-like fury; "frost forms" (89) when she moves. "It's a little cold where the nurse just went past," says Chief, "and the white tubes in the ceiling circulate frozen light like rods of glowing ice, like frosted refrigerator coils rigged up to glow white" (130) in her wake.

Ratched's actions are rote gestures that testify to her failure of imagination: she takes off her hat and puts on her nurse's cap in exactly the same way each day; she dispenses medicine at the same hour to the sound of the same monotonous recording (actions reminiscent of the mechanical lovemaking in "The Waste Land"). By pursuing her particular brand of order and enforcing her mindless regimen with such monomaniacal zeal, she is indeed like a "ratchet," the pawl-like instrument whose teeth move in one direction and one direction alone. Her ratchetlike power to bend others in any way she chooses appears almost absolute. An essential cog in the ward's machinery,[35] she too at first seems a giant, an almost superhuman figure in Chief's eyes. "She's too big to be beaten" (101), he says.

But Ratched's name also connotes "wretched," an allusion to the quality of life on the unit that she runs. When McMurphy mispronounces her name as "Rat-shed," he reinforces the Pavlovian nature of that unit, where the men become her personal experiments, conditioned to respond as she has programmed them. Harsher than her ward rules, which by themselves are oftentimes silly (locking up the toothpaste, for instance—otherwise, as McMurphy observes, "people'd be brushin' their teeth whenever the spirit moved them. . . . lordy, can you imagine? Teeth bein' brushed at six-thirty, six-twenty—who can tell? maybe even six o'clock" [85]), is the intractable way she imposes them upon herself and those around her. Although she masks autocracy with democracy, her own failure to bend ultimately causes her to snap.

From her starched uniform to her stiff smile, everything about Big Nurse implies repression and constriction. Early in the novel, in the only reference to her life outside the ward, Harding tries to impress McMurphy with an instance of Ratched's good will; instead he merely illustrates her rigidity. Noting that she "*further* serves mankind" on her weekends off by "preparing a rich array of charity—canned goods, cheese for the binding effect, soap—and presenting it to some poor young couple" (58), he seems unaware of the implications of his remark. Ratched's volunteer work in the community is, by his very description, an extension of her momism on the ward: even her charity is mechanical (like the "canned goods" she bestows), sterile (like the "soap"), and constrictive (like the "cheese for the binding effect"). And her charitable presence is no doubt as guilt-evoking to the young couple as her purportedly cathartic group sessions are to the inmates.

More complete than her emotional repression is her sexual repression. Yet while Ratched's sublimation is the opposite of McMurphy's lust, she too is a symbol for the excesses of sex. When she reads his record (including his arrest for having relations with a fifteen-year-old girl) on the day he is admitted, she subconsciously skips a section that McMurphy immediately calls to the staff's attention: "The nurse left this part out while she was *summarizing* my record. Where it says, 'Mr. McMurphy has evidenced re-*peated*'—I just want to make sure I'm understood completely, Doc—'*repeated* outbursts of passion . . .' " (46). Such passion is exactly what Ratched has eliminated from her life and her ward, and its reemergence in the figure of her new admission is highly threatening.

Markedly unfeminine, she looks and moves like a robot; even her handbag, which resembles a toolbox with its hemp handle, is full of "wheels and gears, cogs polished to a hard glitter, tiny pills that gleam like porcelain . . . there's no compact or lipstick or woman stuff" (10). To Chief the contents of her purse resemble the fragments of the men she has methodically and mechanically eviscerated. The only element impeding the smooth functioning of her machine is her gigantic chest. Anyone could tell, thinks Chief, "a mistake was made somehow in manufacturing, putting those big, womanly breasts on what would of otherwise been a perfect work, and you can see how bitter she is about it" (11). Tangible symbols of her femininity, Ratched's breasts betray her vulnerability; and McMurphy takes advantage of this weakness at the end of the novel when he assaults her. By ripping her starchy white uniform and exposing her chest in full view of all of the men—inmates, orderlies, and doctors—around her, McMurphy succeeds in asserting his dominant sexuality and forces Ratched to acknowledge the femininity—and the very humanity—she has repressed. Without the sterile wrappings of her uniform to shield her, Big Nurse loses her intimidating presence as well as her authority.[36] Her only recourse is to invoke the now-diminishing power of the Combine: by having McMurphy lobotomized, a last attempt at castration (though admittedly an irrevocably successful one), she becomes the ball-cutter he accused her of being. Yet her victory is Pyrrhic: McMurphy has already passed his strength and manhood on to the other inmates so that not one phoenix but several rise out of the wasteland's ashes in his stead. As the inmates begin to check themselves out or request transfers to other wards, she is voiceless—and powerless—to prevent them. The silenced Madame Sosostris cannot rule the wasteland any longer. Her icy facade melted by the heat of McMurphy's passionate defiance, Big Mom is no more.

A further negation of Ratched's sexuality is demonstrated by her attitude toward and treatment of other women. Manipulative, authoritarian females, such as the aging Army nurse who serves as the asylum's administrator, and Mrs. Bibbit, Billy's domineering mother, become her allies. She uses them for support in her ongoing battle for supremacy of the ward. They are, however, largely reflections of Ratched herself (the former, a model of efficiency who approves of Ratched's successes on her unit without questioning her methods; the latter, a mother who causes, not resolves, problems of sexuality and guilt for her son) and thus they are nonthreatening.

Moreover, both, by virtue of their ages and their independence from men, are symbols of sterility. This is particularly true of the widow Bibbit, who has kept her son incarcerated in the asylum since his adolescence.

But for most other women, especially young, attractive ones, Ratched has nothing but scorn and contempt, based on the jealousy she sublimates as fully as she does her own humanity. Candy and Sandy exude passion and fertility, the very qualities she despises in McMurphy. Ratched considers them slatternly and socially inferior, and she subtly demeans their type, urging her "boys" to avoid the temptations of their Pandora's boxes. After all, for Big Nurse, the only healthy sexuality is a repressed sexuality, a sexuality bound as tightly as her own bosom under her white uniform. She frightens and manipulates the religious Miss Pilbow by telling her in a seemingly offhanded remark to beware of Mr. McMurphy's raging hormones: "Oh, one more thing before I leave it [the ward] in your hands tonight, Miss Pilbow; that new man sitting over there, the one with the garish red sideburns and facial lacerations—I've reason to believe he is a sex maniac" (75). Ratched's warning causes such hysteria in the younger nurse that when McMurphy tries to get acquainted and to lend a hand with the pill she has dropped (unfortunately, down the neck of her uniform), she pops the cross hanging around her neck into her mouth, clinches her eyes, and turns paper-white. " 'Stay back!' she warns. 'There are two aides on the ward with me!' . . . 'Stay back' . . . 'Oh, stay back, I'm a *Catholic!*' " (76).

Women like Mrs. Harding, caught between the extremes of asexual Ratched and loose-moraled Candy, are in some ways the most interesting in the novel. Vera Harding, like Ratched, is big-breasted and disguised with cosmetics; and like Ratched she contributes to the diminishing of her husband's masculinity. However, she flirts openly with McMurphy and, instead of repressing it, she is aware of her sexuality and enjoys flaunting it. So "despite her dubious methods and her own lack of perception about her plight, her harsh qualities are mitigated somewhat," writes Leeds. "Although Vera has damaged her husband's sense of sexual identity, he has failed her in similar fashion by abdicating too readily the responsibilities of the male role. It is one measure of the qualified hope Kesey offers for future male-female relations in America" that by the novel's end Harding is able to accept some of this responsibility and try again, armed with a new honesty derived from his contact with McMurphy.[37]

Big Nurse's therapeutic discussions focus frequently on Harding's marital problems with Vera, but her deprecations extend to all women and involve other inmates as well. She forces Billy Bibbit, for example, to remember and to relive his painful experience with his only girlfriend, a degradation made even greater because Ratched has learned of the relationship from his mother. (Mrs. Bibbit, who continues to infanticize her son, works in the same institution as Ratched and receives from her regular reports on Billy's progress; Big Nurse in turn terrorizes Billy by the mention of what his mother will say about his conduct.)

Since he is already a victim of momism at the time that he is hospitalized, Billy is an easy prey for Ratched, who is described as a "buzzard" poised to strike. His speech defect began with the first word he said; significantly, that first word was "m-m-m-m-mam-ma" (119). Years later, when he proposed to his girlfriend, he could not even manage to articulate a complete question: " 'Huh-honey, will you muh-muh-muh-muh-muh . . .' till the girl broke out l-laughing" (121). By linking Billy's disability with his relationship to the girl he loved, Ratched further humiliates and emasculates him and shows that he, like the other inmates, is unable to function satisfactorily with women—and gives him the subliminal message that he should not even try. Billy's situation is only exacerbated by the fact that he is a virgin. Though over thirty, Billy (like another Billy, Vonnegut's Billy Pilgrim) remains the perpetual child, answerable to a double despot—his real mother, Mrs. Bibbit, and his surrogate mother, Big Nurse.

The novel is brought full circle when Billy becomes enamored of and has his first intercourse with McMurphy's prostitute girlfriend. The experience emboldens him and makes him a man, so that when Ratched finds the two of them in the Seclusion Room the next morning, Billy makes no effort to move or to get up or to button his pajamas; he merely reaches protectively for the girl's hand, grins, and says—with no trace of a stutter—"Good morning, Miss Ratched . . . . This is Candy" (263). In that moment, Billy comes of age.

But the moment is brief indeed. Big Nurse quickly reduces him to a child again and plays on his guilt: "Oh, Billy Billy Billy—I'm so ashamed for you. . . . What worries me, Billy . . . is how your poor mother is going to take this. [She's] always been so proud of your discretion. . . . This is going to disturb her terribly. You know how she is when she gets disturbed, Billy; you know how ill the poor woman can become." At the same time that it causes Billy to regress, Ratched's skillful manipulation of him fuels the fires of her machine. His manhood diminished, now fearful of Ratched's disclosure to his mother, Billy starts to stutter again. "Like a kid that's been promised a whipping just as soon as a willow is cut" (263–64), he rubs his hand up and down his pant leg and shakes his head in panic. Ratched comforts her "poor little boy" and leads him down to the doctor's office to separate him from his male cronies. Left alone, suffocated by guilt, he cuts his throat.

When Billy's suicide is discovered and Ratched retaliates against McMurphy, he confronts her with slow, mechanical gestures, oddly reminiscent of her own. Only "it wasn't the nurse that was forcing him" to react, explains Chief; "it was our need that was making him push himself slowly up from sitting, his big hands driving down on those leather chair arms, pushing him up, rising and standing like one of those moving-picture zombies" (267). In an instant McMurphy destroys the machine that she symbolizes. His large red hands around her throat crack her frozen smile and deprive her of her voice, and he rips open her uniform to expose her sexually and to reveal her mechanical failure. No indestructible set of wheels and cogs, she is merely a woman, pink-breasted and frightened of his strength.

Yet even in her more womanly role, as "mother" of the ward, she proves a failure and is forced into further submission to McMurphy, the father figure for the inmates in the unit (almost all of whose problems are related to their relationships with mothers or other women). Her own perverse momism with Billy, who more than the other inmates is her "boy," is defeated by the vulgar paternalism of McMurphy, who facilitates Billy's sexual initiation and makes him a man (albeit briefly). Her attempt to get Billy to repudiate his sexual act results only in his death and her own demise, after which there can be no restoration of the old order: her authority is lost as irrevocably as Billy's virginity. Moreover, even her familiar battle armor is rendered obsolete. The white uniform that McMurphy has torn cannot be replaced; she must purchase a new one—smaller, tighter and more starched—which can no longer conceal that she is a woman.

Ratched and McMurphy's contest over Billy, more than a battle of wills, is explicitly sexual: his overt sexuality triumphs over her sublimation. The final contest is not, however, the only encounter of theirs that is sexual in nature. McMurphy has repeatedly "penetrated" her nurses' station. His steady assaults on it throughout the novel prefigure his final attack on her, just as they anticipate Chief's escape through the broken hospital window.

The nurses' station is the center of Big Nurse's cold matriarchal world, a safe retreat from extended or direct contact with her charges. It is almost womblike, with its ever-polished glass forming a protective membrane through which she surveys her boys, and the medicine locked and administered from within it a soporific, a kind of mad mother's tranquilizing milk. Male inmates are prohibited from invading the station's sanctity. McMurphy rightly calls it a "Hothouse," since it is the center of a sterile environment which makes the inmates dependent and thus unable to survive in the outside world.[38]

The first time McMurphy puts his fist through the station's window, it is a calculated, deliberate, sexually symbolic act. Then, to show Big Nurse that the first penetration of her "impregnable" chamber was anything but accidental, McMurphy feigns ignorance that the glass has been repaired and puts his fist through the window again. Repulsed by having to administer first aid to her own assailant, she deliberately jerks the adhesive bandage tight so as to inflict pain—and a kind of symbolic castration—on the very symbol of his potency.

As with all of his other rebellious actions, McMurphy (like Yossarian) provides an example that other inmates emulate. Replaced after his second penetration, Ratched's glass is quickly broken again—this third time by Scanlon, who bounces his basketball through it. While the shards of glass puncture the ball and cut it exactly as McMurphy accuses Ratched of cutting the inmates' testicles, her authority is further lessened as her most private area is violated. Big Nurse, the Earth Mother in reverse who once took a perverse phallic pleasure in subduing men with her needles, is no longer insulated from unwanted exposure and cannot hide her vulnerability.

Even the pervasive animal imagery intimates the sexual nature of the conflict between Ratched and McMurphy and of the emasculation of the patients on the ward. Early in the novel, Harding describes the plight of the inmates. "All of us in here are rabbits of varying ages and degrees, hippity-hopping through our Walt Disney world. Oh, don't misunderstand me, we're not in here *because* we are rabbits—we'd be rabbits wherever we were—we're in here because we can't *adjust* to our rabbithood. We *need* a good strong wolf like the nurse to teach us our place" (61). He explains that they are unable to support each other and to defy Ratched because "it's not the rabbit's place to stick up for his fellow. . . . We mustn't be afraid of our own behavior; it's the way we little animals were meant to behave. . . . Most of us in here even lack the sexual ability to make the grade as adequate rabbits. Failures, we are—feeble, stunted, weak little creatures in a weak little race. Rabbits, *sans* whambam; a pathetic notion" (61–63). Victims of a matriarchy, they nevertheless require Big Nurse's mothering. At the end, however, Harding realizes how much they have learned from McMurphy's tutelage. Speaking of his fellow inmates, he admits "They're still sick men in lots of ways. But at least there's that: they are sick *men* now. No more rabbits, Mack. Maybe they can be well men someday" (257).

The inmates are also frequently referred to as "birds": "cuckoos" in a nest; a "flock of dirty chickens"; "pullets" trying to crow. McMurphy, the newly crowned bull goose loony, tells them that by failing to assert themselves and stand up for their rights, they behave like a "bunch of chickens at a peckin' party": "The flock gets sight of a spot of blood on some chicken and they all go to *peckin'* at it, see, till they rip the chicken to shreds, blood and bones and feathers. But usually a couple of the *flock* gets spotted in the fracas, then it's their turn. And a few more gets spots and gets pecked to death, and more and more. Oh, a peckin' party can wipe out the whole flock in a matter of a few hours, buddy, I seen it. A mighty awesome sight. The only way to prevent it—with chickens—is to clip blinders on them. So's they can't see" (55). Yet McMurphy gets the inmates to react precisely by showing them how to resist Ratched, the "monster chicken" of them all, the consummate pecker; and he helps the men to feel as "cocky as fighting roosters" (202). Eventually, most become powerful enough to fly the coop. As in the rhyme Chief's grandmother taught him—"one flew east, one flew west, and one flew over the cuckoo's nest"—they take their leave in various ways: the voluntaries sign out, the others request transfers, and Chief escapes through the shattered window into the night.

If the other inmates are most closely associated with rabbits and birds, Chief's totem animal is the dog. Early in the novel, the dog is "out there in the fog, running scared and lost." Although he sniffs in every direction, he "picks up no scent but his own fear, fear burning down into him like steam" (13). Chief too has a keen sense of smell, but at first it produces only fear as he smells the machinery inside Big Nurse. Later, during his recovery, he begins to register natural odors as well.[39] When he comes out of the fog he is able to detect the sweet smell of sweat under Mack's bed and eventually the fragrance of the autumn breeze through the hospital window. "Seeing lots of things different," he even notices a young, gangly mongrel pup outside, sniffing squirrel holes at night "just to get an idea what they were up to" (140, 142). He watches the dog as it lopes through the field toward the highway following the scent of some geese flying to Canada. (The geese, in their V-formation, symbolize McMurphy, who—even though he dies—still manages to escape the cuckoo's nest. Their honking outside the asylum window awakens Chief to the real world and helps to bring him out of his fog, just as McMurphy's laughter did—and just as the sound of a goose honking brought him out of the fog on the battlefield during World War II. And the "Canadian honkers up there" [86] remind Chief of how his crafty father got the best of the government agents by focusing their attention on the geese and not on the treaty they were trying to negotiate.) Once Chief is restored to his full strength, he breaks out of the asylum and takes long, loping strides "across the grounds in the direction I remembered seeing the dog go" (272). No longer "a dog on a leash" (237), he becomes a hunting hound following his natural instincts, a "dog [that] don't heel" (238). Though he is not completely out of reach of the machine (just as the dog he observed earlier was "making for the same spot of pavement" [143] as a car), he is nevertheless free.

As the many symbols and images indicate, the central theme of *One Flew Over the Cuckoo's Nest* is the restoration of the inmates' individual and collective potency. But potency, for Kesey, is much more than mere sexuality: it is the strong assertion of identity and the firm belief in the strength of the individual as sufficient to challenge mindless regimen. McMurphy saves the men from being swallowed up in the technological horror and anonymity of the institution by making them aware of their own manhood, in the sense of both their masculinity and their humanity.[40] To read the novel literally as a diatribe against women and a celebration of white male chauvinism, as some commentators and critics have, is to neglect this second dimension; such a narrow reading also overlooks the fact that Kesey is questioning, not describing or applauding, such societal stereotypes.

Nevertheless, it is often on these grounds—the novel's harsh treatment of women and Blacks—that *One Flew Over the Cuckoo's Nest* is criticized. Marcia L. Falk, for example, considers the book to be full of the most basic sexist and racist assumptions of our society—that Blacks are "stupid and malicious" and that "women are either dumb and silly (like the quivering young nurse, terrified of McMurphy; like the squealing, wiggling prostitutes who come to build up the men's egos) or they are shrewd, conniving, and malicious (castrating wives, dominating mothers, and a super-powerful domineering nurse)." This characterization of women reduces them to "demonic" figures who exercise dangerous control over men, and Falk argues that "with a pseudo-radical posture, [*One Flew Over the Cuckoo's Nest*] swallows whole hog all the worst attitudes toward women prevalent in our society and delivers the pig right back to us, suitably decorated and made righteous."[41] Elizabeth McMahon argues that "the Big Nurse happens also to be the Big Victim when viewed with an awareness of the social and economic exploitation of women" and implies that Kesey should have been more sympathetic to her point of view.[42] Robert Boyers believes that "in Kesey's view, modern society is a reflection of womanish values—archetypically responsible, cautious, repressive, deceitful, solemn. One must look to the spirit of the whore if one would know what is best in women, and what can best bring out what is vital in men." He concludes that Kesey "labors under a most reactionary myth, involving the mystique of male sexuality, which sees men as intrinsically better than women in terms of the dynamism and strength they can impart to the universe."[43] Even Raymond Olderman, who finds much to praise in the novel, is at times disappointed in Kesey's use of caricature rather than character. He writes that the " 'flat' portrayal of women and of Blacks is more stereotypic and uncomfortable than funny or fitting with his cartoon character pattern. It borders too much on the simplistic."[44]

While it is true that Big Nurse is a towering machine who dwarfs the men and erodes their confidence and self-esteem, her threat lies not in her sex but in her consuming quest for power, which connects her to the all-powerful Combine. The fact that she resorts to traditionally *un*feminine ways to increase her authority suggests, according to Ronald Wallace, that women's—and men's—roles in the novel are anything but stereotypic and that the deliberate reversal is part of larger comic pattern. "Male and female roles are comically reversed. If men have traditionally oppressed women, now the women oppress the men. In the asylum, the weak, ineffectual men are controlled by strong, domineering women, rendering the sexual roles themselves comic. Indeed, Kesey takes the worst male stereotype available—that of overweening power, control, force, manipulation—and imposes it on the women in the book, and the worst female stereotype—pettiness, bitchiness, lack of self-confidence, anxiousness to serve—and imposes it on the men."[45]

And just as the traditional female and male roles are reversed, "so are the traditional black-white roles. Whereas the blacks were traditionally the slaves of white masters, now the whites are the slaves of black masters, and Washington, named for the father and capital of our free country, is their leader."[46]

These role reversals are consistent with other relationships in the novel, most particularly McMurphy and Chief's. Theirs is no Lone Ranger-Tonto affair: it is McMurphy, after all, who has to reintroduce Bromden to the wonders of the natural world and who lays down his life for his friend, not the more stereotypic reverse.[47] And Chief is no timid sidekick: he acts boldly and decisively after McMurphy's lobotomy, and he alone strides out into the wilderness, following no master but himself, at the novel's end.

Taken together, all of these comic role reversals emphasize the underlying principle of ironic contrast and the reason for the novel's universal appeal: that in the contemporary world, madness is sanity and sanity is madness. It is the inmates who are sane, yet they must sign themselves into the institution as "voluntary" admissions in order to learn that. The nurse whose role it is to restore their health only aggravates their situation; the doctor who has authority over the nurse is in fact her underling. The Combine's order is actually chaos, and the random natural elements of the world outside provide the only real meaning and order in life. A lobotomized redeemer lives only by dying. In short, so long as Ratched is in her station, nothing is right with the world—and order is not order until the inmates are running the asylum.

Big Nurse is not a repugnant person because she is a woman; rather, she is repugnant because she denies both her femininity and her very humanity for the sake of a smoothly running routine. The

Japanese nurse—another woman—is, on the other hand, among the most likable characters in the book because she does not subscribe to the system's wholly mindless regimentation. After the shower fight, when Mack and Chief are sent to "Disturbed," she sympathizes with their plight and assures them "It's not all like her ward" (234). She wishes she could keep them in the safety of her unit, but knows she can't, given Ratched's seniority. When she assumes supervisory responsibility in Big Nurse's absence, she allows the men "to change a lot of the ward policy" (268) and even to resume their card games in the tub room. Furthermore, McMurphy, the novel's raging bull, is softened and humanized somewhat by his gentler, feminine qualities: Chief is impressed by the fact that Mack paints delicate pictures and writes letters with a beautiful, flowing hand (simultaneously the symbol of his potency).

Even the argument of latent racism that several critics have raised has a strong counterargument. As Barry Leeds has demonstrated, the fact that the process of selecting the right three Black orderlies has taken many years to accomplish makes it clear that Kesey is not making simplistic judgments against a particular racial group. "In conjunction with the plight of Chief Bromden, the black aides' rage against white people is shown to be a *result* of racism, and thus Kesey makes an indictment against racial prejudice as a self-perpetuating process."[48] By contrast to the three aides, Mr. Turkle, the Black night orderly, is (like the Japanese nurse) among the most sympathetic characters in the book. He is kind to Chief: he sometimes unties him during the night so he can move around his bed without restraints and even pulls him out of his fog: "You havin' a bad dream, Mistuh Bromden. . . . Back to sleep now, Mistuh Bromden" (82). Later, Turkle helps smuggle the whores and liquor onto the ward for the final party and offers McMurphy the key to escape in the morning so he won't get caught. Turkle's humanity balances the other aides' inhumanity and demonstrates that the behavior of Ratched's threesome, who rely on violence and perversion to maintain control, is unusual indeed. Therefore, to fault Kesey for his treatment of women and Blacks is, as Ronald Wallace correctly concludes, "to miss the comedy of a device that has informed comic art from Aristophanes to Erica Jong."[49]

The majority of readers of *One Flew Over the Cuckoo's Nest* have not missed the comedy of it, as evidenced by the novel's tremendous and enduring success. First made popular by a generation that saw in

McMurphy's rebellion against the Big Nurse and Chief's escape from the ward an allegory for the struggle of the Vietnam years, the novel continues to appeal to a new generation of readers, equally frustrated by institutions that have abused their authority and betrayed those whom they were designed to protect. As symbols of resistance to a repressive system, the mad heroes McMurphy and Bromden merely corroborate what another nonconformist, Emily Dickinson, wrote more than a century ago: "Much Madness is Divinest Sense." It is through their almost divine madness that the real insanity of the asylum—and of contemporary society—is exposed.

CHAPTER 4

All this happened, more

or less.

. . . .

And he dreamed millions

of things, some of them

true. The true things were

time-travel.

Slaughterhouse-Five

Pilgrim's Regress:

Slaughterhouse-Five

J. MICHAEL CRICHTON, reviewing *Slaughterhouse-Five* for *New Republic*, observed that Kurt Vonnegut writes about the most excruciatingly painful things, including "our deepest fears of automation and the bomb, our deepest political guilts, our fiercest hatreds and loves." Nobody else, Crichton concludes, writes books on these subjects: "they are inaccessible to normal novelistic approaches. But Vonnegut, armed with his schizophrenia, takes an absurd, distorted, wildly funny framework which is ultimately anaesthetic."[1] As the victim not only of technology but also of a historical schizophrenia, Vonnegut is indeed the ideal spokesperson for the peculiar insanity of the contemporary age.

Most decidedly a Midwesterner and "native son of America's more conservative and self-professedly wholesome heartland,"[2] Vonnegut was born in Indianapolis, Indiana, on Veterans' Day (then called Armistice Day), November 11, 1922. The coincidence of his birth on a day commemorating those seasoned by military experience and marking the cessation of hostilities foreshadowed a great deal about what was to be central in his life.[3] His father and grandfather were successful local architects; his family was large and comfortable, abounding with aunts, uncles, cousins (just as, a generation later, Vonnegut's immediate family was extended after his sister's death in 1958, when he took in three of her four children to raise as his own). In fact, as Jerome Klinkowitz noted, Vonnegut's "was a child's ideal world—before the Great Depression, before the Second World War—and it prompted no doubts in him about identity or the threat of the future."[4]

But, in the aftermath of the stock market crash and the dawn of the atomic age, Vonnegut's family situation, like that of so many others nationwide, changed dramatically. His father, unable to secure a job for almost a decade, wanted to guarantee a better life for his second son and urged him to study sciences, a field in which he believed there would always be employment. Kurt eventually started studies in chemistry at Cornell, but his first love was writing, and he regularly wrote for the *Cornell Daily Sun*, a commercial enterprise associated with the college. After a hospitalization for pneumonia during his junior year cost him his draft deferment, Vonnegut enlisted as an infantry private in the army. Sent overseas as an advance infantry scout attached to the 106th Infantry Division, he survived the Battle of the Bulge but was taken prisoner by the Germans, shipped to Dresden, and put to work in a factory that made malt syrup for pregnant women.

On February 13, 1945, while he and other prisoners of war spent the night in the underground slaughterhouse that served as their temporary barracks, the Allied Forces, led by the R. A. F., attacked Dresden. The bombardment, astounding in its grotesque technical wizardry, rapidly annihilated at least 135,000 people, a death toll greater than the subsequent bombing deaths in either Hiroshima or Nagasaki. Within a matter of a few hours, the city of Dresden, a center of culture and beauty that had been declared "open" and had no military value whatever, was virtually leveled: "a terrible thing," Vonnegut later commented, "for the son of an architect to see."[5] He described it in the introduction to *Mother Night.* First "high explosives were dropped on Dresden by American and British planes"; then "hundreds of thousands of tiny incendiaries were scattered over the kindling, like seeds on freshly turned loam. More bombs were dropped . . . and all the little fires grew, joined one another, became one apocalyptic flame. Hey presto: fire storm. It was the largest massacre in European history, by the way."[6] The bombardment touched Vonnegut's soul and burned itself indelibly into his memory, eventually finding its way into most of his major fiction.[7] But beyond the immediate issue of the insane cruelty of the Allied firebombing was the larger question of moral response. American newspapers carried nothing about Dresden's destruction; for Vonnegut, such absence of both notice and indignant reaction was a demonstration not just of dishonesty but of a loss of moral sense. Recognizing that people "were capable, probably eager, to wipe out life on earth,"[8] he felt responsible in conscience to say something. As one of the few to survive, he knew that somehow he must move past his own cynicism and despair and bear witness to the disaster and to the abject disregard for humanity and human achievement that it represented.

He returned home in 1945 and, without having graduated from Cornell, started graduate school in anthropology at the University of Chicago. While he eventually was awarded his master's (the university accepted *Cat's Cradle* as his thesis in the early seventies), he soon left Chicago without a degree to write publicity for General Electric in Schenectady, New York, where his older brother Bernard, a research physicist, was employed. Public relations work brought him close to one of the centers of technology responsible for the dreary sameness of life that he had always decried. "Profit motives, he saw, were couched in sentimental tributes to pure science," writes Richard Giannone; "individual freedom was sacrificed for professional advancement; and research was conducted without regard for its necessity or desirability. He saw that technology was developed in a moral vacuum."[9] And he was constantly reminded of technology's capacity to create that vacuum, to destroy rather than advance the cause of civilization, as had occurred in Dresden. Brought up to believe that science and technology would ennoble man, he watched instead as they debased man and magnified his brutishness, not his compassion.[10] In a speech at Bennington in 1970, he articulated his disappointment: "I thought scientists were going to find out exactly how everything worked, and then make it work better. I fully expected that by the time I was twenty-one, some scientist, maybe my brother, would have taken a color photograph of God Almighty and sold it to *Popular Mechanics* magazine. . . . What actually happened when I was twenty-one was that we dropped scientific truth on Hiroshima."[11]

During the day he wrote copy praising the merits of electricity; on his own time, he continued to study science and to write stories, which he sold to *Collier's, Redbook, Cosmopolitan,* and the *Saturday Evening Post.* And, as he had done with the Midwest, Vonnegut used upstate New York as a setting for much of his fiction: Schenectady became Ilium, a city distinguished by its inability to live up to its heroic name and by its surrender to decidedly unheroic values. Around this time, already having made several starts at a novel about Dresden,[12] he contacted the Air Force requesting details about the raid—who ordered it, how many planes were involved, why they attacked, what desirable results they achieved, and so on. As he writes in *Slaughterhouse-Five*, "I was answered by a man who, like myself, was in public relations. He said that he was sorry, but that information was top secret still. I read the letter out loud to my wife, and I said, 'Secret? My God—from *whom?*' "[13]

By 1950, Vonnegut had quit GE to devote himself to writing full-time on Cape Cod. Although his more serious work lacked a wide audience, his popular stories and soon his novels, several of which were first published as paperback originals, sold steadily enough to support his large family. Yet the memory of Dresden still haunted him. Rather than attempt to obliterate it, however, Vonnegut chose to make that memory his vehicle for interpreting human history and for contemplating the future. In his earlier novels, especially *Player Piano* and *The Sirens of Titan*, he had written of fictitious revolutions and disasters; now he felt it was time to confront one both real and familiar.

After a 1967 visit to Dresden on a Guggenheim Fellowship—and fueled by the horror of America's increasing involvement in the undeclared war in Vietnam—Vonnegut completed his "famous book about Dresden" (18). Published in 1969 by the independent publisher Seymour Lawrence, whom Vonnegut at one point addresses directly in the first chapter, *Slaughterhouse-Five* had a special urgency, particularly for a generation born in the aftermath of one war and coming of age in another. It became an instant critical success as well as a cult classic, full of antiwar sentiment and absurdly dark jokes. The book was, in part, the legacy of his German-American parents. Vonnegut once said they lived with a constant sadness that the world they loved had been destroyed by war; but fortunately "they were good at making jokes." And they taught him both the joking and the "bone-deep sadness"[14] that became his literary trademarks. Indeed in his fiction the laughter often negates the hurt and serves, in his words, as "an analgesic for the temporary relief of existential pain."[15]

The title page of *Slaughterhouse-Five* is an interesting example of this fusion of laughter and pain. A kind of pun that reads somewhat like a short prayer, the title page not only affirms the author's personal connection to the narrative that follows (itself a prayer that no more Dresdens will occur to haunt future generations) and to the unusual "telegraphic schizophrenic" manner in which it will be told; it also begins Vonnegut's story before its actual beginning.

Even the page's typography, which forms the outline of a bomb with the all-important word "peace" at its tip, serves as a comment on the violence of war.

"Slaughterhouse-Five; or, The Children's Crusade: A Duty-Dance with Death," the triple titles on the title page, synthesize the novel's major events at the same time that they suggest the insufficiency of any one title to encapsulate the experiences Vonnegut describes. "Slaughterhouse-Five" is, of course, *Schlachthof-fünf*, the actual address of the one hundred American prisoners of war in Dresden; they were housed in the fifth building of an old slaughterhouse, originally built as a shelter for pigs about to be butchered. But "the slaughterhouse wasn't a busy place any more," Vonnegut explains later. "Almost all the hooved animals in Germany had been killed and eaten and excreted by human beings, mostly soldiers. So it goes" (152). The slaughterhouse nevertheless provides an effective metaphor not simply for the dehumanizing world at war, in which young men like Vonnegut himself become the meat that feeds the war machine, but also for the increasingly brutal quality of all of life, whose violence merely culminates at regular intervals in such organized chaos as the slaughters in Dresden, Auschwitz, Hiroshima, and Vietnam. (Ken Kesey used the slaughterhouse metaphor for similar purposes several times in *One Flew Over the Cuckoo's Nest*. The inhuman rhythm of Big Nurse's ward was likened to the movement of "carcasses from the cooler to the butcher . . . in meat houses" [80]; and the use of shock treatment to tranquilize asylum patients began after "two psychiatrists were visiting a slaughterhouse, for God knows what perverse reason, and were watching cattle being killed by a blow between the eyes with a sledgehammer. They noticed that not all of the cattle were killed, that some would fall to the floor in a state that greatly resembled an epileptic convulsion" [163]. Postconvulsive states produced temporary physiological calm, and so the principle of the slaughterhouse was applied to institutionalized patients.)

The first subtitle, "The Children's Crusade," which shows how language falsifies war by transforming its cruelty into sentimental heroism and its calculation into innocence,[16] is based on a conversation Vonnegut had with Mary O'Hare, the wife of his war buddy Bernard. Hoping to spend a relaxed evening at the O'Hare home swapping war stories, Vonnegut arrived to find Bernard reluctant to speak and Mary visibly angry and suspicious of her guest's intentions. She refused to provide "two leather chairs near a fire in a paneled room, where two old soldiers could drink and talk" (12–13), and instead led Vonnegut to the rather sterile surroundings of her kitchen. There she denounced what she assumed would be the approach he would take in his novel: "You were just babies in the war . . . . But you're not going to write it that way, are you. . . . You'll pretend you were men instead of babies, and you'll be played in the movies by Frank Sinatra and John Wayne or some of those other glamorous, war-loving, dirty old men. And war will look just wonderful, so we'll have a lot more of them. And they'll be fought by babies like the babies upstairs" (14). Vonnegut, however, appreciated her moral indignation and realized that his responsibility was not just to tell the same old stories in the same old way, but to reinvent the form itself.[17] He promised Mary that if he ever completed his book, he would call it "The Children's Crusade," in honor of her babies, who he hoped would never have to go to war, and for the many other babies, not so fortunate, already killed in battle. Afterwards, Bernard read to them the story of the real Children's Crusade, started in 1213 by two monks who saw an opportunity for profit by selling armies of children from Germany and France. Thirty thousand children, thinking they were heading to Palestine, had volunteered for the crusade. About half eventually drowned; the other half reached North Africa, where they were sold. But due to a misunderstanding, a few reported for duty in Genoa, where no slave ships were waiting; they were fed and sheltered by some Genoans and sent back home. " 'Hooray for the good people of Genoa,' said Mary O'Hare" (16) at the conclusion of the account, harsh parallels of which can be found in the many military crusades of the twentieth century, all—according to Vonnegut—fought by children for causes they usually are unable to understand. (It is hardly surprising that Vonnegut dedicated *Slaughterhouse-Five* to Mary as well as to Gerhard Müller, the German cab driver who happened to pick him and Bernard O'Hare up at the airport, upon their 1967 return to Dresden, and who drove them to their former barracks in the slaughterhouse. Like Mary, Müller seemed to have touched Vonnegut deeply: he had been a prisoner of the Americans during the war, and his mother had been incinerated in the Dresden firestorm. After their visit, Müller sent a postcard wishing Vonnegut and O'Hare peace and freedom and the hope of meeting again in another taxi, "if the accident will" [2]. And indeed, like Mary's imprecation to the author about honesty in storytelling, Müller's "if the accident will" became a crucial theme in Vonnegut's tale.)

"The Children's Crusade" comes up again later in the novel, when the British colonel who hosts the Americans in the German POW camp says to Edgar Derby, "We had forgotten that wars were fought by babies. When I saw those freshly shaved faces, it was a shock. 'My God, my God,— 'I said to myself, 'It's the Children's Crusade' " (106). The appropriate subtitle, like Müller's philosophic (if syntactically fractured) sentiment, thus links the autobiographical portion of the novel's introductory chapter with the more "fictional" text that follows.

"A Duty-Dance with Death," the book's second subtitle, also reveals much about Vonnegut's novelistic approach as well as his intent. The actual phrase alludes to Céline, the French soldier and novelist about whom Vonnegut was reading en route to Dresden. Céline believed that no art is possible without an awareness of death: " 'The truth is death,' he wrote. 'I've fought nicely against it as long as I could . . . danced with it, festooned it, waltzed it around . . . decorated it with streamers, titillated it . . .' " (21). Slaughterhouse-Five, which for years Vonnegut felt compelled to write, had similarly caused him to confront death—the actual deaths of soldiers and civilians exterminated in war as well as the moral and spiritual death attendant upon the purveyors of a technology whose only purpose is to kill. The novel became for Vonnegut not just an artistic endeavor but a *summa*, a catharsis—and an obligation, or duty-dance, as Céline had suggested. In *Palm Sunday*, Vonnegut recalled "I only now understand what I took from Céline and put into the novel." In particular, the need to say "So it goes" every time a character in *Slaughterhouse-Five* died was "a clumsy way of saying what Céline managed to imply so much more naturally in everything he wrote."[18]

James Lundquist offers still another possible explanation for the subtitle, "A Duty-Dance with Death." He argues that the problem Vonnegut faced in his novel was "the increasing gap between the horrors of life in the twentieth century and our imaginative ability to comprehend their full actuality"—the same problem faced by the correspondent for the London *Times* who reported on Belsen, the first Nazi prison camp to be exposed to world scrutiny. "*It is my duty*," wrote the correspondent, "to describe something beyond the imagination of mankind."[19]

In describing the concurrent events at Dresden, events equally beyond mankind's imagination, Vonnegut moves from the autobiography of the title page and of the opening and closing chapters of *Slaughterhouse-Five* to biography in the intervening eight chapters. The shift from Vonnegut's own predicament to that of his central character alters the novel's perspective from introspection to observation: giving a biblical resonance to the moral aspect of his movement out of his own self-absorption into the suffering of another, it allows Vonnegut to serve as a sometimes detached but sympathetic observer of the catastrophe that he describes. He becomes a confirming witness to the testimony that his fictional protagonist silently provides.[20]

That character, a soldier and virtual walking corpse whom Vonnegut claims to have met en route to the prison camp in Dresden, is Billy Pilgrim. Having served honorably in the war, Billy (whose tall, slender shape gives him the appearance of a Coke bottle) returned home without apparent injury to marry the hefty, doting Valencia Merble. Valencia's father, Lionel, owner of the lucrative Ilium School of Optometry, had set him up in business. As Billy's story begins, he is a prosperous optometrist. Moreover, like Ben in Mike Nichols's popular film *The Graduate,* Billy knows where the future of America is: he lives in an all-electric home in the comfortable suburbs, practices his trade in shopping malls, and invests in Holiday Inns and Tastee-Freeze stands. He drives a Cadillac festooned with bumper stickers which serve as a map of his social and political convictions ("Visit Ausable Canyon," "Impeach Earl Warren," and "Support Your Police Department"); owns a dog named Spot; and has two children: a son, Robert, a former juvenile delinquent who has channeled his aggression into war and emerged a decorated Vietnam War Green Beret, and a daughter, Barbara, the caring if overbearing wife of an optometrist who, in the family tradition, has established his practice through his father-in-law Billy's generosity. Solidly middle-class, Billy's is the perfect life. Perfect—except, perhaps, for episodes of extreme violence such as the plane crash that kills all of the other convention-bound optometrists on board and that Billy rather ghoulishly foresees. "He knew it was going to crash," writes Vonnegut, "but he didn't want to make a fool of himself by saying so" (154). Perfect—except for the memory of poor honest Edgar Derby, a high school teacher who entered the war out of pure motives and whose execution over a teapot made him a symbolic human extension of Dresden.[21] That memory reverberates in Billy's consciousness like the chorus of a Greek tragedy and causes him to weep quietly to himself for years. Perfect—except for Billy's kidnapping, on the night of his daughter's wedding, to Tralfamadore, where he is held captive in a mating zoo as an audience of aliens resembling green plumber's helpers eagerly awaits his performance.

Superficially Billy's life is so traditional that it almost parodies the very vision of contemporary success it fulfills; but that success, as Richard Giannone has observed, has an "underside [which] follows the other formula of our time: mental breakdown, shock therapy, emptiness."[22] The almost schizophrenic duality of Billy's existence—the surface stability and affluence of his personal life in Ilium supplanted by his wild, otherworldly adventures, which take him out of the essentially unpleasant present—reveals that there is a flip side to the American dream, whose absolute validity Vonnegut questions as much as Kesey, Heller, Kosinski, and Styron did. Judging by Pilgrim's regress, what passes for the American dream may in fact be an American nightmare. In Vonnegut's earlier novel *God Bless You, Mr. Rosewater*, as Max Schulz observed, that dream had "materialized into a junk yard by way of the glories of technology";[23] Eliot Rosewater (who reappears in *Slaughterhouse-Five*) says that it had "turned belly up, turned green, bobbed to the scummy surface of cupidity unlimited, filled with gas, went *bang* in the noonday sun."[24] In *Slaughterhouse-Five*, Billy similarly notes its failure; finding the American dream as illusory as the beauty of Dresden, he rejects it and the values it purports to represent for the alternative reality of Tralfamadore, a dream ironically more real to him—and more satisfying.[25]

Billy's hospitalization before his marriage to Valencia and his brain surgeries after his accident suggest that he is not merely "unstuck in time" but rather just plain crazy. And he certainly has every reason to be. His war experiences, after all, have wrenched him from a naive, if sometimes troubled, adolescence and catapulted him into a world of bombs and bullies, both capable of a hideous strength. As a pacifist chaplain's assistant, "customarily a figure of fun in the American Army," writes Vonnegut, Billy "was powerless to harm the enemy or to help his friends." Nothing more than a valet to a preacher, he "expected no promotions or medals, bore no arms, and had a meek faith in a loving Jesus which most soldiers found putrid" (30–31). The unpopularity of his role is exacerbated by his appallingly bad timing: replacing a young man killed in action, Billy joins his regiment as it is in the process of being destroyed in the Battle of the Bulge. He does not have a chance to meet the chaplain to whom he was assigned; he "was never even issued a steel helmet and combat boots" (32). On his feet are the cheap, low-cut civilian shoes he had bought for his father's funeral from which he was returning when he received his orders to ship out;[26] the shoes, now lacking a heel, cause him to bob foolishly as he moves. His unsteady gait not only impedes Pilgrim's progress but also provides a sharp visual image of the topsy-turvy, somewhat arbitrary nature of morality—or at least what is perceived to be morality—in the modern world. Literally out of step with his peers, Billy is also out of sync with the cruelty of his environment. The incongruity of his situation is echoed by the plight of others, also victims, around him: the elder Mr. Pilgrim, who is shot during the war not by an enemy force but by a deer-hunting friend; Edgar Derby, sentenced to death for finding wonder in a commonplace object which survived the holocaust; Private Eddie Slovik, court-martialed and shot for failing to obey the rules of war in a war in which no rules apply; and the residents of Dresden and Hiroshima, annihilated simply for being there.

Unlike most of his regiment, Billy survives the Battle of the Bulge, only to be beaten severely by fellow American Roland Weary.[27] The troubled Weary has fantasized that he is part of "The Three Musketeers," an elite fighting unit distinguished by the "great services they rendered to Christianity" (51), and he blames Billy for its break-up. Yet in fact that unit is as fanciful as the Children's Crusade was false. Billy bears no responsibility for its dissolution: the other two of the would-be Musketeers, both skilled scouts anxious to escape the Germans, have ditched Weary because they don't want to be constrained by his slowness and ineptitude. However, it is they who are ultimately ambushed and killed; Billy, spared by the enemy from Weary's wrath, watches with a dopey fascination and detachment as the scouts' blood turns the surrounding snow the color of raspberry sherbet. Yet while Billy's German captors rescue him from his compatriot's violence, they take him captive as a prisoner of war—an act that places him in the underground barracks and ostensibly saves his life yet again. (Lawrence Broer calls such juxtapositions examples of the "principle of ironic contrast," which he correctly suggests informs the whole novel.[28])

After being loaded onto a box car along with other captured Americans to be shipped to a prison camp in Germany, Billy is given still another unenviable task: he becomes a "dumper" responsible for handling, literally, the waste of those around him. Each tightly locked car, Vonnegut writes, was transformed into "a single organism which ate and drank and excreted through its ventilators. It talked or sometimes yelled through its ventilators, too. In went water and loaves of black-bread and sausage and cheese, and out came shit and piss and language. Human beings in there were excreting into steel helmets which were passed to the people at the ventilators, who dumped them" (70). The distinctly scatological image of Billy's world as a large toilet bowl, an image that recalls the rawness and vulgarity of the slaughterhouse, is hardly an isolated one. It is repeated in scenes like the extravagant *Pirates of Penzance*-like production mounted by the British POWs for their American guests, after which all of the Americans experience a severe attack of loose bowels in the makeshift loo.[29] The toilet image is augmented further by the description of the Tralfamadorians as plumber's friends. To Billy, only they comprehend the cosmic happenings and assist him in understanding the contemporary cesspool into which he is thrust. They alone, as Patrick Shaw contends, perform the symbolic function of cleaning the pipes of his perception, unclogging his vision and imagination by disabusing him of historical, sociological fixations. "Roland Weary tries quite literally to 'beat the living shit' out of Pilgrim," writes Shaw, "but only the Tralfamadorians, through unsentimental, sardonic logic, succeed in removing the waste from Pilgrim's mind. Himself a bit of human waste sticking in the cosmological pipes, Pilgrim comes 'unstuck in time' and simultaneously unclogs his own perceptions so that he realizes the 'negligibility of death, and the true nature of time.' "[30]

After arriving in Dresden and being put to work in a malt syrup factory, by mere coincidence (or, as Müller would say, because "the accident will[ed]"), Billy and his fellow Americans escape the city's incineration. In another of the novel's many ironies, the more than 135,000 largely civilian residents die while their prisoners of war, those destined for the slaughterhouse in which they were interned, survive. The morning after the Allied Forces' attack, Billy recalls "seeing little logs lying around. There were people who had been caught in the fire storm. So it goes" (179). The landscape, he says, resembled that of the moon, and the subsequent remembrance of this atrocity launches Billy on other extraterrestrial voyages, both forward into the fourth dimension and backward into his youth.

After the war, he returns to Ilium not a heroic warrior completing a successful odyssey but a shell-shocked victim exhibiting the classic characteristics of postcombat stress and depression, and checks himself into a mental hospital for veterans, even though "Nobody else suspected that he was going crazy. Everybody else thought he looked fine and was acting fine." The doctors recognize the symptoms of his condition but blame Billy's instability on his childhood. Unambiguously Freudian in their analysis, "They didn't think it had anything to do with the war. They were sure Billy was going to pieces because his father had thrown him into the deep end of the Y.M.C.A. swimming pool when he was a little boy, and had then taken him to the rim of the Grand Canyon" (100). Though they dismiss too quickly the obvious and immediate trauma brought on by the Dresden holocaust (deliberately undocumented and thus ignored for many years), the doctors are not completely wrong in their diagnosis. His father's unconscious aggressiveness in fact establishes a pattern of violent acts which Billy must endure throughout his youth and which culminate for him in the accidental devastation of Dresden, just as the violence is reenacted in his numerous personal tragedies, from the plane crash to his assassination, after the war's end.

In the hospital, Billy copes the only way he can: by withdrawing from others. As long as his mother remains at his bedside, he covers his head with a blanket and refuses to come out. "It wasn't that she was ugly, or had bad breath or a bad personality. She was a perfectly nice, standard-issue, brown-haired, white woman with a high-school education" (102), a woman who, like so many Americans, was "trying to construct a life that made sense from things she found in gift shops" (39). Perhaps because he associates her with subtle cruelties from his childhood (such as the gruesome, clinically faithful crucifix she attached to his bedroom wall and which made Billy as familiar with torture as Roland Weary was) or perhaps "because she had gone to such trouble to give him life, and to keep that life going" even though he doesn't really like life at all (102), he always feels much sicker until she goes away. (These feelings are shared by another Billy, Kesey's Billy Bibbit, who is debilitated by the mere mention of his mother.)

When Billy finally peeks out from under his wraps, his mother is gone, replaced by a figure even more frightening—Valencia Merble, wearing harlequin-framed glasses trimmed in rhinestones and looking "as big as a house because she couldn't stop eating. She was eating now" (107). The vision of Valencia is particularly unsettling to Billy because of the memories that it evokes. The "Three Musketeers Candy Bar" that she is devouring, for instance, forces him to fixate at least momentarily on Weary's like-named merry band of marauders, one of the very experiences he has entered the institution to forget. Valencia's diamond engagement ring is a further reminder of traumatic times; itself a booty of war, the diamond was sewn into the pocket of the harlequinish red-and-black coat he was issued by his captors. "Billy didn't want to marry ugly Valencia. She was one of the symptoms of his disease. He knew he was going crazy when he heard himself proposing marriage to her, when he begged her to take the diamond ring and be his companion for life" (107).

In the stream of Billy's distorted consciousness and in the telegraphic schizophrenic narration of the novel, the unpleasant moments sparked by Billy's mother and fiancée are linked to other moments, some equally unpleasant, some happier, yet all intricately interconnected in the book. Valencia's appearance with her candy bar at his bedside, for instance, recalls an earlier episode related in the autobiographical opening chapter. While working at the Chicago City News Bureau (a harsh practical internship in real human behavior diametrically opposed to the theoretical and more humane study in anthropology he had undertaken in graduate school in Chicago), Vonnegut had to phone in the story of the death of a young veteran. The veteran, who ran an old-fashioned elevator in an office building, had caught his wedding band in the door's ornamental ironwork—an iron twig with two iron lovebirds perched on it—and was crushed by the elevator as it descended. When Vonnegut returned to the office, the tough woman writer who had taken his story was seated at her desk eating a Three Musketeers bar. When she asked "what the squashed guy had looked like" (9), he answered simply that he'd seen worse in the war. Valencia similarly presses Billy to share with her the gory stories she overhears him telling her father—an action that links Billy to the author and associates the randomness and brutality of everyday life with the violence of war. Moreover, like the dead vet, physically trapped by his wedding band, Billy is metaphysically trapped in his marriage to his fat and fatuous wife; there is no way on earth for him to escape her, even in his drunken but abortive attempt to make love to another optometrist's wife atop a washing machine during a party or his inebriated fumblings in the back of an automobile.

Valencia's appearance in Billy's hospital room immediately after his mother's departure is likewise no accident: both Mrs. Pilgrims share many oppressive qualities. Yet at the same time that Billy hides from his mother, he has unexpressed longings for her—Oedipal and erotic fantasies fulfilled not by Valencia, with whom he stays because it will be at least "bearable all the way," but by his Tralfamadorian mate, Montana, whose name suggests an untamed wild-west quality so different from Billy's tame Ilium existence. Not surprisingly, Billy has to go out of this world to score with her and to achieve one of the few truly happy moments in his life. Merely thinking of Montana causes Billy to have a wet dream, just as his mother's touch—notably at the edge of the Grand Canyon—causes him to wet himself as a boy. Yet even Montana cannot quell his painful memories; her request to "tell me a story" jars Billy out of his otherworldly happiness and thrusts him back to wartime Europe, just as Valencia forces him to relive moments of his Dresden horror and as the woman writer in the news office forces Vonnegut to recall his.

All of these "random" episodes are thus intertwined: Billy's contradictory feelings for his mother; Billy's loveless but devoted relationship with his wife; Billy's passionate liaison with Montana, his surrogate wife, who embodies both the fantasies Valencia is unable to fulfill and the nurturing the elder Mrs. Pilgrim was unable to provide. Even the dead veteran and his wife and their now fatherless baby are connected to Billy, himself a fatherless vet emotionally deadened by his experiences in Dresden and Ilium, the perpetual child of a dead marriage, perpetuating his own dead marriage.

After his plane crash Billy again seems to withdraw into silence and depression. He says little about the news of Valencia's death and does not respond to his son Robert's visit (a trip comparable to Vonnegut's own return home, after his mother's suicide, just before he was to ship out for overseas duty); the doctors talk about another operation on his brain to improve the circulation of his blood and to remediate his vegetablelike state. (Like McMurphy, he already sports a huge surgical scar across his forehead, a badge of his nonconformity.) Billy's hospital roommate, Bertram Copeland Rumfoord, Harvard history professor, retired Brigadier General, and official Army Air Force Historian, keeps wondering aloud, "Why don't they let him *die?* . . . That's not a human being anymore" (190). He concludes that Billy, who persists in interrupting Rumfoord's conversations about Dresden to insist that he was there, is suffering from echolalia, the "mental disease which makes people immediately repeat things that well people around them say" (192). Rumfoord's assessment is accurate, symbolically if not clinically: like Yossarian, Billy sees everything twice—and sometimes more often. He visits and revisits moments in his life, and his journeys are as reflexive as the nonsensical limerick about Yon Yonson which Vonnegut recounts in the opening chapter.[31] Yet echolalia is also a good description of the larger societal malaise: Rumfoord and his contemporaries are afflicted by a narcissism that echoes through their shallow hearts and minds. T. S. Eliot called such people the wasteland's hollow men, while another Eliot—Rosewater—characterized them as "gutless wonders," emotionless robots programmed only for rote and mindless actions.

When revisionist historian Rumfoord finally realizes that Billy really *was* in Dresden, he makes evident his sympathy for the victimizers, not the victims of the disaster. With a military logic, he urges Billy to "pity the men who had to *do*" the bombing (just as Höss rationalizes his actions in *Sophie's Choice*). Yet Rumfoord's thinking is hardly without precedents in Vonnegut's novel. For instance, in the foreword to *The Destruction of Dresden*, a book that Rumfoord is reading, Lieutenant General Eaker concludes that the deaths of five million Allies in the fight against the Nazis were far worse (substantively, not just numerically) than the 135,000 killed in Dresden. And in the opening chapter Vonnegut recalls his conversation with a faculty member from the University of Chicago; after hearing of his experience of the Dresden raid, Vonnegut writes, the professor "told me . . . about how the Germans had made soap and candles out of the fat of dead Jews and so on" (10). Such false attempts to balance one atrocity with another, to neutralize both, and thereby to expiate all guilt fail resoundingly,[32] and Vonnegut finds them particularly deplorable. "The kind of morality that trades slaughter for slaughter," as Raymond Olderman observed, "ultimately leads to justification of Dresden and to a tricky sense of righteous revenge . . . [and makes] it easier to find just and good causes for total cataclysm."[33] Like Vonnegut, who responds to the Chicago professor with "I know, I know. I *know*" (10), Billy (whose Tralfamadorian insights are more absolute than even Army Air Force wisdom) replies with a studied resignation to Rumfoord that "it was all right. *Everything* is all right, and everybody has to do exactly what he does" (198).

As Rumfoord misuses both history and logic, Billy's daughter misuses affection. Barbara seems to find excitement in "taking his dignity away in the name of love" (132). Drawing attention to his failure to turn on the heat, change from his nightwear, answer the doorbell, or listen to people when they talk to him, she treats him altogether condescendingly and attempts to reverse their parent-child roles. After she threatens to put him in a home with his antique mother, Billy escapes her petticoat tyranny long enough to return to his office. There he manages to see just one patient (a young boy whom Billy assures—Tralfamadorially speaking—that his father, who was killed in Vietnam, is still very much alive in moments the son would see again and again) before the boy's mother reports to "the receptionist that Billy was evidently going crazy" (135) and Barbara is called to take him back home. (The image of the fatherless boy echoes not only the infant son of the veteran squashed to death by the elevator but also the young German guard whose father is incinerated in the Dresden raid and the young Derby left fatherless after Edgar's senseless execution.)

Billy's Tralfamadorian vision also allows him to foretell his own death, less than nine years after the ostensible end of the book, at a convention where he is lecturing[34] on flying saucers and the true nature of time; Paul Lazzaro keeps his promise to execute Billy, and the assassination occurs coincidentally on the thirty-first anniversary of the Dresden firebombing. It is also the nation's bicentennial year, ironically a celebration of independence brought about by military revolution. While the scene inside the convention hall is reminiscent of the raucous Chicago Democratic presidential convention, the actual assassination recalls the murders of other pilgrims who advocated peace and truth, especially Martin Luther King Jr. and Robert Kennedy, to whom Vonnegut alludes in the novel's final chapter. (Vonnegut reportedly finished *Slaughterhouse-Five* the day after Kennedy's death.)

But Billy is no simple schizophrenic or delusional individual; though intermittently institutionalized, he is, like McMurphy and Yossarian before him, quite possibly the sanest man around. His sanity is evidenced, among other things, by his sheer endurance. He survives many of those more belligerent or more clever than he: Derby, his surrogate father; Mr. Pilgrim, his real father; Lionel Merble, his father-in-law; Colonel Wild Bob; Roland Weary; and Valencia. He survives his dog, Spot—and, of course, all the residents of Dresden killed so suddenly and so ignominiously that February night. *Slaughterhouse-Five*, in fact, is full of deaths—by starvation, rotting, incineration, squashing, gassing, shooting, poisoning, bombing, torturing, and hanging, and even relatively routine death by disease. As Lawrence Broer demonstrates, "We encounter individual deaths; the deaths of groups en masse; accidental, calculated, and vengeful deaths; recent and historical deaths."[35] Some of the most hideous are within Billy's own family—Valencia's carbon monoxide poisoning, his father's hunting accident, his father-in-law's plane crash. Billy, a virtual corpse himself, is surrounded by perhaps more corpses than anyone in any other contemporary novel and no longer separates the horrors of war from the pain of contemporary life. In one particularly moving scene, he mistakes the Austrian ski instructors who come to rescue him at Sugarbush Mountain for German soldiers, and—thinking he is back in the war—he whispers to them his Dresden address: "*Schlachthof-fünf.*"

In addition to being a survivor, Billy is a visionary who, despite his corrective trifocals, sees things others cannot. His special sense is implied by the numerous visually oriented images in *Slaughterhouse-Five*, just as contemporary society's reliance on the visual and its emphasis on appearance instead of substance is suggested by the many television images in *Being There*. Billy's sense is not a madness, as it may initially appear,[36] but rather an ability to perceive the madness around him and find some meaning in it. Whereas Billy's wartime service roles as chaplain's assistant, "dumper," and prisoner of war are symbolic, his profession of optometry is even more so, since it is he who measures how well others view the world and he who literally provides the frames as well as the lenses for most of Ilium. At one point, he falls asleep behind an "owl," the optometer in his office which represents his newfound cosmic understanding. (Earlier, in another interesting connection between owls and his otherworldly experiences, Billy had mistaken the Tralfamadorian saucer's whirl for the hoot of an owl.) His patient startles him by asking, "You were talking away there—and then you got so quiet . . . . You see something terrible? . . . Some disease in my eyes?" (56) Indeed Billy does see something terrible, though not what his patient suspects; he sees a spiritual consumption which keeps men from being kind,[37] keeps them oblivious to reality and clinging to illusion, like the blind innkeeper outside of Dresden who waits for guests to arrive even though he knows that the city has been reduced to smoldering ash. To allay foolish earthly fears about death and put chronological time into a better perspective, Billy decides to share his Tralfamadorian vision with newspaper readers and talk-radio audiences; his "prescribing [of] corrective lenses for Earthling souls" (29) who were lost and wretched because they could not see as well or as far as his little green one-eyed friends could is simply an extension of his optometry. He hopes, with these new insights, to help others achieve the peace of the Alcoholics Anonymous credo which hangs on his office wall: "God grant me the serenity to accept the things I cannot change, courage to change the things I can, and wisdom always to tell the difference." (However, as Vonnegut writes, undercutting Billy's good intentions, "Among the things Billy Pilgrim could not change were the past, the present, and the future" [60].) That same popular prayer is later repeated, inscribed on a locket that hangs between Montana Wildhack's sensational breasts, the only place Billy achieves such serenity.

Just as the Tralfamadorians give Billy a unique vantage point from which to view his experiences, Billy provides a similar function for his author by allowing Vonnegut to project his own condition and live with his wartime nightmare. A fictional construct quite distinct from Vonnegut, Billy nevertheless affords the frame for Vonnegut's very personal tale. "Billy the optometrist who fits people with glasses," writes David Goldsmith, "has fitted Vonnegut with a pair which, if not exactly rose colored, have enabled him to see things in their proper perspective."[38]

In contrast, though their sight is far reaching and multidimensional, the Tralfamadorians' vision is limited. By concentrating only on the happy moments of life, they ignore the unhappy ones; and they do not deal with ugly incidents, like Billy's stupid responses to their teaching or Montana's screams of fear and displeasure upon arriving in the dome. Instead they choose a form of self-blindness: they flip their little hands over their lone eyes (also a symbol of the limitations of their vision) and isolate themselves from rather than integrate themselves with the event. Richard Giannone likens their reaction to a child's shutting his eyes to control his environment and making unwelcome sights disappear.[39] The action liberates the beholder from immediate pain but sets him apart from the universe. For the Tralfamadorians, the tranquility that results from their detachment provides a privileged glimpse into time future or past. Yet their focus on "moments" rather than continuum eliminates the need for causality, and it encourages them to abdicate responsibility for their actions.

Billy learns from the Tralfamadorians, but he uses their lessons constructively: he wants not to escape from responsibility but merely to cope. What others perceive to be Billy's illness is actually, for him, a way of expanding his perception. By becoming unstuck in time, he is able to withdraw to be healed and return to face the present situation. In this regard, he is less like the absurdist hero of experimental novels and more like the traditional monomythic hero discussed by Joseph Campbell, who develops his consciousness in stages of departure, initiation, and return, or like the "American Adam" of R. W. B. Lewis, who sees things as if for the first time, as Chance in *Being There* does. Pilgrim's name certainly suggests his Adamic dimension, as do the several allusions to Adam and Eve and to Billy's Adamic function as the first man on Tralfamadore, who fathers his own race with Montana, his Eve.

Billy handles the tragedies and horrors that surround and threaten to overwhelm him by stopping the clock and moving, in flashbacks or flashforwards, to other places, other times—places and times that allow him to understand more fully what is happening in the present. His disconnections are never random: like Walter Mitty's fantasies, Billy's time travels[40] have threads of continuity that link them, one to another. Rather than permitting his psyche to unravel, Billy holds himself in check through his travels and stitches together the fragments of his existence into a less tenuous, more integrated whole.

Moreover, the rather far-out philosophy he learns on his journeys helps him to make sense out of an otherwise senseless reality. In a letter to the *Ilium News Leader*, he notes that "the most important thing I learned on Tralfamadore was that when a person dies he only *appears* to die." There is no reason to grieve for him because the person is still very much alive in the past. Tralfamadorians know that all moments, past, present, and future, have always existed, and they will always exist. So "when a Tralfamadorian sees a corpse," says Billy, "all he thinks is that the dead person is in bad condition in that particular moment, but that the same person is just fine in plenty of other moments. Now, when I myself hear that somebody is dead, I simply shrug and say what the Tralfamadorians say about dead people, which is 'So it goes' " (26–27). Thus the phrase "So it goes" follows every mention of death in the novel: Lot's wife, Müller's mother, the elevator-operating veteran in Chicago, the plane full of optometrists, Private Eddie Slovik, the scouts who deserted Weary and Billy, Martin Luther King Jr., Robert Kennedy, the young men fighting in Vietnam, the dead in the cellars of Dresden, the flat champagne after Barbara's wedding, the two cowboys in the picture pasted on the television tube of Billy and Montana's dome-home in Tralfamadore, the Universe, even the bacteria and lice on the war prisoners' clothes after disinfection. The phrase, which Raymond Olderman likens to Pynchon's "keep cool but care,"[41] is so conspicuous that it works against continuity at the same time that it reduces all tragedy to a sameness. As Richard Giannone demonstrates, "it breaks the action right at the point that seems to require extension if we are to understand death with more than Tralfamadorian disregard." Giannone considers "So it goes" to be "a close translation of *amen*, which is Hebrew for 'truly' or 'it is true' "; thus the repetition of the phrase in the novel "deepens from an initial sign of resignation to a refrain, one that conveys not an asservation of divine presence but an indictment of divine absence."[42] Interestingly, as Jerome Klinkowitz points out in his most recent study of Vonnegut, the novel's antiphonal response to death is anticipated more than two decades earlier: in a letter dated May 29, 1945, and written from a French repatriation camp, Vonnegut described for his family his experiences since being taken prisoner of war. He followed each mention of death with a conditioned response of survival (first "But I didn't [die]" and later "But not me") comparable to that which he used later in his novel.[43]

In *The Sirens of Titan*, the Tralfamadorians undercut the most significant human achievements: man's greatest monuments, from Stonehenge to the Great Wall, it turns out, were not hallmarks of civilization but merely Tralfamadorian communications to one another. (Stonehenge, for instance, was a message meaning "Replacement part being rushed with all possible speed" [271].) In *Slaughterhouse-Five*, the Tralfamadorians offer a similarly humbling cosmic context for Earthlings' inflated view of their own power and importance. The world ends not because of man's bellicose tendencies but because a Tralfamadorian test pilot, experimenting with new saucer fuels, "presses a starter button, and the whole Universe disappears" (117). When Billy ponders the prospect of such an ignoble end—a prospect only slightly more frightening than the thought that all American life and letters could be judged by the standard of Jacqueline Susann's *Valley of the Dolls*, the one English book in the Tralfamadorian museum—he asks if there is no way to keep the pilot away from the button. His hosts blithely reply that "he has *always* pressed it, and he always *will*. We *always* let him and we always *will* let him. The moment is *structured* that way" (117). The Tralfamadorians consider it pointless to try to prevent cataclysms or wars since wars, like glaciers—though inevitable, as even Vonnegut admits—are merely brief moments that soon will pass. Ironically, the Tralfamadorian pilot's "accident" is not so far removed from the devastating but very preventable firebombing of Dresden, and it therefore acts as another link between Billy and Vonnegut, both victims of one of the most egregious accidents of our age.

While he appreciates much of the Tralfamadorian philosophy, Billy is still able to see its inherent violence. The Tralfamadorians' apocalyptic calm, born of total indifference, is disguised by their genial manner. Because they do not change, as Billy and other humans do, they have no ethical referent.[44] Therefore, even though they are responsible for the extinction of the universe, they do not feel compelled to offer any apology for their conduct (a reaction analogous to the Allied Forces' lack of recognition—or assumption of responsibility—for the virtual extinction of Dresden). Since Billy is human and caring—sometimes too human, too caring—he finds it impossible to be as dispassionate as his Tralfamadorian hosts. When the Tralfamadorians express their scorn at his stupidity, he argues earnestly that advanced knowledge needs to be shared so that planets can "live at peace" (116). He even dies trying to share his newly found truth.

Though Vonnegut has frequently been misread by those who

believe he advocates the Tralfamadorian approach to life as an admirable alternative to human shortsightedness, his message, in fact, is to *not* adopt their extraterrestrial outlook. The Tralfamadorians take their cosmic coolness to an extreme and lose the very conscience that Vonnegut endorses and applauds. Conscience— humanity—is why Lot's wife looked back at Sodom and Gomorrah (cities, like Dresden, subjected to a firestorm). Saved from destruction, she turned a final time to see "where all those people and their homes had been," even though God explicitly ordered her not to. She was transformed into a pillar of salt for defying the highest authority (the same reason Derby and Slovik were shot), but Vonnegut writes "she *did* look back, and I love her for that, because it was so human" (22). Like Billy, Lot's wife "endured a great deal but knew little" and "suffered from the warmth of her own mercy." The Tralfamadorians are her opposite: "they know a great deal but care not at all. They play God but without his merciful concern for creation. The Tralfamadorian self embodies this scientific ideal and thereby exposes its shortcomings."[45] Vonnegut states explicitly in the novel that he would not like it if the Tralfamadorians turned out to be correct: "If what Billy Pilgrim learned from the Tralfamadorians is true, that we will all live forever, no matter how dead we may sometimes seem to be, I am not overjoyed" (211). Rather than emulate the Tralfamadorians' icy detachment, Vonnegut advises us to recognize ourselves in them, to understand that they are "appropriate symbol[s] for the mechanistic insanity of our own planet, an extension into the future of our own warlike globe."[46] And accordingly he urges his own sons to act on the free will that the Tralfamadorians deny; he warns them specifically to resist taking part in massacres, no matter how inevitable they may be, or to support in any way those who "make massacre machinery" (19).

Although the Tralfamadorians try to teach Billy about the relative unimportance of time, earth time is so primitive a concept to them that they can apprehend it only metaphorically, equating temporal vision to encasing Billy's head in a steel sphere that he can never remove, giving him just one eyehole through which he can look, and then welding to that eyehole six feet of pipe. Despite their insight that all time is all time, that it simply is, like the "amber" of the moment (86), Billy remains a temporal being; and in *Slaughterhouse-Five* clocks are everywhere, from the pocket watch Billy's father wears in the cavern to the electric clocks that the Tralfamadorians have set up in Billy and Montana's dome to make them feel at home.[47]

Though often inadvertently, Billy himself links time to material success. As he returns from his time travels, he determines what year it is by the amount of money he is making, the type of car he is driving, the dollar value of his gifts to Valencia, and the number of his investments. Even in the prisoner of war camp time has a similar magical property. The huge clock above the stage strikes midnight and the surrealistic American Cinderellas are transformed into puking, wailing, diarrhetic invalids, who in their haste for relief knock over the latrine buckets. (Those buckets, stationed like obedient sentinels, mock their misery, just as the Americans' behavior mocks the Brits' admonition, crisply written in pink paint and nailed to the shed: "Please leave this latrine as tidy as you found it!" [125].) And at the end of the war, when all of the freed prisoners are collecting war booty, one Brit jealously guards his treasure: a clock ensconced in a gaudy plaster model of the Eiffel Tower. It is as if he thinks that by gripping the clock he will somehow recover the years he lost in the never-never land of German captivity. Likewise, looting Americans, for whom time has brought much horror but little wisdom, "had gone into empty houses in the suburb where they had been imprisoned" (194) and removed a stuffed owl and a mantel clock. And the blind innkeeper's family wind their "clock [which] ticked on," despite the fact that "Dresden was gone" (181) and there is little life left to measure.

For others, time is a weapon. Paul Lazzaro, brother-in-arms to the tortured torturer Roland Weary, uses it for creative revenge: after being bitten by a dog, he cuts out the springs of a clock, sharpens them, and imbeds them in a steak, which he then feeds to the miserable animal, who tries to bite his own insides out to alleviate the pain.

Even Céline, the narrator notes, was obsessed by time. A "brave French soldier in the First World War—until his skull was cracked," Céline (like the narrator and Billy) could no longer sleep at night. "There were noises in his head." He became a doctor, treating people in the daytime, and he wrote "grotesque novels all night." In one novel, "He screams on paper, *'Make them stop . . . don't let them move anymore at all . . . There, make them freeze . . . once and for all! . . . So that they won't disappear anymore!'* (21).

Tralfamadorians, of course, can freeze action by concentrating on a particular moment. Even their novels transcend all notions of clock time. Written in clumps of symbols separated by stars, they are a collection of brief, urgent messages (Billy likens them to telegrams) meant to be read all at once. "There is no beginning, no middle, no end, no suspense, no moral, no causes, no effects. What we love in our books," say the visitors from another planet, "are the depths of many marvelous moments seen all at one time" (88).

The Tralfamadorian novels sound suspiciously like Vonnegut's own, especially *Slaughterhouse-Five,* in which he tells the reader that "there are almost no characters in this story, and almost no dramatic confrontations" (164) and in which he parodies traditional structure by revealing in his opening chapter how the novel begins and ends. Moreover, the novel, organized like its Tralfamadorian counterpart and narrated in a "telegraphic schizophrenic manner," depends on its form to suggest its content. But woven into the seemingly random and discontinuous snippets of Vonnegut's narrative are recurring images that provide the story's unity. In addition to the use of the phrase "So it goes," a refrain haunting because of its frequency, is the repeated mention of certain other words and phrases. "Mustard gas and roses," for example, is how Vonnegut describes his late-evening breath. "I have this disease late at night sometimes, involving alcohol and the telephone. I get drunk, and I drive my wife away with a breath like mustard gas and roses" (4). Midway through the novel, on the eve of his daughter's wedding, just as he is about to depart on his first time travel, Billy walks into his daughter's empty room and picks up her ringing Princess telephone to find "a drunk on the other end. Billy could almost smell his breath—mustard gas and roses" (73). On the final pages, Vonnegut brings together again the novel's two most important characters, himself and Billy, through their common experience. In the days after the attack on Dresden, he writes, "There were hundreds of corpse mines operating by and by. They didn't smell bad at first, were wax museums. But then the bodies rotted and liquefied, and the stink was like mustard gas and roses" (214). The mustard gas and rose breath is thus the vestige of the firebombing which Billy remembers and which Vonnegut carries with him still and hopes to purge by finally articulating it in his Dresden book.

Color images also recur throughout the novel. "Blue and ivory" are the colors of Billy's feet after the oil burner in his house has quit; though the temperature is falling, he is oblivious to the cold because he is busy at work composing a letter about the Tralfamadorians. The "cockles of Billy's heart, at any rate, were glowing coals," hot with the belief "that he was going to comfort so many people with the truth about time" (28). On the night of his first trip to Tralfamadore, he gets out of bed in the moonlight feeling spooky and luminous, "as though he were wrapped in cool fur that was full of static electricity. He looked down at his bare feet. They were ivory and blue" (72). His anxiousness to embark on his interplanetary voyage is reminiscent of his feelings on his first afternoon as a prisoner of war, which he found "stingingly exciting. There was so much to see—dragon's teeth, killing machines, corpses with bare feet that were blue and ivory" (65). But his excitement dissipates quickly after he witnesses too much killing and sees too many corpses, including the hobo whom he befriended on the train to the German camp. Somebody had taken the hobo's boots, and his "bare feet were blue and ivory" (148). On that train, Billy almost became a corpse himself as he was forced to lie in a position of crucifixion on the corner-brace, "holding himself there with a blue and ivory claw hooked over the sill of the ventilator" (80).

"Orange and black" have similar connotations, reminding him of the colors of the locomotive and the last car of the trains heading to the German compound (the orange and black banners indicated that the train was not fair game for airplanes since it contained prisoners of war); the colors of the dragger which passes only a few feet from the balcony of his honeymoon apartment with Valencia; and the gaily striped tent set up in his back yard for Barbara's wedding. And Vonnegut writes that, in outlining his Dresden book, he once used the back of a roll of wallpaper: "The destruction of Dresden was represented by a vertical band of orange cross-hatching" (5). Yellow is also significant for Billy. Though the yellow chairs of Sugarbush Mountain, which he observes as he is being taken to the hospital after his plane crash, make him suppose "that they were part of an amazing new phase of World War Two" (157), the "yellow contour chair" he later rides aboard the Tralfamadorian-bound saucer is a far more pleasant diversion, as is his yellow lounge chair in the dome-home he shares with Montana. As Jerome Klinkowitz demonstrates, "Vonnegut takes care with these colors because they will be used to trigger the reader's own time-travel." Because specific colors are repeated, "readers feel the passages belong together" and therefore make the associations subliminally. This creates a deep impression "that this novel does have a principle of order to it, even if that principle cannot be articulated."[48]

Other images also unify the narrative. In the dark of the POW camp, the starving Russian soldiers, whose days are numbered, have faces like "radium dials" (91), as ghoulish as the radium dial of Billy's father's pocket watch, which frightened him as a boy in the dark of Carlsbad Cavern. The partial denture that he finds sewn into the lining of his impresario's coat along with Valencia's diamond is still in his cuff link case at his home in Ilium more than twenty years later; and even on Tralfamadore, Billy's own partial denture links his present happiness to his past sorrows by evoking less enjoyable moments in time. As spastic in space as Billy is in time, the cripples who sell magazine subscriptions door to door for a corrupt distributor in Ilium make him think of the crippled men and boys impressed into service to guard the American prisoners, themselves "crippled human beings" (150). Only four of those guards survived the firebombs; in the subsequent confusion they opened their mouths to speak but could say nothing. Looking "like a silent film of a barbershop quartet" (178), they reminded Billy of the barbershop quartet singing on the plane just before it crashed and of the singing optometrists, the "Febs" ("Four-eyed bastards"), who entertained at Billy's anniversary party years later. (There is, in their description, also the faint echo of the hearty but ludicrous Brits singing "Hail, Hail" upon the Americans' arrival at the POW camp.) And the image of "nestling like spoons" permeates all of his memories: as the train carried him eastward, Billy nestled like a spoon on Christmas night with his hobo friend who later, even in death, tried "to nestle like a spoon with others" (148); the theater in the British compound, which resembled a funeral service, "was paved with American bodies that nestled like spoons" (144); as Billy and Valencia nestled like spoons in their big double bed, he traveled in time back to a different train ride, "from maneuvers in South Carolina to his father's funeral in Ilium" (126).

In *Slaughterhouse-Five*, as in *One Flew Over the Cuckoo's Nest*, the numerous animal images comment on human behavior and provide still further links between the vignettes. Like Vonnegut's dog Sandy, Billy's dog Spot is his faithful late-night companion. Perhaps it is his familiar bark that Billy hears intermittently in the background throughout the novel. But whether it is Spot or not, the repetition of the line "Somewhere a dog barked" helps to root the surreal events of war in a more mundane, comprehensible reality, much as the noise "ta-pocketa-pocketa-pocketa . . ." does in Thurber's tale of Walter Mitty. The German soldiers' ferocious-sounding shepherd Princess (associated by her name to the ringing Princess phone in Billy's home, which, like the barking, disturbs the silence of his evening) "had been borrowed that morning from a farmer" and, like Billy, had "never been to war before" (52); another dog, the victim of Weary's wrath, also mirrors Billy's plight.

While the dogs actually materialize, the bats, on the other hand, never do. Billy merely imagines these omens of evil: roaming the dark of the cavern he visits with his parents, flying through the holes left by Weary's father's Derringer in the bodies of his victims, menacing him as he awakens from his morphine-induced sleep. The "vampire bat," as terrifying to Billy as the crucifix from his childhood, turns out to be nothing more than the fur collar of his own coat hanging above his hospital cot.

Horses appear several times. After the firebombing, Billy and a few of his colleagues find two hitched to a cart which they use to ride around the city looking for souvenirs. Treating their transportation "as though it were no more sensitive than a six-cylinder Chevrolet," the Americans hadn't noticed that "the horses' mouths were bleeding, gashed by the bits, that the horses' hooves were broken, so that every step meant agony, that the horses were insane with thirst" (196). When a couple, two childless obstetricians married to each other (curious symbols of infertility in the wasteland of Dresden), apprise Billy of the animals' condition, it crystallizes for him the brutality of war.[49] He "burst into tears. He hadn't cried about anything else in the war" (197). (His weeping continues, quietly and privately, like the lowing of the cattle in the novel's epigraph, for years.) The penultimate image of the novel occurs after Billy, released from his stable-barracks to discover that "somewhere in there was springtime" and that World War II in Europe was over, sees an abandoned "green and coffin-shaped" wagon drawn by two horses (215).

If the horses typify the pain of war, the pony suggests an animal passion of a much different kind. Roland Weary carries with him a picture of a woman attempting sexual intercourse with a Shetland pony, allegedly a print made from the first dirty photograph in history, which he forces Billy to admire. The unlikely half equine, half human pair of lovers is "posed before velvet draperies which were fringed with deedlee-balls" (40). Years later, Billy discovers the same photo, complete with drapes and deedlee balls, at a pornographic bookshop, where he also finds blue magazines and movies starring Montana Wildhack, who is engaged in equally bizarre bestial acts.

The book's final image is of yet another animal, a lone bird calling out to Billy. Vonnegut gives it the last word: *"Poo-tee-weet?"* That word is either a note of endurance or the dying cry of the canary released below ground to test the level of oxygen in a coal mine and the capacity for sustaining human life.[50] Earlier in the novel Vonnegut had predicted that it is always quiet after a massacre, "except for the birds . . . [who say] all there is to say about a massacre, things like *'Poo-tee-weet?'* " [19], and like the bird's song, Vonnegut's novel is "short and jumbled and jangled . . . because there is nothing intelligent to say about a massacre" (19).

The bird itself, like the horse-drawn, coffin-shaped wagon that Billy sees only a moment before he hears the bird's song, is a symbol of both apocalypse and rebirth. *"Poo-tee-weet?"*—a question and not a statement—suggests the ambiguity of its message and the conflict inherent in Billy's condition. (Is he sterile cuckoo or wise old owl?) Richard Giannone calls the bird "an image of twittering unintelligibility summing up what the dispersed narrative momentum anticipated in many ways—refusing to reach a crisis or resolution, in fine, to clarify itself or its intention for the reader."[51] But Raymond Olderman has a different interpretation. Noting that a similar small bird, Vonnegut's symbol for a kind of detachment, also appears in *Cat's Cradle* and *God Bless You, Mr. Rosewater*, Olderman considers the final song in *Slaughterhouse-Five* to be quite affirmative. The bird's question, he writes, might mean " 'so what' [as well as] 'I see the dimensions of human life and I survive!' " He concludes that "the nonsense words become especially moving . . . [because] we are witnessing a moment of balance in Vonnegut's own life, when he finds himself capable of dealing with the intense pain of his Dresden experience and ready to go on with the delicate business of living."[52] Billy hears the sound of the bird again at another critical point in his life: in the veterans' hospital where he is recuperating, the bird sings *"Poo-tee-weet?"* outside his window.

And, of course, there is the presence of trout—Kilgore Trout, a fish of a completely different stripe, like the atomic carp of the opening chapter. Trout is a prolific but largely unread writer of science fiction who wanders metaphysically through many of Vonnegut's works, as do other familiar characters, including Eliot Rosewater, Howard Campbell, and Bertram Rumfoord. But Trout is special; he is another persona for Vonnegut, who uses him to parody himself and to make cameo appearances in the novel, the way Alfred Hitchcock did in his films. ("Trout's unpopularity," writes Vonnegut in *Slaughterhouse-Five*, "was deserved. His prose was frightful. Only his ideas were good" [110].) Like Vonnegut, Trout puts "everything that happens" (172) to him in his novels, and he creates a new reality through his fiction. John Somer sees a particular kind of reflexiveness in Vonnegut's use of Trout: "Just as Vonnegut, in his twenty-second year, picked his way through the rubble of Dresden, Billy Pilgrim, toward the end of *Slaughterhouse-Five*, picks his way through the squalid ruins of a pornographic shop and finds there the inarticulate wisdom of Kilgore Trout, one of Vonnegut's masks, finds his 'impossible hospitable world.' Just as Vonnegut, twenty years later, is struggling to leave his autobiography and to enter his own fictive world to seek Billy out, Billy is pursuing Vonnegut in the guise of Trout with the same relentless tenacity."[53]

Fellow inmate Eliot Rosewater, assigned to the next bed at the Veteran's Hospital, introduces Billy to Trout's work. Rosewater and Billy, who "were dealing with similar crises in similar ways," had both found life meaningless, partly because of what they had seen in war. Eliot had accidentally shot a fourteen-year-old fireman he mistook for a German soldier; and now, like Billy, he is trying to reinvent himself and his universe. Such reinvention is no easy task. At one time, "everything there was to know about life," Eliot tells Billy, "was in *The Brothers Karamazov*"; but "that isn't *enough* any more." These days, Eliot contends, psychiatrists "are going to have to come up with a lot of wonderful *new* lies, or people just aren't going to want to go on living" (101). Eliot finds his answer and his consolation in science fiction, especially in the novels of Trout, which he gladly shares with his roommate. (In *God Bless You, Mr. Rosewater*, Eliot attends a science fiction convention and announces to the people there: "I love you sons of bitches. You're all I read any more. You're the only ones who'll talk about the *really* terrific changes going on" [18].)

Picasso claimed art is a lie that makes us realize the truth;[54] and Trout's fiction, most of which deals with "time warps and extrasensory perception and other unexpected things" (175), provides Billy with some wonderful new lies to compensate for the old, failed truths of technology. Because of their relevance to Billy's life, Trout's books have an immediate appeal. *The Gutless Wonder*, for example, deals with a robot with bad breath who dropped burning jellied gasoline from airplanes onto human beings below. The robot, whose description recalls the "mustard gas and roses" of the narrator's breath and of the Dresden corpse mines as well as Billy's robotized mother going through the motions at his bedside, has no conscience and no circuits to allow him to imagine what is happening on the ground; moreover, since he looked human, could dance, and even went out with women, "nobody held it against him that he dropped jellied gasoline on people. But they found his halitosis unforgivable" (168). Once he cleared that up, though—one of the benefits of "better living through chemistry"—he was welcomed into the human race. Trout's story, supposedly written in 1932, is fascinating to Billy because it is a sanitized, only mildly fictionalized, and above all prescient vision of pure technology's pseudotriumph in Dresden, where robots without consciences employed weaponry advanced because of, and despite, its capabilities. Implicit in the description of Trout's book—and in *Slaughterhouse-Five*—is a denunciation of contemporary society, which considers killing acceptable while bad breath is not. Similarly, a woman's spinsterhood (Valencia's big worry before her engagement to Billy) is deemed reprehensible, whereas dropping bombs on innocent citizens (especially when unreported in the press, as was the case initially with events in Dresden) is not. "Gutless wonder" is, for Vonnegut, a description not just of the robot programmed to commit such crimes but also of the people who build and then use him to cover up their own unconscionable acts and of the anonymous institutions that glorify technology at the expense of humanity.

Another of Trout's novels, *The Big Board*, features a man and woman kidnapped by extraterrestrials, who put the captives on display in a zoo on a planet called Zircon-12. They give them a big board purportedly showing stock quotes and commodity prices as well as a million dollars to invest, but the board and ticker tape are not genuine, "simply stimulants to make the Earthlings perform vividly for the crowds at the zoo" (201)—as Montana and Billy do, in their hermetically sealed dome. The fake stock market paraphernalia represent man's greed and moral bankruptcy, which lead to wars and massacres and barely tolerable marriages based on financial security, like the Pilgrims'. Billy's escape to Tralfamadore is also curiously reminiscent of Trout's *Maniacs in the Fourth Dimension*, in which people's mental diseases can't be treated because their causes exist in the fourth dimension, which "three-dimensional Earthlings can't see" (104).

But Trout's most controversial novel is *The Gospels from Outer Space*, in which he formulates an improved, higher octane theology. After an extraterrestrial shaped like a Tralfamadorian studies Christianity to understand why Christians find it so easy to be cruel, he concludes that the trouble in part is slipshod storytelling in the New Testament. The gospels, which intended to teach people to be merciful, even to the low, "actually taught this: *Before you kill somebody, make absolutely sure he isn't well connected*" (108–09). The flaw in the Christ stories, realizes the visitor, is Christ: people know that he is well connected, and so when they come to the crucifixion they say, "*Oh, boy—they sure picked the wrong guy to lynch* that *time!*" (109). But that thought has a brother, that there are *right* people to lynch. So the visitor gives Earth a new gospel, in which Jesus really *is* a nobody; he still says all the lovely things he said in the other gospels, but lacks powerfully divine support. When he is crucified by a public who fears no repercussions, God announces rather thunderously through the heavens that he is adopting the bum as his son, and that anyone who torments a bum in the future will be horribly punished.

Trout's theology—so shocking to some that they called for the banning of Vonnegut's novel[55]—holds out hope for the compensation of those wrongs committed in the name of justice, of those transgressions sanctioned by a mere show of authoritarian might, not right. The new gospel has more meaning than the old: according to its tenets, the execution of Edgar Derby for plundering a teapot and Weary's pummeling of Billy without cause won't go unpunished. (Billy, it seems, is attacked for the same reason as Dresden—simply for being there.) Divine retribution will be exacted for these wrongs and others perpetrated on life's honest clowns. Like the Tralfamadorian philosophy of time and history, the new theology makes allowances for the ironic contrasts in life and recognizes that things are not always as they may seem. So the weak may in fact be strong, the insane may possess the greatest insight, and those bound for the slaughterhouse may be the only ones destined to survive.

In his discussion of Trout's fiction, Vonnegut makes a case not only for a broader interpretation of Christianity, science's main

130

rival, but also for the survival of the novel as an art form—a survival that parallels both Billy's and his own, since the problem of living through the Dresden firebombing is rivaled by the problem of writing about it. For him, the form of life relates to the life of form.[56] He demonstrates this again in a wonderful scene in which Billy, who is waiting for the Tralfamadorian saucer to collect him, watches a war movie. Realizing that if his life is to make any sense, he must reinvent it by escaping from linear time, as Trout does through his science fiction, Billy does just that—by playing the movie in reverse. He reinvents reality by recasting it in art, whose restorative power subverts the destructive power of war (a process that again parallels Vonnegut's writing of *Slaughterhouse-Five*).[57]

American planes, full of holes and wounded men and corpses took off backwards from an airfield in England. Over France, a few German fighter planes flew at them backwards, sucked bullets and shell fragments from some of the planes and crewmen. They did the same for wrecked American bombers on the ground, and those planes flew up backwards to join the formation.

The formation flew backwards over a German city that was in flames. The bombers opened their bomb bay doors, exerted a miraculous magnetism which shrunk the fires, gathered them into cylindrical steel containers, and lifted the containers into the bellies of the planes. The containers were stored neatly in racks. The Germans below had miraculous devices of their own, which were long steel tubes. They used them to suck more fragments from the crewmen and planes. But there were still a few wounded Americans, though, and some of the bombers were in bad repair. Over France, though, German fighters came up again, made everything and everybody as good as new.

When the bombers got back to their base, the steel cylinders were taken from the racks and shipped back to the United States of America, where factories were operating night and day, dismantling the cylinders, separating the dangerous contents into minerals. Touchingly, it was mainly women who did this work. The minerals were then shipped to specialists in remote areas. It was their business to put them into the ground, to hide them cleverly, so they would never hurt anybody ever again. (74–75)

At the end of the movie, Billy extrapolates that Hitler turns into a baby and "all humanity, without exception, conspired biologically to produce two perfect people named Adam and Eve" (75). His vision, reminiscent of his epigraph ("Everything was beautiful, and nothing hurt" [122]), is of regression to paradise—a paradise he achieves not on Earth but on Tralfamadore, where he becomes Adam to Montana's Eve and their new baby.

Billy again uses art as a way of examining his own history. When he crashes a talk show in New York City on which several critics are discussing the function of the novel in modern society, he listens to their pompous pronouncements on Norman Mailer (by name), William Styron (by inference), and the purpose of the novel in general (for example, "to provide touches of color in rooms with all-white walls"; "to describe blow-jobs artistically"; "to teach wives of junior executives what to buy next and how to act in a French restaurant"), then tells them about flying saucers and Montana Wildhack and the true nature of time. Regarded as mad, he "is gently expelled from the studio during a commercial" (206); his nonfiction fiction and new realism are apparently more than the critics can handle. In this episode—one of the most humorous scenes in any novel *about* the novel—Vonnegut seizes the opportunity to turn the critical tables on some of his own reviewers, who dismissed his fiction as unliterary. Especially his early reviewers failed to recognize, as Leslie Fiedler did, that *Slaughterhouse-Five* was not about "the death of the novel that threatened literature in the 1960s" but rather about "the death of the elitist art novel"; thus it marked a new art form based on new, genuine myths.[58]

The real madness in *Slaughterhouse-Five,* though, is ultimately not Billy's or Rosewater's or even Trout's. Jerome Klinkowitz rightly observed that "the madness in Vonnegut's cosmos goes beyond the clinical illness."[59] The truly insane are those who, as Mary O'Hare tells Vonnegut, refuse to see the reality of war and who perpetuate it by romanticizing and glorifying it. Those, like Valencia, who associates sex and glamour with war. ("It was," say the Tralfamadorians, "a simple-minded thing for a female Earthling," especially one carrying in her womb the seeds of a future Green Beret conceived on her honeymoon night, "to do" [121].) Those, like the British prisoners of war, magical fairy godmothers who transform its ugliness into "the most popular story ever told" (96). Adored by the Germans, who thought the POWs were exactly what Englishmen ought to be, the captive Brits "made war look stylish and reasonable, and fun" (94) even after four years as hostages. Or those, like Wild Bob and Roland Weary, who see war as a forum for macho camaraderie.[60] Or those, like Bertram Copeland Rumfoord, who realizes he probably should "put something about [Dresden]" in his twenty-seven-volume *Official History of the Army Air Force in World War Two* but worries "that a lot of bleeding hearts might not think it was such a wonderful thing to do" (191). Or those, like Howard W. Campbell, American-turned-Nazi, who exploits war for his own profit. Costumed in an extravagant uniform of his own design (a white ten-gallon hat which would have made Wild Bob proud, black cowboy boots with swastikas and stars, a blue body stocking with yellow stripes, a shoulder patch with Abraham Lincoln in profile, and a red and white armband with another swastika on it, this time in blue), he tries to recruit men for his German military unit called the Free American Corps and writes about the shabby behavior of American prisoners of war. All these hopelessly programmed glamorizers of war are, as Broer concludes, "fully automated boobs, ready to conform to the most convenient mold, whether in the mistaken interests of survival or friendliness or out of the lack of imagination to do anything better; thus"—like the inmates on Big Nurse's ward, the soldiers caught in the military's Catch-22, or the benumbed television generation of *Being There*— "they become the ready slaves of whatever anonymous bureaucracies, computers, or authoritarian institutions take hold of their minds."[61] The real soldiers are babies, innocent children slaughtered on a false crusade. As the German war widow who cooks for the slaughterhouse workers affirms, "All the real soldiers are dead" (159).

The superficial glamour of war is further dispelled by the tragicomic reality of Billy's appearance and demeanor. "It was Fate," Vonnegut writes, "which had costumed him—Fate, and a feeble will to survive" (151). Fate apparently had a great sense of humor but little sense of fashion: still in his civilian shoes, lacking a helmet, boots, and weapon, Billy "didn't look like a soldier at all. He looked like a filthy flamingo" (33). But he doesn't have the flamingo's sense to duck: when he is shot at, he stands politely and permits the marksman a second chance. Later, he is the only one given a coat from a dead civilian; unlike his colleagues' brass-buttoned and tinseled overcoats, Billy's has a flare at the waist, a crimson red lining, and a dead animal frozen to the collar. When the British see him, they are filled with pity. "This isn't a man," they say. "It's a broken kite" (97). Later still, after he drapes himself in the stage curtain (as azure as

Valencia's face when she died) and dons the silver boots from the Cinderella production, "The boots fit perfectly. Billy Pilgrim was Cinderella, and Cinderella was Billy Pilgrim" (145).

His grin is almost as goofy as his garb; when the Germans throw him into the shrubbery to photograph him as part of their propaganda film, they have to tell him to stop smiling. Yet somehow, like his surrogate father Edgar Derby, Billy—despite his chronic innocence—manages to make enemies wherever he goes. No one wants to sleep near him because his dreams are so vivid and so disturbing. And he provokes Weary to such an extent that even the blasé German soldiers are "filled with a bleary civilian curiosity as to why one American would try to murder another one so far from home, and why the victim should laugh" (51).

As a sometimes-institutionalized visionary, Billy Pilgrim resembles McMurphy in *One Flew Over the Cuckoo's Nest,* another deliverer from social ills. But Billy's strongest literary equivalent is Chance in *Being There.* Kosinski's novel about the effects of television on contemporary culture, like *Slaughterhouse-Five,* is an allegorical work which draws no real conclusions; Billy, like Chance, is a nonperson, essentially uninteresting because he lacks depth and emotion. Yet Vonnegut and Kosinski are able to take these nonpersons and "hold our attention . . . by forcing us to think about their emblematic exaggerations"[62] and the shallowness of the society that produces them. Each ultimately creates his own reality: Billy through his Tralfamadorian fantasies, Chance through his collective fantasy of television.

Like Billy Budd and Billy Bibbit, his namesakes in American literature, Billy Pilgrim is a perpetual innocent, stammering simultaneously in several dimensions. His pilgrimage is one of retreat as well as of expansion; Pilgrim progresses as he regresses: his journeys into his past, like his flashforwards, help him to cope with and understand the present. Yet in a lunatic world in which cosmic accidents occur, incinerating tens of thousands of innocent people in a matter of seconds, and in which good men are executed by evil men with more authority, the "unstuck" Billy may well be the sanest man around. His mentor Kilgore Trout wrote about Earthlings who learn more about themselves as they venture into another dimension. Billy achieves such self-knowledge each time he enters a new dementia and returns holding more keys to unlock the asylum's secrets.

CHAPTER 5

Chance would do exactly

what he was told or else

he would be sent to a

special home for the

insane where, the Old

Man said, he would be

locked in a cell and

forgotten.

Chance did what he

was told.

Being There

Happening by Chance:

Being There

A N editorial in the *Journal of the American Medical Association*, commenting on a study by D. L. Rosenhan about "the blurring of the line between sanity and insanity—between normal behavior and actual mental illness," found that "the line of demarcation between mental health and mental illness, between saneness and unsaneness, is unclear and often defined by environmental circumstances." The editorial concluded by referring readers to a particular novel—Jerzy Kosinski's *Being There*—"as a supplement to scientific study."[1] It was the first time that *JAMA* had ever endorsed any work of fiction, and the endorsement quickly brought over 10,000 sales of the novel to doctors interested in its illustrations of aberrant ("unsane") behavior.

Being There (1971) is indeed an excellent portrait of contemporary insanity, especially of the social effects of the benumbing medium of television, an all-powerful American institution which renders individuals incapable of intelligent and free choice and thus creates a force as collectively supreme as the Combine in *One Flew Over the Cuckoo's Nest* and as totalitarian as the military machine in *Catch-22*. *Being There* decries in particular the condition of video idiocy—or "videocy," a term coined by Kosinski—which affects young and old Americans alike, who allow the artificial world of TV to become their only reality. "Imagining groups of solitary individuals," Kosinski has said, "watching their private, remote-controlled TV sets is the ultimate future terror: a nation of *videots*." In "a society founded [as ours is] on the principle of passive entertainment,"[2] such detachment from reality leads easily to the usurpation by others of the privacy and integrity of the individual self, a central concern in all of Kosinski's fiction. Kosinski's celebrated first novel, *The Painted Bird*, was a parable of demonic totalitarianism, "of that form of Nazi bestiality which is not a politics but a violence of the soul and blood." But, according to John Aldridge, "*Being There* has to do with a totalitarianism of a much subtler and even more fearful kind, the kind that arises when the higher sensibilities of a people have become not so much brutalized as benumbed, when they have lost both skepticism and all hold on the real, and so fall victim to those agencies of propaganda which manipulate their thinking to accept whatever the state finds it expedient for them to accept."[3]

Kosinski was personally familiar with the adverse effects of both totalitarianism and propagandism. Born in Łódź, Poland, in 1933, he was sent at the age of six away from the city to the relative safety of faraway Polish villages in order to save his life from the invading Nazis. Separated from his foster mother soon after being placed in her care, Kosinski managed for several years to eke out an existence among the often primitive and sometimes brutal peasants, events that he fictionalized in *The Painted Bird* and to which he alluded in other novels. An impressionable child, he moved from the black magic of witchcraft to the white magic of Christianity, from Nazism to Communism, and alternately embraced the various ideologies that parallel the grim road travelled by Western man. But each ideology proved disappointing,[4] and ultimately he learned that the only escape from the evils inherent in any system lies in illusion-free self-reliance and independently created values.

The wartime terrors took their toll on him; he became mute in 1942 and remained mute for six years, until a skiing accident restored his speech. After being reunited with his parents, who found him—still mute—in an orphanage in 1945, Kosinski worked his way quickly through high school and went on to the university, where he completed *magister* (master's) degrees in political science and history and began work "as a sociologist, as a social scientist . . . [abstracting] certain social forms into meaningful formulas which could be perceived by others in an act of self-recognition."[5] While continuing study and research at the Institute of the History of Culture in Warsaw and at Lomonosov University in Russia, he realized the impossibility of satisfying his creative needs in a totalitarian state and started to plot his escape, all the while living the life of an "inner émigré." Using "the creaking bureaucracy and the confusion of the aftermath of the Hungarian revolution, and Khrushchev's bent for liberalism, to obtain a passport,"[6] Kosinski said that he invented academicians who would endorse and sponsor his proposed research study abroad. With letters written on official-looking stationery which he had printed himself, he was determined to get out of Poland; yet in order to protect his parents, he chose not to tell them about his plans. Carrying (Kosinski claimed) a cyanide capsule in case his scheme failed, he secured a passport and plane ticket and embarked on the fictitious "Chase Manhattan Bank Fellowship" he had so elaborately orchestrated. (Kosinski's version of the events has been disputed by some critics and compatriots, who allege that his departure was less dramatic and less byzantine than he has reported.)

However he left his native land, Kosinski arrived in the United States in December of 1957 and undertook a succession of odd jobs—doing scab labor, scraping paint, cleaning bars, driving cars and trucks, working as a parking lot attendant. By 1958 he had secured a real fellowship, from the Ford Foundation, which allowed him to pursue doctoral study at Columbia University. A fellow student who was impressed by Kosinski's Russian experiences encouraged him to write about them. Kosinski did, in two nonfiction books—*The Future Is Ours, Comrade* (1960) and *No Third Path* (1962)—both published by Doubleday, serialized by the *Saturday Evening Post*, and condensed in *Reader's Digest*. The books were well received, especially in an era of cold war, and generated much fan mail. One letter came from Mary Hayward Weir, the widow of steel magnate Ernest T. Weir. Mary was a wealthy woman, with a Park Avenue apartment, houses in Hobe Sound and Southampton, a floor at the Ritz in Paris, a suite at the Connaught in London, a villa in Florence, a huge staff, and the use of corporate planes, yachts, and automobiles.[7] They met (after Mary played a trick on him by impersonating her own secretary—a trick that is fictionalized and recounted in *Blind Date*) and, in 1962, they married. Once he became a part of Mary's world, Kosinski discovered a life as sensational as that of fiction. "I had lived the American nightmare," he said, "now I was living the American dream"[8]—and he used those American-dream experiences as the basis for many of his nine novels.

Being There, Kosinski's third novel and the first to treat an American protagonist in an American setting, is his vision of that dream turned into a bizarre video nightmare. Drawing on his perspectives as a foreigner and an outsider observing the sociopolitical landscape of his new country, especially the uniquely American obsession with celebrity and power, Kosinski was able to comment incisively on the willingness of many contemporary Americans to sacrifice their individuality to the institution and their reality to a collective fantasy. In *Being There*, he even alluded to people from his own life. Benjamin Rand, for example, the wealthy financier who welcomes the protagonist Chauncey Gardiner into his home, is based at least in part on Ernest T. Weir, the multimillionaire "lone wolf" of American industry who died in 1957, ironically the same year Kosinski arrived in the United States. Weir was chairman of the National Steel Corporation and one of the founders of the modern steel industry; for Kosinski he was also a curious model for the autonomous self.[9] Born poor on the north side of Pittsburgh in 1875, a generation after Mellon, Carnegie, and Rockefeller, Weir found employment at the age of fifteen with the Braddock Wire Company. Doing work that no one else wanted to do and earning a mere three dollars per week in salary, he rose quickly through the ranks, becoming chief clerk of the Monongahela Tin Plate Mills and then general manager of Monessen Mills, both subsidiaries of the American Steel and Tin Plate Company. Soon after Weir joined J. R. Phillips in the reorganization of a decrepit tin plate company in Clarksburg, West Virginia, in 1905, Phillips died and Weir assumed the presidency. The company, renamed Weirton Steel, in the town renamed Weirton, grew and prospered, and by 1929, after several successful mergers, became the National Steel Corporation.[10] A man "who would give in only to time," Weir lived nearly eighty-two years, married three times (the last to Mary, who was more than forty years younger than he), and died solitary, as he had lived. Even his funeral, without a eulogy or pallbearers, was bare.[11] Yet Weir's was essentially a Horatio Alger story of success, a success that Kosinski eventually shared through Mary.

There are numerous intimations of Weir in the immense wealth and power of *Being There*'s Ben Rand. The chairman of the board of the First American Finance Corporation and a benign and benevolent figure to Chance, Rand is also a kind of lone wolf in American industry: resolute, quirky, crusty, and powerfully connected. However, Kosinski's portrait of him is more satiric than biographical, and possibly the most stinging satire concerns his benevolence toward his young guest. Rand sees in Chance the image of himself—a consummate businessman, overburdened by taxes, exploited by politicians, misunderstood by the general public,[12] and suffering at the hands of lawyers and others who regulate and limit the exercise of free enterprise. The great irony in Ben's distorted democratic view

139

is that he himself is as far removed from the masses he purports to defend as Chance is from true genius. Living regally in the American equivalent of a palace or chateau, Ben is an autocrat and an experienced kingmaker with little use for the common man. Though his capacities are diminished—and rapidly diminishing further—he continues to wield an inordinate amount of political and financial power and to impress his opinions on others. Because of his kinship with Chance (he even adopts Chance's garden metaphors ["I feel like a tree whose roots have come to the surface" (42)], much the way Sophie adopts both Nathan's and Stingo's colloquialisms), Ben makes him his protégé and personally chosen successor. But in reality their respective assumptions of power are as different as their backgrounds and beliefs. Rand's climb to the top of the corporate world, for example—a rough, political climb typical of the older generation of entrepreneurs—contrasts sharply with Chance's rapid ascent to the pinnacle of American celebrity. Conversely, the success that Chance achieves, like his prominence in politics and society, is not earned but accidental, as his very name suggests—a sort of cosmic joke like those played by the Tralfamadorians in *Slaughterhouse-Five*.

Whereas Ben is a Wall Street guru, Chance is an innocent Gulliver possessed of a Lilliputian intellect, a contemporary Candide who wants only to cultivate his own garden. His knowledge of the world is restricted to the yard that he tends and the television set that he watches in his room. Although never specified, Chance's origins are somewhat suspicious: there is the suggestion that he is the Old Man's child by one of the young women in his employ. Once the Old Man's house is closed, Chance is thrust onto the street where he is soon struck by EE Rand's limousine, which pins and injures his leg. After EE insists that Mr. Chauncey Gardiner (Chance the gardener) recuperate in her home, he watches dispassionately as his new "program" unfolds. "Everything that happened had its sequel" (38), and the many coincidences that follow—from Chance's purportedly trenchant analysis of the economy, which is repeated by the president, to his instant Kissinger-like star status—are highly amusing. But because they illustrate the hollowness of a culture so narcotized by television[13] that it values image over substance, those events are also terrifying in their implications.

In *The Art of the Self* (a commentary on his second novel, *Steps*),

Kosinski wrote of "the inability to escape from others who prove and prove again to you that you are as they see you."[14] Contemporary Americans were, for him, the best example of such lack of selfhood. Possessed of little self-knowledge or self-worth, they readily adopt the view of the world that the fairy-tale magic of television creates for them; in short, as McLuhan suggested, the medium becomes the message. Raised "to the ultimate power of electronic derangement," says John Aldridge, they perceive life wholly in terms of television situations and "create the personages they see on the screen in the image of their hopes for themselves, their wishful projections of transcendent glamour, wisdom and financial success." As a result, they are vulnerable to seduction by whatever powers happen at any moment to be in control of the mass media. Their experience of a public figure is shaped by the manner in which that person is video packaged, and they accept the image as a reliable index of his true identity. "A person," writes Aldridge, "is what he appears to be, and he can be made to appear to be almost anything his sponsors . . . wish him to be. He can also be created quite literally out of nothing. He need have no actual history or identity, no record of failure or accomplishment, and the result will be the same."[15] So it is with Chance, whose lack of the usual records—medical and dental histories, tax files, driver's license—gives him a brief history at best and makes his very existence a triumph of the mindless image over the intellectual challenge, a celebration—and elevation—of media hype over substance.

Duped, even brainwashed, by television, itself a collective fantasy that Kosinski described as "subjected to various collective influences, collective editing, collective simplifying, collective sponsorship,"[16] people accept Chance on the basis of his appearance and connections as a wealthy businessman and a presidential advisor; they attribute to him many positive qualities, including great intelligence, linguistic ability, impeccable manners, and social presence. Though his only actual political assets are that "he's personable, well-spoken, and he comes across well on TV,"[17] such superficial charisma is sufficient to qualify him for a position of high authority, even as a leader of the country. The fact that he never responds to the specific question posed to him is easily overlooked; ironically, his evasiveness is hailed as directness and lauded as a political and social virtue. He has, says his dinner companion, an "uncanny ability of reducing complex matters to the simplest of human terms" (106). Similarly, his inability to reflect or calculate is praised as a "naturalness" absent from most public figures.

Both the media and their audience become quickly enamored of Chance because he is the fulfillment of their shallow expectations. Hungry for balms, they seize his literal remarks and transform them into profound metaphors; yet his "insightful" comments—such as that spring follows winter and that gardens need tending—are no more than their invention, echoes of their own hollowness. (Kosinski documented this tendency of Americans to accept without question or challenge what others offer as reality. One week, in a course on "Creativity and Reality" which he taught at Yale University, he announced that, at the next class, teachers from a professional dance studio in New Haven would come and teach all the students how to tap dance; after the dance session, he would have a point to make. As Adrienne Kennedy, a student in that course, recalls: "The following week the dance teachers came and gave us lessons in basic tap steps. We practiced for more than an hour. When the lesson was over, Mr. Kosinski told us we had just had a lesson in reality. He pointed out that, as inept as the teachers had been, *because* he told us they *were* dance teachers, none of us, not one, had even questioned it. The dance teachers were, in fact, undergraduate students at Yale. It had all been staged."[18] Little wonder then that Kosinski repeatedly criticized the American college student, a modern "dead soul on campus" who has succumbed to the collective impulse and no longer thinks for himself.)[19]

Being There makes clear that being *there*, in the right place at the right time, can itself assure success in contemporary society. The enviable fantasy of Chance's rapid elevation to American icon and A-list celebrity so obfuscates the reality of his passivity that Chance becomes, for viewers, synonymous with the image they have of him; "by looking at him, others could make him be clear, could open him up and unfold him" (14). Particularly after his image is legitimated by the president's reference to his views on the economy, by his accidentally savvy performance on the *This Evening* show and during other media events, and by his simple presence among a circle of powerful friends, no one dares to form his own impression of Gardiner as a man or as a political figure. Although Chance recites the same short script of garden wisdom to all he encounters, people seem not to notice or to care. Since "being there" with Chance, in the artificial world of sound bites and klieg lights—the TV world of happy endings—beats "being here" in a more mundane reality, almost everyone is anxious to bask in his reflected glory.

Kosinski was therefore rightly concerned about "the fatal power of the media" to confer instant celebrity simply by exposure, because the ability to influence and control the thoughts and actions of others automatically follows the attainment of such celebrity.[20] With luck and with proper handling, even an imbecile like Chance or a madman (like Hitler or Mussolini, other notable "nobodies of the twentieth century" who were able to manipulate the media)[21] can be presented as sufficiently charismatic to be mistaken for a potential leader or a culture god. As historical events have demonstrated, television's imagery so fully saturates political thinking as to encourage nonthinking. John F. Kennedy, for example, proved in the nation's first televised presidential debate that it is at least as important to look good as to sound good, while Ronald Reagan's skillful manipulation of the press by choreographed "occasions of state" and carefully orchestrated photo opportunities—augmented by infrequent speeches aimed at the lowest common denominator—confirmed that even a grade-B actor can find success on the international stage in a well scripted role. Moreover, as with Chance, the longer Reagan played that role, the more he became his own creation.[22] Similarly, having learned a valuable lesson from his mentor about the effect of television in shaping political opinion, George Bush turned his timely if largely inaccurate tale of Willie Horton into a parable for the nineties. And Ross Perot added a true Chance-like dimension to the political process by campaigning almost exclusively on TV.

Kosinski's novel is thus a sharp and critical portrait of a growing constituency, the new generation of watchers and followers who suffer a Big Brother dependency on television and whose minds are picture pasteboards—video without audio, all reception, no perception.[23] Chance is their kindred spirit, the "quintessential screen" upon which they can act out their dramas, a mirror that, lacking depth itself, merely reflects and duplicates the images presented to it—a quality emphasized by the many mirror images in the novel. "The figure on the TV screen," for example, writes Kosinski, "looked like his own reflection in a mirror" (6); and so Chance defines himself by his resemblance to television characters. When Chance recalls his last meeting with the Old Man—"There was no

TV then"—he remembers catching "sight of his reflection in the large hall mirror" (7). The image is especially apt since Chance is, after all, a reflection of the Old Man's munificence—and possibly of his guilt as well. But with the Old Man dead, Chance has no home and no identity, reflected or otherwise; he observes sadly the shrouded furniture and the "veiled mirrors" (7).

At the Rand estate, his new home, Ben cautions him just before the president arrives to hide his mind because the president's security officers often confiscate "sharp objects." The advice is deeply ironic, since the sharpest thing about Chance's mind is its absence. But even more ironic is the realization that such stellar vacuousness will soon inform the chief executive's economic policy. Wondering about Ben's remark and almost coincidentally with the assumption of his accidental but new identity as Rand's advisor and confidant, Chance looked at the mirror, "liked what he saw," and "turned on the TV" (48–49). Before appearing on the *This Evening* show, he sits in front of a mirror as a man makes him up with a layer of powder, just as the nurse had earlier disguised Rand's near deadness. "Chance was astonished that television could portray itself; cameras watched themselves and, as they watched, they televised a program. This self-portrait was telecast on TV screens facing the stage and watched by the studio audience. . . . only TV constantly held up a mirror to its neither solid nor fluid face" (63). At the novel's end, caught up in the blur of EE's society friends, he is blinded by the "blaze of photographers' flash-guns" (139–40) and seeks his own image once again in the garden. It is mirrored in a pool of rain water just beyond the door, perhaps too liquid now ever to be reclaimed.

Chance also serves as a mirror for the other characters in the novel. For EE, "there were innumerable selves that he evoked in her" (74) as he showed her how truly to be free. On the television talk show, "the viewers existed only as projections of his own thought, as images," just as "Chance became only an image for millions of real people" (65). Since he reflects Ben's views on business and on life, there is discussion that Chance soon "may fill Rand's place" (93)—a trick done by mirrors, to be sure. Much of Chance's conversation is nothing more than an aural reflection of what others have said to him. And in the screenplay for the film, Kosinski added another interesting mirror image: Ben explains,

"When I was a boy, I was told that the Lord fashioned us from his own image. That's when I decided to manufacture mirrors."[24]

The mirror images are particularly appropriate, however, given the mythic dimension of the protagonist as a contemporary Narcissus. Chance echoes the shallow and narcissistic values of his society, which in turn makes him a legend in his own time. The original Narcissus was a youth so handsome that every woman who saw him longed to be his, yet he scorned them all. As punishment, Nemesis caused him to become so enamored of his own image, reflected in a pool of water, that he gradually pined away and metamorphosed into the flower that bears his name. Echo, the fairest wood nymph, who fell in love with Narcissus, had been similarly punished by Hera: she could never use her tongue except to repeat what was said to her. But when he spurned her, she hid in a cave and wasted away from unrequited love; only her voice remained,[25] an echo of his image.

Since Narcissus continues to be a relevant prototype for self-loving and self-indulgent contemporary man, Kosinski modernized the myth accordingly. He replaced Narcissus' symbolic pond of water with a television set, a synthetic symbol that offers the same ultimate meaning as its natural counterpart. As Narcissus was drawn to the water, Chance is drawn to his own fluid but somewhat unreal image reflected on television's screen for confirmation of his authenticity. "Though Chance could not read or write, he resembled the man on TV more than he differed from him. For example, their voices were alike" (6).

Ironically, television becomes Chance's surest and most constant measure of reality; "by changing the channel he could change himself" (5). Likewise, people "began to exist, as on TV, when one turned one's eyes on them. Only then could they stay in one's mind before being erased by new images" (14). In the real world, Chance is "bewildered: there was clearly no place to which he could run away. He searched his memory and recalled situations on TV . . ." (76). When he is approached sexually by a male guest at a party, "he tried very hard to recall seeing something like this on TV but could remember only a single scene in a film in which a man kissed another man" (110). After EE asks Chance to make love to her, he feels that "EE should no more have wanted to be touched by him than should the TV screen have wanted it" (113–14). His life revolves around TV: he falls asleep by it each evening, watches it while traveling from point to point in Rand's car, and even defines his conduct by particular programs that he recalls. While dining with the Rands, for instance, he makes a most fortuitous selection: "the TV program of a young businessman who often dined with his boss and the boss's daughter" (39). Television, with all of its distortions, soon becomes his primary vision of the world, and his reliance on it is an effective symbol of his removal from the real.[26] Nevertheless Chance, himself a kind of human void who resembles the politician Kosinski stereotyped in "The Lone Wolf" as merely "a television image, a product of his own public relations men,"[27] fills society's collective void. An absolute blank of a person, he is elevated to power by the narcissistically reflected dead souls around him[28] who hail television's artificiality as the ultimate reality and look to their sets, and to him, to provide the very values they lack. Those dead souls are no more than mere receptors—echoes to Chance's Narcissus.

The duplicating images of the garden and the water, integral to the Narcissus myth, are significant to an understanding of Kosinski's novel as well. The garden is Chance's idyllic place; he relates to its simple beauty, and it provides him with a prelapsarian bliss and wholeness, just as it did for his archetypal predecessors: Adam, Eve, Buddha. But when that wholeness is destroyed, Chance too is expelled. So, after the Old Man's death, Chance must seek a new benefactor and a new garden in which to work and live. Fortunately for him, his pastoral imagery of changing seasons and cyclical growth takes root in the otherwise infertile American imagination, and he becomes America's "last chance." But while others revel in his purportedly profound garden "metaphors," Chance's yearning remains more literal: he wants to return to the actual garden—to its natural, uncomplicated order so different from the social pretense and artificiality beyond its boundaries, and to the innocent happiness he finds there.

Since in myth and symbol Narcissus illustrates the denial of all repression in society and stands as the absolute challenge to social values, a figure who opposes by showing another way, who challenges simply by "being there," he serves as an ideal prototype for Chance. Narcissus cannot be cured of self-absorption by saturation;[29] he is too much of a "blank page" (which, incidentally, was Kosinski's working title for the book[30]). But unlike the Narcissus popularized by John Barth in the stories of *Lost in the Funhouse* (1968), who himself becomes a fabulator *regressus in infinitum*, recounting his tale which involves multiplicity and winds back to the incontrovertible source of being,[31] Chance harkens back to the Ovidian Narcissus, whose very existence is a passive rebuttal to established social values.

A second important mythic dimension in the novel is the biblical one. Kosinski's contemporary parable is written in seven parts and occurs over a period of seven days, paralleling the seven days of creation. The Old Man, in whose home Chance resides, is portrayed as a distant but godlike figure; after he dies, Chance is expelled from his garden paradise into the fallen world and must find a new benefactor and a new Eden. Rand's wife, EE, whose name is actually Elizabeth Eve, tries to tempt the Adamic Chance and corrupt his innocence.

In Kosinski's parable for the new age, however, the higher power is no longer a traditional one. Contemporary society's newest god is TV, whose filmic images are modern miracles revered by those who worship celebrity. Chance, as television's child, is symbolic of what Jack Hicks terms "a new sort of telegenic being and generation,"[32] begotten of the medium and marketed as the great hope for the future.

Chance is Adamic from not only a mythic but also a literary perspective. He is "the American Adam in his New World Garden," a figure characterized by R. W. B. Lewis as "an individual emancipated from history, happily bereft of ancestry, untouched and undefiled by the usual inheritances of family and race; an individual standing alone, self-reliant and self-propelling, ready to confront whatever awaited him with the aid of his own unique and inherent resources." A type of his creator, he creates language itself "by naming the elements of the scene about him."[33]

Lacking ancestry (no one knows his parentage); unburdened by inheritance (so much so, in fact, that the combined forces of the CIA, FBI, and KGB can turn up little more about him than the name of his tailor); innocent (perhaps permanently so, by freak of birth)— Chance indeed fits the archetype. Newly arrived on the political and financial scene, he too is a type of the creator giving voice to his society. He experiences everything as if for the first time, from the incredible beauty of the natural garden before his expulsion to the inexplicable wonder of the postlapsarian world beyond the Old

Man's walls. This new American hero, for whom a small garden was once his whole world, soon finds that the whole world is his garden. Only he can restore it—or, perhaps more significantly, others believe that he can. To them, consequently, Chance emerges as a kind of miracle-working redeemer, risen from the ranks, redefining the way to prosperity and salvation (qualities too often perceived as synonymous). This image of Chance as redeemer is conveyed especially strongly in the ending of the movie version, whose screenplay Kosinski wrote.

Like Kosinski's earlier protagonists, Chance is an outsider. While his assimilation problems do not spring from philosophies that are alien to him (the plight suffered by the Boy in *The Painted Bird*) or from his own foreignness (though EE does, at one point, say to him that he is obviously "European" in his lovemaking and later that his unwillingness to exploit others is not really "American"), Chance is nonetheless estranged from the society of *Being There*. His passivity results in detachment. Never fully a part of the Old Man's home, he feels a similar isolation at the Rands' estate: though in Ben's inner circle, he is neither the caretaker tending the metaphoric Wall Street garden nor the presidential economic advisor he is assumed to be. He merely longs for a retreat from the limelight which he never sought and cannot fully understand—but he is too passive to achieve his end. Yet this very passivity constitutes much of his appeal as a contemporary Everyman by allying him to the anonymous masses of Americans who learn from an early age to avoid engagement by isolating themselves in front of television sets or by participating in communal activities that require no individual thought or response (such as rock concerts, another type of misguided idolatrous worship, decried by Kosinski later in *Pinball*).

Like Sophie Zawistowska's, his estrangement is not simply physical; it is also linguistic. But whereas Styron's Sophie deliberately withholds the truth of her background, Chance is incapable of true communication with anyone, from Louise to EE, from the lawyers to the chief executive. Words simply mean something different to him than they do to others. When Mr. Franklin asks him to sign a legal document, Chance says, "I can't sign it . . . . I just can't" (24). It is Franklin who assumes that he refuses to withdraw his claim against the Old Man's estate; Chance just means that he does not know how to write and therefore is unable to sign anything. When Chance tells Ben, "all that's left [for me] is the room upstairs" (40),

148

he refers literally to the bedroom that he occupies in the Rand home, not the more heavenly space on Ben's mind. When Chance is asked whether he agrees with the president's view of the economy and he responds "Which view?" (65), the talk show host smiles knowingly at the witticism. But Chance's response is nothing more than a request for the most basic information. When Chance says to EE, "I like to watch" (114), he means precisely that: he enjoys watching television. It is EE who concludes that he is interested in kinky sex and who obliges him—and herself—by masturbating while he observes. When he says to a reporter, "I do not read any newspapers" (96), he is not commenting on the intrinsic worth of the print media; he means exactly what he states, that he cannot read and thus does not read the news but watches it instead on TV. It is the reporter who interprets his remarks as a judgment that TV news is superior to news in print and who hails his candor in striking a blow for television. When Skrapinov, his Soviet dinner companion, says to him that "We are not so far from each other," and Chance responds literally, "We are not . . . . Our chairs are almost touching" (89), his response is greeted as a fine metaphor when in fact there is no subtlety to it whatsoever. And when he is extended the recognition of an honorary doctor of laws degree, he dismisses it quickly because "I do not need a doctor" (123). Sometimes even his silences have reverberations. When the Soviet Ambassador speaks Russian to him and Chance raises his eyebrows in bewilderment at the strange sounds, Skrapinov interprets the gesture as one of understanding and approval. Chance is soon admired for being a multilinguist. Skrapinov later sends him a copy of Krylov's fables, which is inscribed "*One could make this fable clearer still: but let us not provoke the geese*" (101)—implying that others ("the geese") are too unsophisticated to appreciate the Krylovian qualities they both share.

This Adamic image "of a rootless, pastless, totally unaffiliated man who sees everything as though for the first time"[34] must have fascinated the author, just as the concept of the "divine idiot," or the idiot savant, and the irony implicit in a character who turns out to be much different than he initially appears did. Examples of idiot savants abound in world literature (Meursault, Gulliver, Candide, to name a few); and even in Kosinski's native Polish literature, there are a number of such characters: Bolesław Prus's Michałko, a strong, hardworking man who saves a comrade from being crushed by a wall on a construction site but is unaware of his heroism; Jozef Wittlin's Piotr Niewiadomski (Peter "Unknowing," in *Sól ziemi* [*Salt of the Earth*], 1936), a naive Polish mountaineer impressed into military duty who cannot understand the new world surrounding him, the world of war; and Tadeusz Dołęga-Mostowicz's Nikodem Dyzma (*Kariera Nikodema Dyzmy*, 1950), an aggressive but stupid dirty trickster whose idiotic witticisms help elevate him to the level of national hero. Many idiot savants also appear in recent American fiction—Vonnegut's *Slaughterhouse-Five*, Purdy's *Malcolm*, Percy's *The Last Gentleman*—and films, such as *Rain Man*, *Big*, *Dominick and Eugene*, and *Awakenings*. Yet few have had the pervasive influence or enduring effect on the American public that Chance, the already-realized "future shock," has.[35]

And few have tapped a source so universal. In fact, when Kosinski wrote *Being There*, he had to search for a device to encompass Chance's existence. First he considered music, but that posed a problem since readers could not "hear" what Chance was hearing. He then considered photography or painting as an analogy for Chance's vicarious life, but that would have required illustration of some sort for the book. With the inspiration of television, a medium everyone shares almost osmotically, the story just flowed.[36]

Kosinski admitted that his own feelings about television were mixed. *WATCH Magazine* wrote that he liked it. "He says a TV set is constantly on when he's at home. But he has no favorite shows, for that would be succumbing to the medium."[37] In an NBC-TV Comment, Kosinski noted that his own attitude toward television "is neutral. . . . The danger is in the use we make of it."[38] In an interview for *Media and Methods*, Kosinski added that "for me, the word 'beneficial' doesn't apply to television. TV is simply a part of contemporary life." Calling the medium "overwhelming," he asked, "how do you judge its role in our political life? The impact of its commercialism? Of its ordering of time? Of its ranking what's important (therefore visible) and what's not (therefore left out)?"[39]

Kosinski made clear that what fascinated him most were the "medium's recipients." He said, "I would rather talk about 'the grammar' of a perceiver, the grammar of an audience. A television set without viewers doesn't interest me. Television as a technical process doesn't interest me either. Yet the role television plays in our lives does interest me very much."[40]

That role, of course, is one of an ultimate disinvolvement which causes an anesthetizing of the mind and of the emotions, a spiritual and psychological catatonia like Chief Bromden's or Billy Pilgrim's or Yossarian's or Sophie's. Unlike the novel—which forces the reader to think, react, assume, project—television, as medium, "takes the initiative: it does the involving." According to Kosinski, "It says, 'You, the passive spectator, are there. Stay there. I'll do the moving, talking, acting.' Frenetic, quick-paced, engineered by experts in visual drama, everything from a thirty-second commercial to a two-hour movie is designed to fit into neat time slots, wrapped up in lively colors and made easily digestible."[41] It offers a neat and pat solution to daily concerns. But the real problem is that those solutions are too neat: TV gives viewers the sense that all they need to do is sit back and wait for the answer to come. The only contact it requires of them is an occasional flick of the wrist. TV does not challenge viewers to confront the chaos inherent in much of life; rather, it provides an easy escape, a diversion.

Whereas the reader is tempted to venture beyond a text, to contemplate his own life in light of the book's personalized meanings, TV demands no such inner reconstruction. Everything is already there, explicit, ready to be watched. The TV viewer can eat, recline, walk around the set, even change channels without losing contact with the medium. In fact, unlike theater or cinema, "TV allows, even encourages, all these 'human' diversions. TV's hold on you is so strong," wrote Kosinski, "it is not easily threatened or severed by 'the other life' you lead. While watching, you are not reminded (as you would be by a theater audience, for instance) that you are a member of society whose thoughts and reactions may be valuable. You are isolated and given no time to reflect. The images rush on and you cannot stop them or slow them down or turn them back."[42]

Some of Kosinski's opinions about the social effects of television seem borne out by his experiences. Subsequent to the writing of the novel, to validate his ideas, Kosinski tried several experiments, which he called "ad hoc sessions . . . crude attempts to find out a bit more about the young."[43] On one occasion, he set up TV monitors in a classroom; a closed circuit TV fed the monitors. He arranged for an intruder to rush into the room during a class session and to pick a fight with him. He found that the majority of children in the room watched the fisticuffs on the monitors instead of watching the men actually fighting in the room. Later, the children explained that they could see the attack better on the screens—the close-ups of the attacker and Kosinski, the attacker's expressions (all the details they wanted)—without being frightened by " 'the real thing' (or by the necessity of becoming involved)."[44]

Another time, Kosinski told students they could stay in class and watch TV or leave to go into the hallway, where something "really incredible" was happening. "I repeated, 'you know *what's outside is really fantastic. You have never seen it before.* Why don't you just step out and take a look?' " Almost every student preferred TV to taking a chance on reality. "There it was: they were already too lazy, too corrupted to get up and take a chance on 'the outside.' "[45]

On still another occasion, he interviewed a number of children in *Tonight Show*-like surroundings. In typical conversations before the cameras started rolling, the young people felt awkward and were hesitant to talk. Yet these same youngsters—so long as they knew the camera was on them—instantly became poised, confident, blasé. Even when questioned about such topics as masturbation or shop-lifting, they performed in familiar talk show style. "Their manners typified the easy warm 'openness,' the total frankness, they've learned from TV,"[46] Kosinski recalled. Like Chauncey Gardiner, the kids felt comfortable with TV mannerisms and chose the specific "program" they would emulate.

As a consequence, Kosinski saw a particular harm in TV's influence on children and pointed out that a number of teachers had commented to him about the resemblance of their young students to Chance. Instead of learning real and lasting values in the natural garden, "a child begins school nowadays with basic images from 'his own garden'—television,"[47] which teaches him that all things are equal, "neither bad nor good, neither pleasant nor painful, neither real nor unreal, merely more or less interesting, merely in better or worse color. It is a world without rank,"[48] one which is there to amuse the audience. If it doesn't entertain, the viewer can simply switch the channel. Problems are solved in thirty or sixty or ninety minutes; victims rarely bleed; heroes rarely die but rise again for next week's episodes; prostitutes usually find love; justice usually prevails; and fantasies are fulfilled by the omnipresent game show hosts or soap opera stars.

The danger occurs when a child grows older and leaves the "TV room." Accustomed to controlling his environment by channel changing, the child is threatened by real people. By the teenage years, he is easily depressed and beaten down, "challenged and often out-ranked . . . instead of coming of age, [he's] coming apart."[49] Frequently he returns to the collective fantasy of TV to escape reality. Television therefore becomes as powerful a force as the Big Nurse and her Combine in *One Flew Over the Cuckoo's Nest* or the Syndicate in *Catch-22* and as much of a fantasy as Billy's Tralfamadore in *Slaughterhouse-Five* or Nathan's alleged Nobel Prize-winning research at Pfizer in *Sophie's Choice*. It is not surprising, as Kosinski noted, that the average working American watches 1,200 hours of TV per year but spends only five hours per year reading books or that young people, weaned on the collective medium of television (their "plug-in drug"[50]), typically seek out other collective media as well, from rock bands to escapist films—any mass activity that allows them to avoid direct contact with each other and continues to shape their impressions and opinions.

Cast as prophet and visionary for such a society, Chance becomes a reluctant messiah, as Yossarian, McMurphy, and Billy Pilgrim before him did. But through his passivity he bears witness to contemporary society's suggestibility; through his very existence, simply by his "being there," he provides an important perspective on that society's folly. And ultimately, through his efforts to return to the prelapsarian innocence of the natural garden, he reveals a meaningful alternative to the artifice of television and the artful dodges of the other media. Chance's peculiar brand of madness, like that of the heroes of Heller, Kesey, Vonnegut, and Styron, may in the end offer the sanest challenge to the larger insanity of a system hostile to the individual.

CHAPTER 6

*This place for a while, it
was like a cuckoo ranch.*

. . . .

*Throughout my life I had
heard about madness,
and considering it an
unspeakable condition
possessed by poor devils
raving in remote padded
cells, had thought it
safely beyond my
concern. Now madness
was squatting in my lap.*
Sophie's Choice

When Dark Gods Prey:

Sophie's Choice

A S Styron makes clear in *Darkness Visible* (1990), madness is a familiar topic to him. In his self-professed "Memoir of Madness," Styron writes eloquently of his own mental illness, an illness fictionalized yet accurately portrayed more than a decade earlier in *Sophie's Choice* as well as in his other novels—an illness characterized by self-hatred, excruciating near-paralysis brought on by anxiety and alienation, and ceaseless thoughts of "oblivion" and of suicide. "In rereading, for the first time in years, sequences from my novels—passages where my heroines have lurched down pathways toward doom—I was stunned to perceive how accurately I had created the landscape of depression in the minds of these young women, describing with what could only be instinct, out of a subconscious already roiled by disturbances of mood, the psychic imbalance that led them to destruction."[1]

It is precisely the pathology of madness, a metaphor for the disabling and disorienting threats to individuality inherent in contemporary society, which *Sophie's Choice*, Styron's long-awaited fourth novel,[2] explores so fully and chronicles so well. The novel is replete with images of madness, ranging from the universal (the bureaucratized institutions that demand complete conformity, like the society of editors at McGraw-Hill, and that, taken to the extreme, create systematic oppression of individual liberties, even organized murder, as at Auschwitz and in slavery in America) to the personal or particular (Stingo's moments of blinding lovesickness and "insane lusts," or Nathan's drug-induced outbursts of extreme violence).

Published in 1979, *Sophie's Choice* was selected by the Book-of-the-Month Club, spent over forty weeks on the *New York Times* bestseller list, and won the American Book Award for fiction. The praise it received from many important critics was effusive. Paul Fussell (*Washington Post Book World*) deemed it an "American masterpiece . . . in the main stream of the American novel," which "offers splendid comedy, too." Stephen Becker (*Chicago Sun Times*) called *Sophie's Choice* a triumph, "a compelling drama of our age's central horrors . . . . A dazzling, gripping book of the highest intelligence, heart and style."[3] And John Gardner, in a front page review in the *New York Times Book Review*, described it as a passionate and courageous book, "a thriller of the highest order, all the more thrilling for the fact that the dark, gloomy secrets we are unearthing one by one . . . may be authentic secrets of history and our own human nature."[4]

Yet, like Styron's third novel, *The Confessions of Nat Turner* (1967), which also explored the evil of slavery and the nature of redemption, *Sophie's Choice* generated almost as much immediate controversy as it did critical acclaim. Some readers and critics, male and female alike, saw in Sophie's victimization a portrait of what they alleged was Styron's own misogyny and in Stingo's narrative voice Styron's narcissistic appropriation of Sophie's tragedy. Leading the charge was Gloria Steinem, who contended that Styron brought his "liberal *chutzpah* and [an] infuriating bias" to the portrayal of his title character. Although Sophie had survived years of atrocities in a concentration camp, including the deaths of her children, and had vowed to outlive the hated commandant so that he would not triumph, Styron depicts her freely loving "a sexual fascist in New York" and then fulfilling the adolescent sexual fantasies of another chauvinistic lover, who ultimately usurps her experience. Such a portrayal, Steinem claims, demonstrates Styron's galloping sexism, which condones criminally insane behavior as a normal male mating style and takes for granted "female self-hatred, egolessness, and obsession with pleasing men."[5]

Not all feminist critics agreed with Steinem. Carolyn Durham, who draws heavily on feminist literary theory in her analysis of the novel, suggested that Steinem's charges of sexism are a little off the mark. She wrote that Styron's novels "are not oppressive but about oppression, not racist but about racism, not anti-Semitic but about anti-Semitism, and . . . not sexist although, in the instance of *Sophie's Choice* especially, [they] are persistently about sexism."[6] Styron himself could not understand any attacks on the book along sexist lines. Referring to Steinem as a propagandist more interested in sexual politics than in legitimate literary criticism, he dismissed her contention that creation of weak, suicidal women is an indication of misogyny either on his part or on his male protagonist's part; Sophie was the way she was because of her personal and cultural circumstances. "It is true," he writes, "that Sophie responded to men in certain masochistic and supine ways, but that was simply the way she was constituted, and anyone who would construe that as an insult to womanhood is just simply a lunatic."[7] He disagreed further that Sophie's struggle to transcend inherently sexist cultural traditions demeaned her, or womanhood in general; rather he believed it elevated her to a tragic stature like that of Peyton Loftis, the heroine of his first book, *Lie Down in Darkness* (1951), whose unresolved guilt over her troubled relationship with her father, reenacted in part in her own marriage, also leads to her suicide.

Other criticism of *Sophie's Choice* was leveled by several Holocaust scholars, most notably Elie Wiesel, who took umbrage at Styron's very use of the Holocaust as the stuff of popular fiction. Wiesel argued that any writer, but particularly a nonsurvivor, profanes the sacred memory of those who perished in the camps by attempting to capture their experience in mere words. Since Auschwitz is beyond description, he urged silence (a curious appeal for a man who himself has spent a lifetime writing about the Nazi terror). In an article for the *New York Times* entitled "Art and the Holocaust: Trivializing Memory," Wiesel contended that Auschwitz ultimately defeated art, "because just as no one could imagine Auschwitz before Auschwitz, no one can retell Auschwitz after Auschwitz. The truth of Auschwitz remains hidden in its ashes. Only those who lived it in their flesh and in their minds can possibly hope to transform their experience into knowledge. Others"—and Wiesel seemed to be singling out Styron—"despite their best intentions, can never do so."[8] Alvin H. Rosenfeld, in *A Double Dying: Reflections on Holocaust Literature,* offered a similar observation; declaring that Styron spoofs rather than interprets the Holocaust, Rosenfeld insisted that Styron's emphasis on sexual combat reduces the import of the moral tragedy and makes *Sophie's Choice* little more than a fanciful exploitation more aptly retitled "The Erotics of Auschwitz."[9]

Others were offended less by Styron's decision to treat Auschwitz in his fiction than by the approach he took to the subject. They attacked, for example, his focus on a Catholic survivor, through whose eyes the Auschwitz portion of the story is seen and revealed. Alan L. Berger, in *Crisis and Covenant: The Holocaust in American*

Jewish Fiction, writes that Styron accomplishes in the literary world what the "so-called revisionists" who falsify and deny history try to achieve: the "de-Judaizing" of the Holocaust. By failing to understand the Holocaust's Jewish specificity, he argued that Styron deals not so much with an epoch-making event but with human existence in extremity, sexuality, slavery, and stereotype. He declared that by capitalizing on "the Holocaust fad," a novel such as *Sophie's Choice* only "encourages trivialization by ignoring the interconnection between the destiny of Judaism and the fate of Western civilization."[10] And Cynthia Ozick reacted sharply to Styron's comment in his *New York Times* Op-Ed piece, "Auschwitz's Message," that Auschwitz was not only anti-Jewish but also "anti-human. Anti-life." Ozick, in her article "A Liberal's Auschwitz," dismissed such a view as too egalitarian. By shunning specificity and insisting on the "ecumenical nature" of the tragedy, she writes, Styron used the Jews as mere metaphors and made "an abstraction out of human wickedness." As a result, "we will soon forget that every wickedness has had a habitation and a name."[11]

Styron was hardly surprised by such reactions, especially in light of a similar kind of criticism about *The Confessions of Nat Turner*. In fact, Stingo, Styron's persona in *Sophie's Choice*, refers explicitly to the "accusations from black people . . . that as a writer—a lying writer at that—I had turned to my own profit and advantage the miseries of slavery."[12] Even as he worked on the novel during the seventies, Styron was keenly aware of "certain fixed ideas about Auschwitz," particularly that "one should not write about Auschwitz at all" or that it is not "a legitimate topic for any writer who had not himself been a survivor," because writing about such an event and symbol has "to a singular degree—at least in the popular mind—become the property of the Jews."[13] These ideas "were calculated to defeat all but the most resolute novelist from attempting to write a book like the one I had set out to complete." But he contends that one of the key virtues "of the literary method, of literary art, is its ability, its impetus, to go for broke, for a man to write like a woman, to jump racial barriers, to jump sex and sexual barriers. The idea that I would have to be a victim of the Holocaust to write about it is absurd as is its corollary about fictionalizing it."[14]

Sophie's Choice is an honest work in another important regard as well. Styron had based his heroine on a real character in his life, a "beautiful, but ravaged"[15] girl who lived on the floor above his in a

Brooklyn boarding house one summer after the war. "Though her 'choice' was an imagined one," he writes, "the Sophie I knew had suffered cruelly and had been a Catholic."[16] At Auschwitz alone "there were a million and a half Poles who died, some of them in the gas chambers, but others who died as miserably as the Jews on a daily basis." Styron argues that those who ignore the fact that such victims existed and that they endured "as much as any Jew who had survived the same afflictions" (265) are the real betrayers of history, not the historians or the writers like himself who appreciate the validity of the perspective of the "hapless Gentile victim."[17] Philip W. Leon sees another interesting dimension to Sophie's Catholicism: he suggests that since "catholic" means "universal," Sophie's experience touches everyone.[18]

Cognizant nevertheless of the sensitivity of his position as an outsider, Styron felt it was necessary to maintain an appropriate distance from the story he was telling. He did this not only by creating a narrator who, years after Sophie's death, retells and interprets Sophie's life as well as his own but also by avoiding very deliberately the details of "the killings, gassings, beatings, tortures, criminal medical experiments, slow deprivations, excremental outrages, screaming madnesses and other entries into the historical account which have already been made by Tadeusz Borowski, Jean-François Steiner, Olga Lengyel, Eugen Kogon, André Schwarz-Bart, Elie Wiesel and Bruno Bettelheim, to name but a few of the most eloquent who have tried to limn the totally infernal in their heart's blood" (264–65). As Styron acknowledges, "I knew I dare not . . . get myself into a situation where I was describing, let's say, Sophie from the point of view of her barracks experience, the whole bit—the beatings, the tortures, the humiliations, the deprivations, the freezing, the terrible roll calls."[19] He assumed instead a different vantage point, one that allowed him to describe her experience[20] outside the actual concentration camp. Although Sophie smells the Jews being burned, hears the boxcars, the pistol shots and the screams, "the closest she gets is in the Commandant's house, which is outside the compound." By remaining on "the periphery of the experience,"[21] by not describing the indescribable, Styron forces the reader to reimagine the horror and to personalize its meaning so that ultimately the reader's vision is like Stingo's—"necessarily particularized, and perhaps a little distorted, though honestly so" (265). Moreover, as Richard Pearce observes, "by identifying with Stingo, and limiting the reader to his point of view, he compels us to recognize the limitations of our imagination and language in dealing with the historical event we must nonetheless confront."[22]

Stingo tries to make sense out of Auschwitz by creating what George Steiner, in *Language and Silence,* called a time relation to put events into "some kind of bearable perspective."[23] With a mnemonic urgency, Stingo recalls his own movements during Sophie's imprisonment at the camp. He realizes that, as Sophie was arriving at the camp with her children, he was stuffing himself with bananas so that he could pass his Marine physical—not, however, to fight the Nazis, of whose atrocities he was unaware, but to vanquish "the Oriental foe" (264), on whom his racist imagination had focused all its animosity.[24] In creating such a time relation, Stingo discovers, as Steiner did, that his imagination balks at the two orders of simultaneous experience that are so different, so irreconcilable to any common norm of human values. Only as he "particularizes" and personalizes Sophie's experience by superimposing it on his, especially on the slave past of the Old South and the continuing bigotry of the New South, does he acquire any understanding. Only then does his *real* story, not just about the Holocaust but about the nature of absolute evil in the world, emerge. The theme of that story is best stated in Styron's epigraph from Malraux: "I seek that essential region of the soul where absolute evil confronts brotherhood." Sophie confronts absolute evil on the platform at Auschwitz; but many years pass before Stingo truly begins to comprehend it.

Styron's novel, though, is not only about evil; it is also about madness. And madness finds no better expression than in Sophie, whose inescapable personal guilt is effected by the larger horror which leads to her final and most existential choice. Like so many other characters in contemporary literature, from Kesey's Chief to Vonnegut's Billy, Sophie struggles to forge a healthy identity from the fragments of her shattered existence. But the past she tries to bury in order to survive keeps resurrecting itself. The war that destroyed her illusions as well as her sensibility becomes the metaphor for her new experience as well.[25] She continues to be tormented by demons which refuse to be repressed, preyed on by the same dark gods to whom she once turned in prayer, and oppressed by the cultural and social institutions she thought she had escaped.

Stingo senses this latent schizophrenia when, early in the novel, he describes Sophie as a "cluster of contradictions" (265). At once the outgoing, sensual beauty whom he first meets at Yetta's Pink Palace boarding house in Brooklyn and the guilt-ridden survivor whose secrets come gradually to light, at once the passive victim of racial and male dominance and the agent of hatred and destruction, she tries to celebrate life even as her own lies and half-truths hurtle her headlong toward doom. Sophie's psychological fragmentation is perhaps best conveyed by the image of the antlered stag that literally mirrors her disintegration. The stag head is mounted on a wall in the Höss home, midway between the damp, foul-smelling basement in which Sophie and the other prison workers live and the white, sterile attic room that the commandant uses as his study.[26] In the stag's protuberant glass eyeballs which "gave back twin images" of herself, "frail, wasted, her face bisected by cadaverous planes, [Sophie] gazed deeply at her duplicate self, contemplating how, in her exhaustion and in the tension and indecision of the moment, she could possibly hold on to her sanity" (481).

Ironically, while seeking to free herself from old guilts, Sophie plunges herself into further bondage and self-alienation. The enslavement of her self is due in large measure to the fact that her whole identity is relational;[27] lacking confidence and self-esteem ("one of the most universally experienced symptoms" of depression which leads ultimately to madness, according to Styron),[28] she tends to define herself by means of others, especially by the men in her life. However, most of them are "monsters," and all of them treat her with condescension, if not outright disdain, thus exacerbating her passivity and victimization. As Styron observed in an interview with *Psychology Today*, "I don't know of a woman in modern literature who has suffered as much at the hands of men as Sophie has."[29]

Relegated to a subordinate status both in her East European homeland, where traditional cultural values of male dominance prevail, and in her new country, where many of the same oppressively patriarchal patterns are repeated, Sophie learns to live in the shadow of the men she is with. She loses herself so fully in their image that she becomes a reflection of their ideas, prejudices, sexual tastes, even language.

Such lack of self-sufficiency, which seems to be the plight of most women in the novel, is typified by Sylvia Blackstock, the wife of Sophie's employer in Brooklyn. So utterly directionless in her own right, so aimless that her only occupation is spending her husband's money, Sylvia—in the aftermath of a shopping spree—quite literally loses her head (a head she never really used) in an accident on the Triborough Bridge.[30] Conversely, though, even the rare woman who knows her own mind—like Wanda Muck-Horch von Kretschmann—suffers for asserting her independence and competing in a realm in which she has no real title. Caught for her Resistance activities within the Auschwitz camp, Wanda is taken to a prison block for torture, hung on a hook and left to strangle to death. She is thus literally deprived of her voice.

Sophie, alternatively overprotected and pampered like Sylvia and brutalized like Wanda, learns to respond to both behaviors with quiet obedience and subservience, as her "sweet, unthinking, submissive" (306) mother did. Fully accepting the passive role, Sophie feels that her fate is deserved and even begins to blame herself rather than the actual perpetrators for the violence that is inflicted upon her. In this way, her condition as woman and as victim becomes a central metaphor in the novel for the general degradation of self and others.[31]

Sophie's father is the most dominant figure in her life, and the complete fealty she offers him is "part of her bloodstream . . . all bound up in her Polish Catholicism, in which veneration of a father seemed appropriate and necessary" (293). A renowned scholar at the Jagiellonian University in Cracow, Bieganski is a believer in Aryan superiority who endorses *Vernichtung* (the extermination of the Jews) and expounds on his fiercely anti-Semitic ideas in his polemics, pamphlets, and papers. Sophie, as his dutiful daughter and secretary, and—at least professionally—his second self, transcribes in her fluid, elegant German the venomous rhetoric to whose fruition she will later bear heartbreaking witness. Not only is Bieganski monstrous in forcing her to articulate his prejudices; he also refuses to acknowledge her many efforts on his behalf. Sophie, it seems, can never do enough for "the Professor" (the formal manner in which she refers to him). One of her most bitter memories is of the afternoon she spent preparing and editing his manuscript *Poland's Jewish Problem: Does National Socialism Have the Answer?* for publication. The typing had taken longer than she anticipated, and when she arrived at the café where her father sat drinking tea with the printer, he was furious. Ignoring her exhaustion, refusing to get her even a cup of tea—though desperate for a drink, Sophie says "I would never order it myself, never!" (297)—he proceeds to humiliate her over a typographical error and to denounce her stupidity. "Your intelligence is *pulp*, like your mother's," he says with contempt. "I don't know where you got your body, but you did not get your brains from me" (298).

Bieganski so consistently repays Sophie's diligence with disgust, her devotion with cruelty, that violence becomes the metaphor not only of her daily life but of her dreams and sexual fantasies as well. Even in her unconscious mind she longs to be overtaken, to submit to the dominant male. The feelings of worthlessness and helplessness leave Sophie unable to react with any indignation to his attacks; rather she withdraws into silence and tears. Her victimization finds its fullest expression in her self-hatred, a hatred that should appropriately be directed at him—and, later, at his surrogates, her other oppressors, from von Niemand to Nathan and Stingo.[32]

Even after she marries and becomes a parent herself, her relationship with her father never evolves; Sophie remains his obedient daughter, the perpetual child. When Bieganski orders her to accompany him to his meeting with Dr. Walter Dürrfeld, director of IG Farbenindustrie (a conglomerate not unlike the Combine, the military-industrial complex, and other contemporary bureaucracies) so that she can later help recreate their conversation for the Professor's diary, she is "barely able to conquer her boredom but manages to remain attentive" (468). And when he urges her to perform for the Doctor the "trick of mimicry [of various local German accents—a gift similar to Nathan's] which she picked up easily as a child and which the Professor has relished exploiting ever since," Sophie, who detests such demands, smiling "a twisted embarrassed smile, complies" (468).

Unlike her mother, who "retained a faithful love for her husband to the very end" (306), Sophie eventually recognizes the evil Bieganski embodies (an evil symbolized by the serpent ring which her mother despises but dutifully wears because it is a gift from her spouse). Yet Sophie's urgent need for her father's approval, which continues into her early adulthood, and her need for the identity that he provides make her a virtual shadow of him, even of his extremist, controversial beliefs. In fact, when he is removed from the courtyard of the University to Sachsenhausen, her grief is more for her own plight than for his: "her entire sense of self—of her identity—was unfastened" (306). For years afterward she struggles "with the demon of her own schizoid conscience" and, for her sake as for his, keeps uttering the saving lie by throwing upon the Professor "a falsely beneficent, even heroic light" (302). When she finally admits her loathing of him and is able to demythologize him, her new awareness is not regenerative because she fails to develop sufficient sense of self to fill the void created by his loss. In fact, at times she resorts to the very actions of his, including outbursts of anti-Semitism, that she abhors. The realization of her emptiness only intensifies her feeling of victimization. Unlike Sophie's later rage at Höss, which prevents her suicide attempt in Sweden and impels her to survive him, the enslavement by her father (reenacted literally in Auschwitz and again in America) prohibits any reclamation of her self or any liberation from his legacy. He haunts her dreams with his contemptuous reminders of her ineptitude (when she tries to steal Emmi Höss's radio for the Resistance, for instance, his voice, exultant in its contempt—"*You do everything wrong*" [483]—rings in her head) and, even from his grave, he directs her destiny by contributing to her tragic ending. Sophie's unhealthy attachment to her tyrannical father, moreover, contrasts graphically with Stingo's healthy attachment to his sympathetic father, who supports and encourages his independence. Stingo is thus able to establish his own voice, quite literally as a writer—a fact that saves him. But Sophie, unable to make a similar separation[33] and assert any durable identity, is destroyed.

Sophie once said that there could be no better life than "to be able to play beautiful music, and teach and be married to a fine professor like my father" (96). Yet her loveless marriage to Kazik, indeed an extension of her paternal relationship, proves to be anything but satisfying and fosters her personal decline and her eventual descent into madness. A junior professor at the Jagiellonian University, Kazik is Bieganski's witless disciple; like her father, who shames Sophie for her ineptitude and grafts his disappointments onto her, Kazik rationalizes his own inadequacy. Demonstrably weak and unmasculine (he accepts orders without hesitation and parrots the Professor's ideas, in the absence of his own), he soon cannot perform, even sexually, as a man; and he shifts the blame for his sorry condition to Sophie. "You must get this under your thick skull," he tells her, "which may be thicker even than your father says it is. If I am no longer able to function with you, it is, you understand, due to no lack of virility but because almost everything about you . . .

leaves me totally without sensation" (472). Having married very young and being still "a little girl" (98), Sophie reacts to her husband's abuse as she has learned to react to her father's—by silently tolerating it. Publicly, as she had done with the Professor, she paints a rosy picture of Kazik as generous, loving, and intelligent. Even after he meets his demise in Sachsenhausen, appropriately alongside Bieganski, Sophie—whose identity is so inexorably linked to both men—maintains the facade because her only opportunity to feel self-esteem, however vicarious and reflected, is by belonging to men of whom she and others can think well.[34]

After their deaths, Sophie must salvage some portion of her self by fashioning a semblance of new identity. Wanda, the sister of Sophie's lover Jozef (another essentially dysfunctional man) offers her one option: to join the underground movement in support of the Home Army. Participation in the Resistance would allow Sophie to affirm a strong national identity as well as to repudiate her father's murderous views by putting the plight of the Nazi victims, especially the Jews, above her own. But Sophie is cast from different metal than Wanda. Sophie's later selfishness in withholding from the underground the significant information she overhears while working in Höss's office and her fear of making another attempt to steal Emmi's radio—like her subsequent lie about it to Bronek—contrasts with Wanda's selflessness in and eventual martyrdom for the Resistance cause. (Rhoda Sirlin notes, though, that Wanda is childless and risks less than Sophie in defying the Third Reich. And, as a minority—a lesbian—Wanda can afford to be defiant because she is more disenfranchised and has less to lose.[35]) Perhaps only as an excuse to hide her own cowardice,[36] Sophie insists that her primary responsibility is to her children; therefore she cannot get involved in any activity that would compromise their safety. Even after Jozef is murdered and Wanda again pleads for Sophie's help against the Nazis ("I am trying to appeal to your sense of *decency,* to a sense of yourself as a *human being* and a *Pole*" [451]), Sophie refuses: "I *can't* risk it, with children" (452). Electing maternal over national identity, she says, "I have already made my choice" (457).

Ironically, it is the guise of maternity that leads to Sophie's arrest and deportation to Auschwitz, the same fate that befalls Wanda and the other Resistance fighters whom she refused to help. Returning by train from the country, Sophie hides a ham she has bought for her tubercular mother under her clothing and pretends that she is pregnant. Her ruse is so obvious that the German officer leading the round-up cannot conceal his contempt for her "doltish Polack dodge": he inserts the blade of his penknife "with relaxed, almost informal delicacy into that bulgingly bogus placenta," and asks leeringly, "Can't you say ouch, *Liebchen?*" (446). Sophie's failure to deliver the ham, like her failure to deliver herself from the Gestapo, foreshadows her inability to save her children from the impending horror of the camp; her arrest and untimely separation from her mother anticipate her impending separation from her daughter by another agent of the SS, equally contemptuous of her motherhood.

The cruelest test of Sophie's new identity as mother, however, occurs upon her arrival at Auschwitz, on April 1, 1943. Only three days later, orders would be issued forbidding further executions of non-Jews entering the camp. But on that fateful April Fools' Day, Sophie becomes a victim of the dark gods' cruelest joke. Rather than merging unobtrusively with the press of people on the railroad platform, she tries to secure the favor of the Hauptsturmführer, whom Stingo, in retelling her story, calls Fritz Jemand von Niemand. (The name, which has been read by some critics as "nobody" or "from nowhere," is, as John Lang suggests, best translated as "Everyman."[37]) On hearing Sophie's urgent profession of maternal concern ("My children—they're not Jewish either. . . . They are racially pure. They speak German" [588]), von Niemand forces her to exercise her "privilege . . . [as] a Polack, not a Yid," and to make the choice that rips apart the family—and the identity—she has sought to preserve. In response to her expression of belief in Christ the Redeemer, he asks, "Did He not say, 'Suffer the little children to come unto Me'?" Then he tells her, "You may keep one of your children" (589).

In deciding which child to save, Sophie sacrifices the other to certain death. In refusing to choose, she condemns both to the gas chambers. Perhaps because she herself feels so little ego or perhaps because the influence of the cultural chauvinism inculcated in her is still so strong, almost instinctively she keeps her son and thrusts Eva toward the Rottenführer—though, as Styron points out, it is absurd to think that there is a "right" and "wrong" selection.[38] Sophie's action nevertheless explodes her identity as mother by turning her into a Medea, morally guilty of infanticide. "Not only," writes Carolyn Durham, "has she implicitly preferred one child to another in a society in which maternal love is by definition unconditional and all-encompassing, but she whose value as woman is based upon her ability to give life has sent one of her children to death."[39] The choice is made even more repugnant because, in choosing, Sophie allies herself to the Nazis, who regularly decide who will live and who will die at the camps; her decision thus recapitulates theirs.[40]

Durham argues that von Niemand's treatment of Sophie is the logical extension of all male behavior toward women recorded in *Sophie's Choice* up to that point. "Despite Stingo's elaborate attempts to 'understand' the Doctor's action, to offer an explanation that inevitably becomes a defense," she writes, "Jemand von Niemand fits into a clearly established pattern. He makes Sophie the same proposition that virtually every other man in the novel, implicitly or explicitly, has made her—'I'd like to get you into bed with me'—and when she fails to respond, he destroys her. For with tragic irony the perfectly pliant Sophie, who has always understood the necessity of female submission in a male world, fails to react quickly enough at the single moment when the metaphorical survival of the female becomes literal."[41] His behavior is later reenacted almost as cruelly by Stingo: after Sophie tells him the terrible truth of Eva's death, Stingo too wants to go to bed with her.

The choice von Niemand imposes on Sophie bitterly parallels the death sentence Bieganski—whose personal contempt is translated into the larger racial hatred of the Nazis—forced on her with his radical social philosophies. In a commentary after the publication of the novel, Styron wrote that "Sophie, through her father and his anti-Semitism, represents the victim of the wheel of evil which comes full circle."[42] So perceptive about other aspects of the German mind, Bieganski had failed to foresee how the Nazis' "sublime hatred could only gather into its destroying core, like metal splinters sucked toward some almighty magnet, countless thousands of victims who do not wear the yellow badge" (461). Uneasy accomplice to her father's plan for liquidation of the Jews, Sophie thus becomes its victim, along with her children, whom Bieganski had so genuinely adored.

At the camp, in order to save herself and her remaining child, Jan, Sophie turns to the commandant, Rudolf Höss. As part of Höss's personal employ, Sophie schemes to use her proximity to argue for the error of her incarceration and, if necessary, to seduce him in order to secure his support. Hidden in her boot is Bieganski's rabid pamphlet, which she mistakenly believes will prove her allegiance to the German cause; and, on her tenth and final day as Höss's secretary, Sophie seizes the opportunity to make her case.

But rather than helping her, Höss only assaults further her increasingly fragile identity. Dismissing the pamphlet, he rejects her anti-Semitism as posturing. And, though briefly tempted by her beauty, he recovers his bloodless Nazi dignity in time and does not allow himself to be seduced. "Having intercourse with you would allow me to lose myself," he concedes, but it would be risky and "doomed to disaster." Above all, he says, alluding both to his potency and to his power over her, "Pregnancy here would be out of the question" (344).

Nevertheless, as the camp's symphonic sounds of death echo beyond his office window, he (like Dr. von Niemand before him) expresses his crude desire to "deposit my seed within such a beautiful vessel" (343). His words are a grimly accurate assessment of Sophie's status at Auschwitz: she is nothing more than a receptacle for any of his Nazi abuse or perverse sexual pleasure. A mere object, she can be used as the men—and occasionally even the women—of the camp see fit, and she is powerless to prevent it.

Sophie does not need Höss to confirm her plight: earlier that morning, so consumed by the thought of saving her son, so bereft of her own individuality, "she realized that she could not remember her own name. 'Oh God, *help me!*' she called aloud. '*I don't know what I am!*' " [324]) Paradoxically, her only chance for survival was in her complete submission to Höss, her only identity was in her abandonment of all sense of self. By permitting Höss to have his way with her, she hoped to gain some small advantage—in some small way to have her way with him. But, like the Poland her father had described years earlier as "losing its identity with clockwork regularity to oppressor after oppressor," with no hope of finding either "salvation" or "grace" (291) on its own, Sophie inspires little more than Höss's abuse. Significantly, his rejection of her occurs on the anniversary of her marriage to Kazik.[43]

But, like von Niemand's, Höss's rudest assault is on Sophie's maternal identity. He denies absolutely the release she seeks for Jan. Then, after agreeing to give her the chance at least to see her son again (an act that reduces Sophie to such gratitude that she embraces Höss's boots), he reneges for fear of compromising his standing as commandant. Finally, he gives his word of honor "as a German officer" (503) to place Jan in the *Lebensborn* program, in which "they took away the identities of those children . . . changed their names so fast, turned them so quickly into Germans" [599]), but never acts on that commitment either.

While the possibility of repatriation was abhorrent to Sophie in Warsaw, at Auschwitz she sees it as the only chance for her son's survival and for her own redemption. Jan, a bilingual child, "a lovely blond German-speaking Polish boy with Caucasian freckles and cornflower-blue eyes and the chiseled profile of a fledgling Luftwaffe pilot" (368), is an ideal candidate. When Sophie learns from Wanda that Jan has not been transferred into *Lebensborn*, she is crushed and realizes that Höss's promise was a lie, in some ways more devastating than the choice von Niemand had thrust upon her. Von Niemand, after all, had compelled her to act impulsively; she had had no chance to reflect. But with Höss, she had deliberated for weeks, had adopted her father's hateful posture of anti-Semitism and had been ready to prostitute herself. Kneeling before her tormentor, licking his boots, she had become his "torpid tongue-tied slave" (329) and would have killed at his command—"a Jew, a Pole, it don't matter, I would have done it without thinking, with joy even" (350). Yet her intense humiliation has resulted only in failure. She had counted on Höss to be her deliverer; instead he betrayed her before throwing her into deeper hell, both physically, by returning her to the barracks, and spiritually, by falsely raising her hopes to protect her child.

Sophie's experience with Höss, which affirms her tendency to rely on men who just end up destroying her, is mirrored in a parallel incident involving one of Höss's colleagues, Dr. Walter Dürrfeld, the director of the IG Farben plant at Auschwitz. Dürrfeld, who represents the corporate mentality that governs contemporary life— especially, according to John Lang, contemporary American life[44]— has the task of managing the Auschwitz slaves, the non-Jews like Sophie who are not slated for immediate extermination but rather are kept for cheap labor.[45] Sophie first met Dürrfeld when he had been her father's guest in Cracow; she had been attracted to him, aroused by his physical presence and promises of a musical pilgrimage together through Germany. Six years later, on the day she is to be reunited with Jan, she sees Dürrfeld again, outside Höss's office. It is a symbolic meeting place, since Dürrfeld, as a functionary of the impersonal, bureaucratic institution that Höss also serves, is indirectly responsible for her continuing internment. But even more significant than his SS affiliation is his role in her dreams.

Only the night before, immediately after her disappointing encounter with Höss, Sophie had dreamed a curious dream. As she was walking on a beach along the Baltic, a man—possibly a famous *Heldentenor* from the Berlin Opera—approached her, started stroking her buttocks suggestively, whispered lewd things, and disappeared. Suddenly inside a seaside chapel, Sophie felt filled with lust. Standing naked by the altar listening to the sounds of Bach, she saw her mysterious companion again, now with a murderous scowl on his face. Telling her to look down, he commanded her to perform fellatio, during which she experienced a "choking sensation that wilted her with pleasure, while at the same time the Bach chimes, freighted with the noise of death and time, shivered down her spine" (491). Then he pushed her away, turned her around, and—amid the clatter of hoofs and the smell of smoke—entered her violently from behind.

The demon lover, Sophie realizes soon after awakening, is Dürrfeld. The dream about him upsets her for many reasons, but especially because it reveals her tremendous guilt over her supposed complicity with the Nazis and demonstrates her need to be dominated sexually. (Dürrfeld's sadism, though never actually enacted at Auschwitz, is played out by Nathan in Flatbush.[46])

Moreover, as a presence in her dream, Dürrfeld provides the connections to Sophie's past and present that her conscious mind is unable to make. He is a link between Bieganski (who had forced Sophie to "perform" for the doctor six years earlier and who tried to advance his own radical ideas through his acquaintance with him, ideas for which Sophie pays with pounds of her own flesh) and Höss (who that afternoon had fondled Sophie and uttered his crude desire for her); between Sophie's loss of faith (which she says occurred that same day, after the inspiring Haydn hymn of creation emanating from Frau Höss's phonograph and causing her own heart to lift in prayer was terminated abruptly and replaced by the crude "Beer Barrel Polka") and her trip through the contemporary hell of the camp (whose gas chambers, created by the Nazis, spew through their towers the smoky remains of the newly arrived Greek Jews); between her possibilities for redemption (saving her child, helping Wanda and the Resistance) and the certainty of her damnation and despair (her erotic but adulterous thoughts of Dürrfeld, her at-

171

tempted seduction of Höss, the abandonment of her children). Dürrfeld is himself a symbol of Sophie's broken dreams, a hurtful reminder to her of the discrepancy between her hopes and her realities. No longer the attractive man who promised to take Sophie to visit Bach's grave, he is now "a caricature of the romantic figure gone to seed" (497), the fat, jowly company man "answerable to a corporate authority" (495) which brings all of Auschwitz's inmates closer to their own graves. "It was not at all difficult to explain Walter Dürrfeld's role as protagonist in Sophie's terrifying yet exquisite *Liebestraum*," concludes Stingo. "Nor was it really difficult, either, to see why her dream lover became so easily metamorphosed into the devil" (494).

Sophie's dream is also a foreshadowing of her failed prayers for Jan, who is lost to her forever.[47] Even had Jan been selected for *Lebensborn*, Sophie probably would never have seen him again; like the survivor of Ravensbrück whom she meets later at the refugee center, Sophie might have been doomed to search forever for her child, imagining him "in those ruined cities, on every street corner, in every crowd of schoolchildren, on buses, passing, in cars, waving at [her] from playgrounds, everywhere" (600), so that in the end she would have lost Jan hundreds of times over. Had Höss made provision for Jan to be taken from camp into *Lebensborn*, he still might have ended up like the thousands of children of Zamość, whose photos Wanda had shown Sophie before their arrest. Rejected from the Germanization program, the children were placed in trains which were then diverted onto sidings; they were thus left to starve or freeze to death, or both. And had Jan been left at the children's camp to survive the many months of deprivation, he would in the end have suffered an equally gruesome death, as did the other children whom the SS wanted destroyed before the Russians came. Deciding that shooting or burning them alive in a pit would leave too much evidence, they marched the youngsters to the river and forced them to wash their clothing. Marched back to the camp, the children endured a terminal roll call: they stood wet and freezing for most of the night and died, very fast, of exposure and pneumonia. "I think," Sophie later admits to Stingo, "that Jan must have been among them" (600). Her memory of the cruel deception wrought upon those children, who believed the river's waters to be cleansing, not lethal, only makes Sophie's suicide attempt by drowning at Jones Beach years afterward more poignant.

After failing with Höss and losing her son, Sophie is left with little identity other than the tattoo she bears on her arm. When she arrives in America, though, she is sure that she has "experienced *rebirth*" and in fact functions with "the helplessness of a newborn child" (108). Her most childlike behaviors, however, occur after she meets Nathan and are often the result of his sadistic provocation and her complete dependence on him: Sophie sobs like "a bereft child" (55) and starts "bawlin' like a baby" (259) when Nathan shouts insults at her; reacts like "a terrified child clutching at Daddy" (246) after his outburst; and curls up like a baby on Nathan's floor when he leaves in a rage. She also feels a childlike wonderment about the many delights, especially the abundance and variety of food, that the city of New York has to offer. "The privilege of choice"—a privilege that earlier had doomed her—now, at least for a while, resuscitates her and gives her a feeling that is "achingly sensual" (107). But ironically freedom proves to be a terrible burden to Sophie: her new life, a life about which she only dreamed at Auschwitz, requires constant choice-making; and the more choices she makes, the more alone she feels and the more intense is her grief over her irrevocable past decisions.[48]

In Brooklyn, it is Dr. Blackstock, the chiropractor, who first comes to Sophie's aid. Blackstock is so struck by her beauty and her plight that he hires her even though she is a *goy*. The job is a fairly menial one—again as a secretary—but it gives her an income as well as a modicum of freedom and self-esteem. And Sophie is able to converse with the doctor, an amiable old-time Polish immigrant, in her native tongue. (Like Sophie, he has assumed a new identity in his new homeland: "Bialystok" [*bialy* = "white" in Polish] had become Blackstock, just as he had turned himself around from poor Jewish boy to affluent American.) She feels a genuine affection for him, even though his dandyish wardrobe and polite charm remind her of her father; and, after his wife Sylvia's traumatic death, she consoles him with a daughterly devotion. But even this kindly older man contributes to her destruction: after witnessing a grieving Blackstock hugging Sophie, Nathan accuses her of infidelity, an unsubstantiated charge that nevertheless leads to his brutal vengeance.

As she is struggling to hold her "new and transformed identity" (109) together, Sophie is victimized yet again by a terrifying, anonymous act of penetration of her body and her psyche. The incident is all the more harrowing because the threat, as Richard Pearce notes, "derives not from some demonic power but the ordinary."[49] After leaving Blackstock's office and climbing into a congested BMT subway train, she is pushed with brutish force toward the end of the aisle by a crowd of screaming high school baseball players. When the train screeches to a halt and the lights go out, one of them, working with impersonal "surgical skill and haste," digitally rapes Sophie. As the lights come on again, she cannot even identify who has violated her. "A straightforward, conventional rape would have done less violation to her spirit and identity, she thought later, would have filled her with less horror and revulsion" (110); a "classical face-to-face rape," she reasons, no matter how repellent, would have permitted her the small gratification of knowing her assailant, of making him know some of the emotion—hatred, fear, disgust—she registered. But this impersonal stroke in the dark was tantamount to a "looting of her soul" (111). A graphic reminder of how little control she has over her life, of how close she still is to the nightmare world of the camps from which she so desperately tries to escape, it is also, according to Rhoda Sirlin, an example of "how women are often the victims of male sexual aggression, sexuality devoid of tenderness or mutuality."[50] She "who had for so long been off and on literally naked and who, these few months in Brooklyn, had so painstakingly reclothed herself in self-assurance and sanity had again by this act, she knew, been stripped bare" (111), and for the next week she withdraws to the darkness of her room. Her violation makes her yearn for her childhood and especially for "the womblike perfection of that clock into which as a child she had crawled in her fancy" (111). Significantly, in that childish fantasy, Sophie is able to manipulate the clock's levers and dials and thus to control time (much the way in which the Tralfamadorians in *Slaughterhouse-Five* teach Billy to freeze time by concentrating only on life's happy moments and ignoring the unpleasant ones).

Secluded in her room, "she felt herself to be in a somnolent trance, like the enchanted maiden in one of those Grimm fairy tales of her childhood" (106). Only Nathan is able to rouse Sophie's sleeping beauty. He enters her life dramatically—"like a redemptive knight from the void" (380)[51]—and almost cinematically, by rescuing her from the hectoring Sholom Weiss, the intimidating Brooklyn College librarian who is the startling double of the "mirthless German bureaucrat[s] and demi-monster[s]" (123) she had known in Poland. Weiss had berated her for her ignorance about the American poet

"Emil Dickens" and caused her such déjà vu that she swooned and fainted in a pool of her own vomit, as she had swooned and vomited Bronek's figs on the landing of the Höss home in the face of an even more awesome bureaucracy of evil. In Nathan's protective embrace, however, Sophie feels secure from further harm. Though Nathan's ministrations prove to be as victimizing as they are healing (as Emmi Höss's Young Hitlerian methods of first aid were)[52] and though he merely delivers her from one evil into another, she believes that she has been "restored . . . to life" (380).

Sophie does not see Nathan's demented side; he is simply, totally, her Prince Charming, the fulfillment of her childhood dreams. Like the storybook prince, Nathan gives her a new name ("Sophielove," "dollbaby," "sweetie"); a new identity (through his gifts of expensive clothing and elaborate period costumes); and so many of the pleasures for which she has always wished (from the exotic meals which nourish her sickly body to the phonograph and records which nourish her soul). He even moves into a palace with her—the Pink Palace, Mrs. Zimmerman's progressive boarding house. Most importantly, his passion reawakens her somnolent sexuality, stirred and prefigured by the embracing couple she observed on the Brooklyn College campus just moments before Nathan's gallant rescue. Raised Catholic and Polish and a child of her time and place, Sophie had been "a young woman brought up with puritanical repressions and sexual taboos as adamantine as those of any Alabama Baptist maiden"; though she dreamed of oral sex with Dürrfeld, for instance, she had never performed it with her husband Kazik, who found her unattractive and unstimulating, or with Jozef, her virginal lover. Only Nathan, with his liberated sexuality and insatiable appetite for sex (especially while on benzedrine), "unlock[s] the eroticism in her which she never dreamed she possessed" (117) and allows her to bid "adieu, Cracow!" and adieu to the values of her youth. The self-absorbed bliss they find together affords Sophie an "almost sinister final losingness of herself . . . a sucking death like descent into caverns during which she cannot tell whether she is lost in herself or in him" (404). But the very fact that she feels the need to lose herself in *any* fantasy prince suggests both Sophie's tenuous hold on reality and her continuing dependence on men.

As Nathan keeps weaving his spell over Sophie, her hold on reality becomes even more tenuous, her sense of self more precarious. Their life, which has a *carpe diem* intensity, takes on an air of increasingly tragic unreality. Dressing in outfits from the twenties, thirties, and Gay Nineties to enhance the illusion, they frequently retreat to their own private world. The period costumes, all of which predate her camp years, are Sophie's idea, a way of countering the dull sameness that surrounds her. But the eccentric garb is also a rejection of the mandated conformity at Auschwitz to which Sophie is still reacting—and perhaps to the conformity to which Nathan was subjected during his various incarcerations in mental institutions. He too, as Judith Ruderman demonstrates, "takes to this costuming with great exuberance, instructed about clothing by Sophie herself."[53] At other times, they immerse themselves in a marathon of moviegoing and imagine that they are cinematic characters. Nathan, in fact, is alternatively described as being as handsome as John Garfield, as funny as Danny Kaye, as crazed as Ray Milland in *The Lost Weekend*. Sophie is as graceful as Ginger Rogers; as exotic as "a movie star from an earlier time," like Clara Bow, Fay Wray, Gloria Swanson; as "utterly doomed" as Lana Turner. Together they are, as Nathan says, like the "romantic strangers of Hollywood daydreams . . . whose destinies became intertwined from the first twinkling of their chance encounter" (118).

Yet Nathan cannot fulfill Sophie's ultimate fantasy—of familial happiness; in fact, he thwarts it, as fully as Höss did with her dream of being reunited with Jan. And like Höss's broken promise, the proposals of marriage that Nathan makes in his maddest, most manic moments are always withdrawn and followed by accusations of infidelity and episodes of violence. Among the first gifts Nathan gives Sophie is a diaphragm, a symbol of his selfishness and spiritual sterility. Like Höss, he does not want to impregnate her, to restore— if only nominally—what she has lost. (Similarly, Sophie withholds facts about her own children from him. Though she tells Nathan in passing—and only once—of the existence of her son, she never reveals the secret of Eva, much less the circumstance of Eva's death.)

As Nathan transforms Sophie into "the world's most elegant cocksucker" (602), she again becomes a mere vessel for his seed—to use Höss's words—instead of a sacred Grail; and she drops to her knees for him at any time, as ready to lick his penis as she was to lick Höss's boots. Even as Nathan repeatedly hurls at her the ugly epithet, Irma Giese—an allusion to the beautiful but diabolical blonde personally responsible for thousands of deaths at Auschwitz (an identity Sophie, in her guilt, partly accepts)—she is ready to pull off the road to give him the oral gratification he demands. The episode is actually quite similar to Sophie's dream at Auschwitz of degradation, humiliation, and forced fellatio with Dürrfeld, her earlier demon lover.[54]

On their first night together Sophie admits to Nathan that she is "a very uncomplete person" (170). As a result, their relationship soon falls into what for her is a predictable pattern of subservience and abuse—his delight in her beauty and his physical desire for her alternate with an obsessive jealousy that manifests itself in physical harm. The more he debases her, the less she is able to break from his hold and the more she fashions her own life to his. She suffers his many indignities because she feels she is "nothing" without him. After Nathan calls her from the lab one evening and idly mentions a special pastry he had enjoyed, she immediately travels the many miles to Yorkville to satisfy his whim. "My darling," he tells her affectionately after returning home to her surprise, "I think you have absolutely no ego at all." She responds, "I would do anything for you, anything, *anything*" (416). On their flirtation with death in Connecticut—a trip that foreshadows their final coupling on another fall weekend one year later—after Nathan's protracted humiliation of her, which includes his attempt to urinate in her mouth and a brutal kicking which breaks one of her ribs, she again demonstrates her lack of ego by affirming that she would still do anything for him—"*anything!*"

Broodingly handsome (like von Niemand and the younger Dürrfeld) and intelligent (like Bieganski, Kazik, and Stingo), Nathan is both the composite and the culmination of all the other men who have oppressed Sophie by their dominance. He controls her, even to the point of regularly correcting her unidiomatic English and buying her wardrobe, and while he offers her an almost exact replica of her relationship with her father[55]—protection and identity at the price of "childlike dependence" [388]—in his maddest moments he demeans her far more than Bieganski ever did.

Since Nathan is most closely the giver of Sophie's new identity, he is also most able to undermine it. He knows just how to hurt her, as he does when he demands the return of all of the records that she so loves. Moreover, he unwittingly taps into her greatest guilt when, in his "*tempêtes*," he asks why she survived while so many others perished in the camps. His accusation that she prostituted herself at

Auschwitz and his irrational charges of infidelity are significant because Sophie is indeed guilty of being unfaithful—though not, perhaps, in the conventional sense. She is guilty of prostituting herself by prostituting her *self* and by allowing men to use, ravish, even usurp her individuality.

Yet Nathan misdirects his jealousy. As Carolyn Durham notes, the justification for his accusations lies not in her attraction to other men but in their obsessive interest in her: "for every man she encounters, however briefly or infrequently, Sophie becomes an object of desire, a seducible prize. But in the sexist world that Styron portrays, once Sophie has allowed herself to be seduced, she must be degraded as the whore she has become." Her submission to Nathan corroborates the justice of his beliefs, and marriage logically becomes the prize that he proffers or withdraws on the basis of his current suspicions about her fidelity.[56]

Even Stingo, who has lusted after Sophie for months, is taken aback by her "forthrightly lewd" (436) seduction of him on the beach. The episode illustrates with special clarity the double standard to which women are subjected and the inescapable, vicious circle in which they are trapped. Stingo condemns Sophie for her frivolity, capriciousness, and inability to feel: "The shift in mood—the grisly chronicle of Warsaw, followed in a flash by this wanton playfulness. What in hell did it mean?" (437). Yet Sophie is simply enacting the fantasy of her he has had for many months. This double standard under which Sophie labors—men can have lustful thoughts about her, but she cannot respond in kind—is typical of the plight of women in the novel.

Ironically, Nathan is often responsible for precipitating the very actions for which he later condemns Sophie. After he orders Sophie to leave Yetta's, she seeks Blackstock's assistance in relocating; because the doctor helps her, Nathan is convinced of Sophie's infidelity with him. And Nathan's rejection of Sophie and his threats on her life because of her alleged infidelity with Stingo prompt her to escape to the South, where she and Stingo do indeed engage in sexual relations.[57]

In Nathan's dark side, Sophie sees her own "badness"; in his madness, Sophie sees a mirror of her own. That her identity is a reflection of his is symbolically conveyed by the fact that they often make love in front of a mirror.[58] Even after she learns from Stingo that Nathan is an impostor who has fabricated most of his illustrious history, she can easily forgive him because she knows she too has been less than honest about her past. When she realizes she can neither live with Nathan's continuing violence and threats nor live without him, she makes her most existential choice yet—to die with him. Their suicide is their ultimate flight from reality and from faith. Dressed in their fanciful costumes from another era, they rest happily, if anachronistically, entwined on top of Sophie's apricot bedspread, and freeze the illusion of their peaceful, tender love, as Emily Grierson did with her lover Homer Barron in Faulkner's great Gothic tale, "A Rose for Emily." As she had fantasized about doing since her childhood, Sophie at last is able to stop time. "Their joint suicide," notes Rhoda Sirlin, "makes total psychological sense; both are unable to bear the burden of their knowledge and experience."[59] As the Holocaust claims two more victims, their deaths unite Jew and Gentile in a way their lives never could.

While Nathan heals Sophie when she is wounded and ill, it is Stingo who fills her need for a spiritual confessor—though he lacks the power of absolution.[60] "Unbeknownst to herself she was questing for someone to serve in place of those religious confessors she had coldly renounced," says Stingo, and she divulges to him things "which she could never in her life tell Nathan" (177). As Gwen Nagel points out, she turns to Stingo "to get in touch with that self that she has left in the past. This process of self-discovery is, to some extent, Sophie playing the Prince to her own past by verbally recreating it for Stingo."[61] She tells Stingo more and more, however, only as her relationship with Nathan becomes increasingly threatening.[62]

Sophie confides in Stingo because he understands her situation in a way Nathan is unable or unwilling to. She sees in the young Southerner, especially in his affecting childlike innocence which so diametrically opposes Nathan's drugged-out brutality, an echo of herself and of her past. Moreover, both she and Stingo are Gentiles in Brooklyn's "Kingdom of the Jews" (1), nominal Christians who have lost their faith; both are dazzled by the same man; and both must confront the ethnic stereotypes that limit their vision.[63] They also share a certain guilt over the genocidal past of their countries. Sophie says to Stingo that "Poland has this strong anti-Semitism and that make me so terribly ashamed in many ways, like you, Stingo, when you have this *misère* over the colored people down in the South" (95). Stingo makes the same association. He calls Poland a beautiful, heartwarming soul-split country which resembled the Old South, similarly proud in the face of "adversity, penury and defeat" (301). However, he notes, "In Poland and the South the abiding presence of race has created at the same instant cruelty and compassion, bigotry and understanding, enmity and fellowship, exploitation and sacrifice, searing hatred and hopeless love" (302). (With those words, particularly in his reference to the splitting of the soul, he highlights the motif of schizophrenia which underlies all of the identity problems in the novel.) The similarities between Sophie and Stingo create such kinship that by the time she has finished sharing with him her whole and true story, he empathizes completely: "I felt Polish," he says. "Auschwitz still stalked my soul as well as hers" (599). The novel, in fact, is replete with parallels between the enslavement of Blacks by whites in the United States and the enslavement of Jews and Poles by the Nazis, and both the American slave system and the Nazi terrors parallel the oppression that Sophie, as woman and victim, feels.

While they have led such different lives, both Sophie and Stingo have been touched by death (Sophie more overtly), particularly the death of loved ones of the opposite sex, and both carry a heavy burden not only of Oedipal fixation[64] but also of survival guilt. At thirteen, Stingo had lost his mother; and for many years he feels a complicity in her death, as Sophie does in her father's. Seven months before she died of cancer, Stingo had left his mother alone and virtually incapacitated in their home while he went with his friends for a ride in a new Packard Clipper automobile; when he returned, he found her "shivering helplessly beneath her afghan, her lips bitter and livid, her face chalky-dry with cold but also fright" (360). Convinced that his irresponsible act hastened her demise, he confesses his irrevocable guilt: "My crime was ultimately beyond expiation, for in my mind it would inescapably and always be entangled in the sordid animal fact of my mother's death" (361). And both Sophie and Stingo experience similar kinds of dreams—erotic, death-haunted fantasies. Sophie dreams of Dürrfeld, who symbolizes her ruin, and recurringly of her father, who she believes wants her to die. Stingo dreams of his mother's cancerous "rain-damp ravaged face" (563) staring at him from her satin vault, an image that finds an eerie parallel in Sophie's dentureless face. (Entering Sophie's room unannounced, Stingo sees "—for a mercifully fleeting instant—an old hag whose entire lower face had crumpled in upon

180

itself, leaving a mouth like a wrinkled gash and an expression of doddering senescence. It was a mask, withered and pitiable" [158].) Stingo also has the most ferociously erotic hallucination of the "poor dead Maria" (132), the beautiful but self-destructive woman he adored and who both resembled and foreshadowed Sophie, seducing him "with the abandon of a strumpet" (52–53); and he wakes from a dead sleep "understanding with a dreamer's fierce clarity that [Sophie] was doomed" (63), a clarity much like Sophie's sense of doom after her erotic dream about her demon lover. An unredeemed sinner who feels guilty that he either contributed to or did not otherwise prevent the deaths of his mother and of the other women he loves, Stingo is thus the appropriately sympathetic soul to whom Sophie can pour out her guilt about her abandonment of her mother during her illness, her abandonment of her own children at Auschwitz, and even her ambivalence over her father's deportation alongside her husband to Sachsenhausen.

But, despite their kinship, Sophie suffers at Stingo's hands because ultimately he is like the other men in her life—men who want something from her, who seek to objectify and dominate her. His first vision of her is as a "flaxen Polish treasure" (59) to be possessed, her behind "as perfectly formed as some fantastic prize-winning pear" (61). She immediately becomes the object of his lust, and even as their relationship deepens he continues to be overwhelmed by sexual thoughts and fantasies of her. In fact, his strongest urges for her often correspond to her least sexy moments, a correlation that suggests that she is most desirable to him when she is most vulnerable.[65] When Stingo initially meets Sophie, in the aftermath of the terrible fight with Nathan, her sorrow is palpable: her face is tear-stained and drawn. Stingo wonders "how one mortal human being could be the vessel to contain such grief" (62). But, more significantly, he dreams about replacing Nathan in her bed. Later, after Sophie has revealed to Stingo the extent of her degradation by Nathan that weekend in Connecticut, he feels "sweltered by lust" (424) rather than by compassion. And, as Sophie collapses from drink and exhaustion in the Washington hotel after escaping Nathan's latest assault, Stingo is again seized by "pure lust" and longs to touch her exposed breast as she sleeps.

Since Sophie's sense of self has been subsumed by Nathan, she is so lost and empty without him that she almost automatically lets Stingo become her new protector. Traveling south to become the

181

chatelaine of the manor at his peanut farm, she passively accepts the new identity he intends to bestow on her: "I'll do whatever you say" (549), she whispers with resignation. Stingo wants to make her his wife—to become her master, just as he will become master of the farm he has inherited. He even contemplates calling their home "Sophia," which, while on the one hand is an expression of Southern gentlemanly courtesy, is also a chauvinistic appropriation of her identity. Yet his grandiose design for their future is both unrealistic and selfish; he barely acknowledges Sophie's pain. As he talks excitedly about the many ways that he will provide for her, including the best wedding dress he can find, he forgets that she is still carrying the wedding outfit that Nathan so recently purchased for her and for their honeymoon trip south.

Rather than feeling consoled by Stingo's plans, Sophie is unsettled even more by this further erosion of her diminishing self, and she continues to fall irretrievably into her dark past. Like other Styron characters too weak to rebel openly (Milton and Peyton Loftis, Cass Kinsolving), Sophie seeks relief for her solitary pain in alcohol, which she hopes will lend "a rosy glow to a drab and depressing world."[66] But alcohol only plunges her into a deeper depression, much like that which Nathan experiences during his postnarcotic downs, and causes the grim memories that still torment her to surface. Her pitiful situation finally becomes clear even to the self-absorbed Stingo after they get separated on the train; he finds her sitting on the floor and crying, the bottle under her arm. "She was hunting for a telephone," the club car clerk tells him. "She wanted to call Brooklyn" (556). The look on Sophie's face is that of a trapped animal. The prospect of never seeing Nathan again, of growing old on a remote peanut farm among proper Virginians who will dictate her morality, is indeed for her the end of the line. She sees herself condemned to another imprisonment, another servitude, another separation from the person she loves the most; the trip to Virginia becomes a repetition, in her mind, of another southbound train, from Warsaw to Auschwitz, years before. The sense of claustrophobia is intensified when they arrive at the hotel in Washington and Stingo registers her as Mrs. Entwistle, wife of the Reverend Entwistle; even in her drunken, exhausted state, Sophie feels the conflict between her own unredeemed "badness" and the new identity of respectability and propriety that Stingo is trying to impose on her.

Inadvertently, Stingo, like the other men in Sophie's life, deper-sonalizes her: he perceives her as the prize, the veritable jackpot that is his payoff for a summer-long adoration from afar. Ironically, en route south, Stingo tells Sophie his "cautionary tale" of greed—of how, as a boy, he literally hit the jackpot at a bus rest stop and then dropped and lost all of the nickels before he had a chance to spend them. Sophie too tells Stingo a cautionary tale. In a desperate attempt to salvage some sense of herself, she says, "I want to write about Auschwitz. . . . I want to write about my experiences there" (553). Yet Stingo ignores the caution and characteristically represses her desire for self-expression and for the self-knowledge that alone might have saved her. In painting his imaginary picture of Sophie raising his children and helping him with his writing, he concerns himself far more with his achievement than with hers. Failing to recognize her need to accomplish something significant in her own right and thus to have a purpose for enduring, he attempts to graft his fantasy onto her reality, as Nathan and other men had. Thus he denies Sophie even the most minimal expression of her selfhood at an especially critical and vulnerable point. This final theft of spirit, this "despair beyond despair," as Styron calls it in *Darkness Visible*,[67] forces Sophie to make her ultimate choice: to return to her life—and death—with Nathan.

Sophie had looked to Stingo as she did to the other men in her life for salvation as well as for identity; instead, he merely causes her to lose more faith. All of her would-be redeemers, in fact, propel her more quickly toward her doom. She believes, for example, that—by teaching her German—Bieganski, "though in his grave at Sachsen-hausen, had provided for her this measure of salvation" (270); yet it is precisely the bigotry of such ideas as her father's that results in her internment. At Auschwitz, she remains convinced that the distillate of his philosophy (his pamphlet) used prudently will be her "corpo-real salvation" (304). In Höss's employ, she fantasizes "all manner of little skits and playlets" in which she and the commandant are drawn into some intimate connection whereby she can "pour out the story that would lead to her redemption" (316). But Höss, a failed believer who "used to have faith in Christ" but now has "broken with Christianity" (277), not only refuses to save her but creates additional trials; he casts her "back into darkness" (345), out of his house into the hell of the camp's barracks. "A bureaucrat with priestly sensibili-ties" (271), Höss hangs in his "monkish cell," whose walls are bathed in almost sacramental light, a portrait of Hitler which in another world "might have been the portrait of Christ" (272). "Beneath the image of [the Führer] his lord and savior" (324), he conducts the diabolical affairs of the camp. Höss's only religion, as John Lang notes, is the state, his only values those of the Nazi bureaucracy he serves.[68] Dürrfeld, Höss's associate, likewise makes promises to Sophie he never keeps. Although he speaks of the pilgrimage they will make together to Bach's grave in Leipzig, he merely brings Sophie closer to her own grave by his abuse of the camp's slave labor force. Their Auschwitz rendezvous is foreshadowed by their earlier trip to the Wieliczka Salt Mine, "an upended anti-cathedral, buried memorial to ages of human toil, plunging giddily toward the underworld" (473). And, in her dream, which is actually about her loss of faith, Dürrfeld violates her at the altar of a chapel.

Von Niemand had also been "a failed believer seeking redemption, groping for renewed faith," but "cracking apart like bamboo, disintegrating [like Höss] at the very moment that he was reaching out for spiritual salvation" (591–92). Sophie's profession of religious faith prompts him to ask her about her trust in Christ the Redeemer—and then to give her the chance to "redeem" one of her children, at the cost of damning herself and the other child. Rather than being the agent of her salvation (and possibly his own), he forces her to commit the unpardonable sin, thus sealing his doom as well as hers. Later Nathan, whom Sophie also "had come to see as her savior," becomes "her destroyer as well" (163). Though she glows "like a madonna" in his arms, he takes her through hell—even as the redemptive promise of the Bach cantata "Jesu, Joy of Man's Desiring" plays, uniting them "just before the darkness" (617). Moreover, Nathan's attachment to fire, from his juvenile tendency toward arson to his fiery passion for and jealousy of Sophie, coupled with the numerous references to his dark side, suggest that he is indeed a diabolical sorcerer who steals her faith as he usurps her identity. Even Stingo, who saves Sophie from suicide by drowning and wants to spare her from the wrath of pious Southerners by marrying her, only plunges her into her own black despair by serving as her confessor and urging her to bare her soul. It is the naming of the unnameable which helps to undo her. After her death, when Larry asks if he should arrange for a priest to officiate at the funeral service, Stingo says no and then wonders if his "blasphemous assumption . . . consigned Sophie to hell" (618).

Christ, too, fails Sophie. Sophie had once been a devout Catholic: in fact, she had been attending Mass the morning the deportation of professors occurred at the Jagiellonian University. But, as her own father is taken, she feels that her heavenly father also turns away from her. The invocation of His name at Auschwitz only draws the Nazis' wrath, as Sophie discovers on the railroad platform. And her subsequent prayers for her own safety and for Jan's go unanswered. "I don't know any more, about *when* God leave me," she realizes. "Or I left Him" (282). As she confesses to Stingo, "I once believed in Christ and His Holy Mother too, but now after these years I was like those Jews who think God was gone forever. . . . Christ had turned His face away from me and I could no longer pray to Him as I did once in Cracow" (102). At the center for displaced persons in Sweden, when she first tries to commit suicide, she makes the attempt in a church. "Like in that dream I told you about, the chapel—I had this obsession with *le blasphème*," she says to Stingo. "I had this idea that if I killed myself in this church, it would be the greatest sacrilege I could ever commit, *le plus grand blasphème*, because you see, Stingo, I didn't care no more; after Auschwitz, I didn't believe in God or if He existed" (499–500). When she sees two nuns in her local bar in Brooklyn, she cannot conceal her hatred for a God she calls a "monster." And her final message to Stingo, left in the bathroom of their Washington hotel, recalls but perverts Haydn's joyful hymn, which Sophie heard playing on Frau Höss's phonograph the day she stopped praying. "FUCK God and all his Hände Werk" (607), she writes. The only real possibility of "salvation" that seems to exist for Sophie is that implied by Wanda's comments on *Lord Jim:* "In the end the hero redeems himself for his betrayal, redeems himself through his own death. His own suffering and death" (576).[69] Yet Sophie's obsession with blasphemy, like her fixation on the language, if not the possibility, of redemption, suggests her inability to reject even that God whom she charges with being so monstrous.[70]

While religion fails Sophie, classical music provides some means of transcending her plight. As Styron said, "the book is filled with music . . . and people who fail to understand that may well fail to grasp the book on one of its most important levels"; a response to classical music is necessary "to get at some of the underlying levels of *Sophie.*"[71] Music, perhaps the only pleasure Sophie retains from her childhood, becomes the way that she remakes herself throughout her later life. Connected to the past, having itself survived, music—according to Frederik N. Smith—"suggests the strength of memory, human continuance, and our ability to construct order out of seemingly unconquerable chaos."[72] After coming to America determined to put "the madness of her past" behind her, Sophie is so moved by the music she has missed during her years of incarceration that she believes she can "reclaim the scattered pieces of her life and compose of them a new self" (105). She admits that "sometime I have thought that I love music almost as much as life" (95).

Her fondest youthful memories are of her mother at the piano: "I would lie awake and hear the music faint and beautiful rising up through the house and I would feel so warm and comfortable and secure" (95).[73] Only later does she understand that her mother turned to music to drown out the cacophonous sounds of her husband's obsessive anti-Semitism and of her own sorrow, as Sophie learns to do.

It is their mutual love of music that intensifies Sophie's attraction to Dürrfeld (whose words were implanted in her memory "with archival finality, as if within the grooves of a phonograph record which can never be erased" [496]) and that brings her closer to Wanda, who had originally come to Warsaw to study voice at the Conservatory. Music also forges Sophie's strong link to Nathan and even often defines the tempo of their relationship. She plays Beethoven's Fourth Symphony, with its "ravishing sweet heartbeat" (44) after they make love; Brahms' First Symphony, full of "sadness and nostalgia" (62), after Nathan leaves; Handel's triumphant Water Music to celebrate his return. After Nathan rescues her at Brooklyn College, she enjoys with him "the gay redemptive music" (176) of *The Marriage of Figaro*. As they race to Morty Haber's party, a hell-bent and narcotized Nathan sings along with the radio the words from *Don Giovanni,* an opera about a descent into the underworld. When Sophie and Nathan reconcile for their final embrace, she turns the phonograph so high that its sound blares several hundred feet from the house. The music, recalls Fink, was not only boisterous but "filled with what seemed to be trumpets" (610), and it washes over the neighborhood for several hours before stopping. While the police conduct an investigation, Stingo notices two of the records still on the phonograph. The first is the larghetto from the B-flat major piano concerto of Mozart, written close to the end of his life and "filled with a resignation that was almost like joy"

(617). The other—the last sound that, Stingo assumes, in their final anguish, or ecstasy, Sophie and Nathan heard—is Bach's song of redemption, "Jesu, Joy of Man's Desiring." By contrast, at their funeral service, a whiny Hammond organ plays Gounod's "Ave Maria"—a peevish, vulgar utterance that makes Stingo's stomach turn because it would offend Sophie's "loving and noble response to music" (619).

Because music is so relevant to Sophie's identity, she also associates it—especially its absence—with painful incidents in her life. Perhaps the most traumatic of these instances involves her father, who, says Sophie, "is everything that music cannot be . . ." (473). While Bieganski in general reduces her to "virtually menial submission" (293), his most significant assault is aimed at Sophie's love of music because it represents her individuality.[74] As an important prelude to her account of her arrival at Auschwitz, Sophie relates a recurring dream in which she explicitly identifies her father's will to deny her music with the death of the self:

> "So in the dream that has returned to me over and over I see Princess Czartoryska in her handsome gown go to the phonograph and she turns and always says, as if she were talking to me, 'Would you like to hear the Brahms *Lieder*!' And I always try to say yes. But just before I can say anything my father interrupts. He is standing next to the Princess and he is looking directly at me, and he says, 'Please don't play that music for the child. She is much too stupid to understand.' And then I wake up with this pain . . . Only this time it was even worse, Stingo. Because in the dream I had just now he seemed to be talking to the Princess not about the music but about . . ." Sophie hesitated, then murmured, "About my death. He wanted me to die, I think" (566).[75]

On the train from Warsaw, Sophie dreams of performing before thousands of onlookers, of "soaring to deliverance on the celestial measures of the Emperor Concerto" (585), but is awakened by the braking stop at Auschwitz, where the welcoming prisoners' band plays an Argentine tango, its off-key "erotic sorrow" (587) a prelude to the aria of pain that follows. And her final vision of Eva is of her being led away, still carrying her one-eyed bear and her beloved flute, its notes eternally silenced, in her little hands. (Earlier, in Warsaw, as a Luftwaffe plane drowned out Eva's flute song, Sophie had felt moved by the notes, which "spoke of all she had been, of all she longed to be—and all she wished for her children" [456]—yet all that she knew even then could never be.) Sophie feels a similar sorrow each time Nathan ostentatiously removes his records from Yetta's, because their removal parallels the withdrawal of his affection. And as she contemplates life with Stingo in Virginia, she asks whether "We *will* have music where we're going, then, Stingo. I wouldn't be able to last long without music" (565).

Even popular songs provide a musical counterpoint to her experiences. At Auschwitz, the noisy "schmaltz" Frau Höss usually plays on her phonograph mocks the grim business being conducted beyond the fence of her home.[76] And in their neighborhood restaurant in Brooklyn, as Sophie tells Stingo the story of her enslavement by Höss, the Andrews Sisters' tune, "Don't Fence Me In," plays on the jukebox.

Unlike music, which usually proves liberating, language becomes another form of oppression and reminds Sophie of her bondage. She is degraded regularly by Nathan's harsh and sexist language, which reduces her to her sexual anatomy[77] ("sweet little ass" [255], "piece of ass" [378], "miserable lying cunt" [55], *première putain* of Flatbush Avenue" [245], "Coony Chiropractic Cunt of Kings County" [252]). And, while Sophie is articulate and intelligent, she is nevertheless reduced to serving as secretary to a succession of men—Bieganski, Höss, Blackstock—and into using their words.

Similarly, though she is fluent in several languages, including French, German, and Polish, Sophie is handicapped by her limited command of English. Yet she finds herself in a situation where she must speak English, the single language in which Nathan, a remarkable storyteller, and Stingo, an aspiring writer, retain total superiority.[78] She learns to imitate them, to echo so much of Nathan's diction that it seems as if he is her dialogue coach. " 'Stinking infinitive!' she blurted affectionately, mocking Nathan's tutorial manner" (191), remembers Stingo; and she refers to a penis as a *schlong* because "it's what Nathan calls it" (438). Sophie even adopts Stingo's Faulknerianisms ("I'm *swooning* with hunger. I am . . . the *avatar* of hunger!" [158]).[79] However, when using her own words, she tends to switch languages midsentence: her difficulty, while charming, is symbolic of the incoherence of her identity.

At times, Sophie is almost "slain" by language (125). Her father's words, "seductively convivial" yet "caustic" (295), wound her; Kazik's are "as excruciatingly hurtful as the sudden slice across her face of a kitchen knife" (471–72). Von Niemand's choice, precipitated by Sophie's response in perfect German,[80] leads directly to Eva's death; Höss's word as a gentleman and a German leads indirectly to Jan's death. Nathan's horrible epithets, abuses that she sometimes can't even understand (for instance, Nathan calls her a cunt and she replies, "You're a cunt too" [55]), move Sophie closer to her own end. And when she tries to articulate her need to write about Auschwitz, Stingo merely says, "Hush, Sophie!" (554)—and then ultimately appropriates her words.

As Durham observes, in *Sophie's Choice* the respective societal roles of men and women are well illustrated by the multiplicity of narrative voices. Since in most cases it is Stingo, not Sophie, who recounts her past, " 'herstory' becomes 'History,' " and "a clear narrative pattern emerges to distinguish the female from the male narrator. Sophie tells her own story only when she is lying or confessing previous lies," such as her creation of a false childhood in Cracow (93–104), her misleading portrait of Nathan as a supportive lover and deliverer (188–93), her malignant representation of Wanda (434–42). Thus unreliability is attributed to the female, while "the male voice becomes in contrast the voice of Truth" (461–62) and is compelled to identify the female as a liar and to correct her account. Sophie's lack of credibility as a narrator is linked to her alleged infidelity, as when she tells Stingo at their first meeting that she had never made love to anyone other than her husband or Nathan—a "fact" she soon contradicts. By contrast, though, the unbalanced Nathan is established as a credible source. The emphasis on "his prescience, his insight, his power to predict correctly" is altogether consistent "with the representation of the male as possessor of knowledge." Moreover, while Sophie remains obsessed with her personal life and story, Stingo seeks to place the former in its historical and theoretical context. Styron thus portrays the male in general as the learned, objective, neutral scholar who provides the statistics, information, facts to balance the female's lies (for example, Sophie's version of her happy marriage, Leslie's profession of uninhibited sexuality). And even the psychopathic liar Nathan, who inexhaustibly researches Nazi anti-Semitism and the Civil War, fulfills this vision as much as Stingo.[81]

Yet almost all of Sophie's lies are about men; typically, she promotes their goodness—Bieganski's kindness, Nathan's gentleness—when they possess little real goodness to promote. By contrast, Stingo's inaccurate assessment of characters and situations (like his rejection of the manuscript of *Kon Tiki* because it was "long, solemn and tedious" [10]), a lack of perception resulting from his own naiveté, is accepted as part of his evolution as a writer and as a man. Even his admittedly "distorted" account of Sophie's experience at Auschwitz is assumed to be valid and true.

Nathan, moreover, is not just the glamorous eccentric Stingo believes him to be: with his multiple personalities, he is clinically schizophrenic. Early in the relationship, Stingo mistakenly attributes Nathan's mood swings to Sophie's power over him. Stingo writes that she was "able to work upon Nathan such tricks of alchemy that he was almost instantaneously transformed—the ranting ogre become Prince Charming" (88). In reality, the reverse is the case: Nathan is the dark prince who dominates Sophie.[82] And his drug-induced, irrational sadism, which extends the more routine, legitimized, efficient sadism of the camps[83] and links political and sexual brutality in the novel, demonstrates to Sophie (who, devoid of a firm sense of self, suffers from a schizophrenia that is metaphysical) that there is no escaping victimization.

Because of his great polymathic knowledge and oratorical skills, Nathan is quite capable of concealing his madness by creating various illusions. Yet his real personality is best conveyed by his own joke: he whimsically claims "to have been in a past life the only Jewish Albigensian monk—a brilliant friar named St. Nathan le Bon who had single-handedly promulgated that crazy sect's obsessive penchant for self-destruction, which was based on the reasoning that if life is evil, it is necessary to hasten life's end" (225). That joke has a serious side, as Gwen Nagel notes, for it shows him deliberately fabricating an identity that is essentially self-destructive. "Nathan's playful identification with this imagined figure," she writes, "conveys his ability to charm by creating fanciful identities for himself, but it also foreshadows his suicide"[84] as well as his complicity in Sophie's death.

A more real—but just as saintly—figure with whom Nathan identifies is his older brother. Larry Landau, a handsome, affluent urologist who lives well in Forest Hills with his beautiful blonde wife, is Nathan's role model. Heir to their father's great wealth, Larry has also achieved his own success through his medical practice and his distinguished wartime military service. Nathan attempts to emulate Larry, even to the point of trying to join the paratroopers despite his 4-F status; and when he fails, he reverts to a life of lies and make-believe modeled on Larry's actual accomplishments. Allen Shepherd suggests that while "we never hear Nathan rail against his brother, . . . one has to imagine that Nathan's murderous outbursts derive in part from his repressed rage and utter hopelessness of ever successfully resisting or competing with Larry. He suffers, cynics might say, from an advanced case of sibling rivalry."[85]

While Nathan's only credentials are a series of expensive sanatoriums and funny farms throughout the country, he convinces both Stingo and Sophie—a blonde as beautiful as Larry's wife—that he is a Harvard graduate. At times he masquerades as a doctor: "Just lie still," he tells Sophie after she collapses in the Brooklyn College Library, "let the doctor take care of everything" [126]. But instead of curing Sophie's ills or his own, he aggravates them, bringing further injury and ultimately death. The only pills he prescribes are the tablets that he and Sophie use to take their lives—tablets of cyanide, like the gas the Nazis used in the camps for extermination. And, though a fake himself, he later demeans Blackstock because he is not a real doctor, merely a chiropractor. Alternatively, Nathan poses as a prominent research scientist at Pfizer who is on the verge of a medical breakthrough. But in that role, too, he fails to do what he professes. Rather than inventing miracle drugs for the cure of polio or cancer, he relies on common narcotics to give himself the euphoric high he cannot find in real life. The drugs help to make his fantasies come true and allow him to drive faster, think better, and make love longer. That Nathan wants Stingo, whom he affectionately regards as a younger brother, to respect and admire him is a reflection of the awe he feels for his older brother—and a poignant reminder that his own dark side keeps him in Larry's shadow and forever prohibits a more traditional fulfillment of his aspirations. (Ironically, Stingo feels some of the same ambivalence about Nathan, who is his rival for Sophie's affection, as Nathan does for his brother Larry.)[86]

Clothing, like drugs, is another way Nathan disguises his real self; he changes his identity simply by changing his outfit. Because his manic states are usually accompanied by clothes-buying sprees, sometimes even weekend-long excursions to Manhattan, clothing is linked to his madness. To celebrate his lab's supposed scientific breakthrough, Nathan buys Sophie an elaborate outfit ("Something chic and sexy . . . and *daring*" [237]) and then appears for the celebration in an equally extravagant suit of oyster-white linen, with heavy oval gold links sparkling on the cuffs of his custom-made shirt. Later he purchases for Sophie "a trousseau fit for a Hollywood princess" (537). As Nagel points out, clothes, including the period costumes he commissions his tailor to sew, are thus more than a hobby for him: they are "the manifestation of Nathan's pathology and Sophie's need to escape her past."[87]

Alleging to be Sophie's "savior" (163,) an adjunct of his fantasy about being "mankind's deliverer" (526) at Pfizer, Nathan turns out to be her greatest tormentor. For, while he brings her back to life, he does not allow her to escape; rather he compels her to face the living death she thought she had eluded.[88] Despite his strong assertion of his Jewishness—"As a Jew, I regard myself as an authority on anguish and suffering" (83)—he is all too often Nazi-like in his brutality toward her. Fink rightly calls him "a golem . . . some kind of *monster* . . . invented by a rabbi" rather than by Frankenstein (70). Not only does he address Sophie with the base insults she endured at the camp but also, by associating her with the larger Polish tradition of anti-Semitism, he alleges that she is a victimizer, not a victim. Yet it is he who fails to comprehend her suffering, even after he learns that she lost her son at Auschwitz, and who in turn victimizes her. In his desperate search for his own authenticity, he assaults the little sense of identity she has been able to preserve by confusing her with his various denunciations and with his professions of love. As a result of his actions, however, he raises Sophie to tragic proportions.[89]

Nathan also reveals his two faces to Stingo, who (like Sophie) has difficulty reconciling them. After Nathan calls Stingo "the Dreary Dregs of Dixie" (252), a dumb "Cracker" (65) and the spiritual twin of the lynch mob that killed Bobby Weed—pejorative remarks about the South which show that he is as much of a bigot as he accuses Stingo of being—Stingo, still in awe of Nathan's generosity and intellect, tries to rationalize his hostility. He attempts to balance the insults with Nathan's interest in Southern history and his desire to travel south to see firsthand the places about which Stingo writes. Nathan's schizophrenic personality is evident in other ways, too. He heaps lavish praise on Stingo's novel-in-progress, hailing his literary influences while extolling his unique voice; then he dismisses the work as cheap and shallow caricature, perhaps the "first Southern comic book" (253). He is a devoted friend who gives Stingo money but who, a moment later, wants to kill him for his alleged infidelity with Sophie. "It is like watching not one but two separate performers" (223), observes Stingo. And, though reluctant to admit it, Stingo is aware of Nathan's schizophrenia long before he hears Larry's actual medical diagnosis.

Yet Nathan is no simple psychopath; he is a complex character who resembles his Old Testament counterpart by acting as a moral touchstone for those around him. As Sirlin writes,

> Just as the biblical Nathan rebuked David for murdering a man to marry his wife, Nathan Landau rebukes the world for the most monstrous horror of the twentieth century—the Holocaust. Nathan is quite literally mad with the knowledge of Auschwitz and is determined to make those around him as obsessed and demonic as he. Although never touched literally by the European genocidal madness, he understands how nobody, Jew or Gentile, can escape the ramifications and consequences of the Holocaust. Although Nathan is literally diagnosed as schizophrenic, we must see his fragmentation and rage as a necessary response to the excruciating horrors the twentieth century has wrought. The biblical Nathan's advice helped save Solomon's kingdom; similarly, Nathan's warning about the evil that is totalitarianism must be heeded if this planet is to survive.

Ironically, his mania about totalitarianism in turn produces totalitarian behavior. He usurps the rights of others and brutalizes those he loves. He "is blinded by his cause, by his own self-righteousness, very much like an earlier Nathan, Nat Turner, a man whose strong sense of morality provoked immorality and violence."[90]

Stingo too is personally affected by the madness of the mad world around him. But unlike Nathan's, Stingo's madness is not clinical; it is peculiarly phallic and adolescent—the horniness of a twenty-two year old *demi-vierge* who translates all of the significant events in his life into sexual terms. In his small, claustrophobic University Residence Club room, the friendless—and womanless—fledgling writer feels like a "half-mad anchorite" (12). His infatuation with Maria Hunt is a "small-scale madness" (50). "I am semi-deranged" (211) with an "insanity of desire" (205), he writes of his first necking session with Jewish-American princess Leslie Lapidus.[91] A subsequent girlfriend, Mary Alice Grimball, makes him "nearly insane" with her passionless and very limited lovemaking, which leads to his almost "suicidal despondency" (529). And with Sophie Stingo experiences a " 'primordial' derangement" (424) of concupiscence, which "obsess[es]" him (509) and stirs inside him "a fretful, unhappy malaise" (498).

Torn by his love for Sophie and his love for and hatred of Nathan, whom he ultimately comes to see through Sophie's eyes as both savior and destroyer, Stingo's hyperbolic adolescent madness becomes at times quite earnest. The "hysteric necessity" (443) he feels after saving Sophie from drowning at Jones Beach becomes a "deep crisis" after he flees Brooklyn with her to save them both from Nathan's murderous wrath. When Sophie returns to Nathan after transforming Stingo's awkward tumescence into ecstasy, Stingo aches all over; a kind of quivering St. Vitus' dance possesses his limbs. And when he tries to continue his trip south without her, his fear for her safety so rattles him that he has to get off the bus and travel back to Brooklyn or risk a complete breakdown. "What, I wondered, would some intern at the local hospital think at the sight of this skinny distraught apparition in rumpled seersucker requesting to be put into a strait jacket?" (612).

Since Stingo's priapic horniness is matched only by his lust to become the Great American Novelist, it is not surprising that he associates sex with writing or feels "an affinity for the written word . . . that was so excitable that it verged on the erotic" (12). Assigned to write blurbs for McGraw-Hill's books, he struggles with his prose rhythms and fights back "the desolate urge to masturbate that for some reason always accompanied this task" (14). As he gazes from his window at his neighbor Mavis Hunicutt, he imagines making breathless love with her. But sometimes "in these demented fantasies," he says, "I was prevented from immediate copulation on the Abercrombie & Fitch hammock only by the sudden arrival in the garden of Thornton Wilder. Or e. e. cummings. Or Katherine Anne Porter. Or John Hersey. Or Malcolm Cowley. Or John P. Marquand" (15–16). When he thinks lustfully of his lost love Maria, he is excited by the prospect of "possessing the heroine of my own novel" (364). With Leslie, an English major who wrote her thesis on Hart Crane, he discusses "scattered books (among them *The Function of the Orgasm*)" (150) and fantasizes about "those 'melon-heavy' Jewish breasts so dear to Thomas Wolfe" (144). The twin impulses to make love and to write coincide especially frequently with Sophie. "I hugged Sophie softly and thought of my book" (547), he says. And at her funeral, he bids her adieu with lines from Emily Dickinson, whose work Sophie adored. Dickinson had brought Sophie and Nathan together. But Stingo reads not from the poem for which Sophie was searching that day in the library (ironically, one about a gentle lover who stops his carriage to escort the speaker past death and to Eternity). Instead, he selects a different verse, which links inevitably love and death and reflects the "womb-and-tomb" nature of Sophie and Nathan's relationship.[92] "Ample make this bed," he reads. "Make this bed with awe; / In it wait till judgment break / Excellent and fair." The lines have a special meaning for him since, he writes, his "entire experience of Sophie and Nathan was circumscribed by a bed" (622).

Stingo's initial impression of Sophie and Nathan, in fact, occurs almost voyeuristically on the first night of his residence at Yetta's as he hears the wild sounds of their crazed, boisterous, marathon lovemaking: "no mere copulatory rite but a tournament, a rumpus, a free-for-all, a Rose Bowl, a jamboree" (43). Stingo had come to Brooklyn to pursue his dream of writing, yet, as he confesses, though he had traveled great distances for one so young, "my spirit had remained landlocked, unacquainted with love and all but a stranger to death" (28). In the unconventional but doomed lovers who regularly rock the ceiling above him he finds both.

The tedious job that Stingo left prior to moving to Brooklyn had threatened to turn him into a "prisoner" (21) of the McGraw-Hill bureaucracy (not unlike the bureaucracy of the military order in *Catch-22* or the asylum in *One Flew Over the Cuckoo's Nest*), to thwart his ambition to write creatively by forcing him simply to edit others' words.[93] Instead of adjusting to the system, he had rebelled: when advised not to read the New York *Post*, he conspicuously displayed his copy of the *Daily Worker*; when urged to conform to the McGraw-Hill "profile," rather than buying the compulsory hat, part of the company "costume," he donned his green Marine "pisscutter," "the kind of cap John Wayne wore in *Sands of Iwo Jima*" (21).[94] After he blows plastic bubbles from his twentieth-floor office window—as Styron himself is reputed to have done before his dismissal from McGraw-Hill—he in turn is shown the door.

Yet his dismissal is liberating: it allows him to pursue in earnest the vocation of his choice. "Call me Stingo" (1), he announces with full awareness of his burgeoning identity as a writer.[95] And to Robert Penn Warren, whose *All the King's Men* influences his own work, he says, "Move over, Warren, this is Stingo arriving" (41). His search for this new self, in fact, becomes the subject of his novel at least as much as Sophie's less successful but parallel quest.[96] *Sophie's Choice*, in part about Stingo's growth and development, is thus a kind of portrait of the artist as a young man—a particularly appropriate comparison, since Stingo wants to do for the American South what Joyce did for Dublin. What gives it such resonance is that it is a novel of *two* Stingos, the naive, aspiring writer who metamorphoses from Stinky to Stingo and beyond, and the older, accomplished novelist who has been able to assimilate the experiences of his youth, fill in most of the gaps, and provide a perspective on the sad tale of contemporary madness. The latter is a husband and father who hates April Fool's Day because it reminds him of Sophie's arrival at Auschwitz, who forgives Leslie Lapidus for her torture and imagines her a multiorgasmic Jewish wife, and who realizes that "no one will ever understand Auschwitz" (623).

Unlike Sophie, who is handicapped by the restrictive role society allows her and by the lack of loving support from those (such as her father and Nathan) to whom she looks for approval, Stingo has a warm, fostering family life. His father, in particular, promotes his goals. He encourages Stingo's new career by boldly affirming, "I think you may be well shut of your employment at McGraw-Hill," which in grand Southern tradition he considers "notoriously little else but the mouthpiece and the propaganda outlet for the commercial robber barons who have preyed on the American people for a hundred years and more" (33), and provides him with a financial and spiritual legacy. Stingo so prizes his father's wit and intelligence that he even incorporates his words into his own novel as a way of understanding himself. When Stingo—following Steiner's principle of time relation—tries to recall where he was and what he was doing on the day that Sophie petitioned Höss for her release from Auschwitz, he is able to refer to his own correspondence from Duke, still in his father's hands. "The letter itself," he notes, was easily obtainable "from a father who has cherished my most vapid jottings (even when I was very young) in the assurance that I was destined for some future literary luminosity" (267).

His father, however, is not the only one to encourage Stingo's literary aspirations. In fact, Stingo enjoys a paradigmatic form of male bonding through art: throughout the novel, as Durham demonstrates, older males, denied writing careers of their own, devote themselves to the support of Stingo as a surrogate gifted "son" or "brother."[97] Farrell, Stingo's senior editor at McGraw-Hill, transfers to Stingo his wishes for his own son, an aspiring young writer who was killed in the Marines during the war. As Stingo prepares to leave, he exhorts him, "Son, *write your guts out*" (28). And Nathan, who at one time had hoped to be a writer ("until halfway through Harvard," he alleges, when "I realized I could never be a Dostoevsky" [137]), acts as a supportive "older brother" (141) and "generous, mind-and-life-enlarging mentor" (227). The only person with whom Stingo shares his work-in-progress, Nathan provides "passionate assurance" and enthusiastic critiques that give Stingo the confidence to keep scribbling away "like a fiend" (227). When Stingo's inheritance is stolen, Nathan even underwrites his literary career with a $200 gift, which Stingo prefers to view as a loan, payable, interest-free, "when and if my novel found a publisher and made enough money to relieve me from financial pressure" (507). Nathan becomes Stingo's big brother to such an extent that, after Nathan and Sophie's death, Larry Landau justifies Stingo's presence in the boarding house by telling police that Stingo is a "member of the family" (616).[98]

While Nathan reinforces Stingo's identity as a writer, Sophie affirms his sexual identity.[99] She helps him to recover from his devastating experience with Leslie, the dream girl who Stingo mistakenly assumes is "free of the horrendous conventions and pieties that afflict this hypocritical culture of ours" (155) and whom Sophie accuses of enjoying "*unearned* happiness" (157). Sophie's passionate sexuality contrasts with Leslie's entirely lingual sex life,[100] just as her real guilt contrasts with Leslie's more fashionably 1940s one. Leslie had reached a "plateau of vocalization" in which, as Stingo succinctly proclaims, "you can say fuck but you still can't do it!" (216); Sophie, on the other hand, has difficulty mastering the English language but exhibits a refreshingly frank sexuality.

And Sophie delivers him from still another English major, who proves to be an even greater devil from sexual hell than Leslie, the "Cock Tease." Whereas Leslie could talk about but never perform specific sexual acts, Mary Alice is too uptight to use or hear dirty language. Yet, as her surname Grimball implies, she is a "whack-off artist" who performs her task with such clinical detachment that Stingo realizes he could do better himself, and "certainly with more affection" (527, 529). The nightly torment of arrested lovemaking that occurs quite literally at her hands causes Stingo to ponder the possibility of his own homosexuality, a worry that Sophie soon dispels. In their Washington bed at the aptly named Hotel Congress, Sophie, demonstrating both appetite and devotion, helps him finally to shed the curse of his virginity and to savor many varieties of sexual experience. However, Stingo's long-delayed moment of ecstasy, which is couched in almost religious terms,[101] "coincides," as Jay Halio observes, "with his fullest glimpse into the horrors that Sophie has endured in the death camps";[102] only later does he realize that her "plunge into carnal oblivion . . . [had been] a flight from memory" and "a frantic and orgiastic attempt to beat back death" (603). More importantly, though, Sophie gives Stingo the reassurance he needs concerning his manhood. "Your such a beautiful Lover I hate to leave," she tells him in her farewell note, "Your a great Lover Stingo" (606–7). She also satisfies his earlier fantasy of possessing Maria Hunt, the heroine of his novel, since at one point in Stingo's fevered dreams Maria metamorphoses into Sophie, who later herself becomes his heroine. And Sophie's personal torment, which helps him comprehend Maria's unresolved guilt and hatred, also gives him the subject and framework of much of his subsequent fiction.

Furthermore, Sophie guides Stingo to a new assessment of his Southern heritage, especially of the system of slavery, which constitutes such a vital part of his identity. In Brooklyn, Stingo literally lives off slave fortunes: the money that supports his writing that summer is the legacy of another Southern artist—the black servant named "Artiste" who was briefly owned by his grandmother when she was a girl. As Stingo's father writes, "Apparently Artiste, who was in the first lusty flush of adolescence, made what your great-grandfather calls an 'improper advance' toward one of the young white belles of the town." For that offense, Artiste was separated from his own family and sold for $800 "into the grinding hell of the Georgia turpentine forests" (35–36). After it was discovered that the girl who accused him was a hysteric and a liar, Stingo's family tried without success to locate him and to rectify the injustice.

The proceeds of the sale of Artiste, converted into gold and hidden until after his grandmother's death, becomes Stingo's legacy in two ways: his $485 share helps to launch his new career, while his acceptance of the money signals his burden—the burden of all contemporary Southerners—to understand and then to make amends for the slave system from whose profits he thrives.[103] Not some isolated, barbaric act of a long-gone century, Artiste's fate, after all, is reenacted all too graphically in the savage murder of sixteen-year-old Georgian Bobby Weed, who was alleged to have "ogled, or molested, or otherwise interfered with (actual offense never made clear, though falling short of rape) the simpleton daughter, named Lula" (86), of a crossroads shopkeeper. After Weed's genitals had been hacked off and stuffed in his mouth while he was still alive and he was branded with a flaming blowtorch, Lula's claim was proven to be as spurious as that made against Artiste. On learning of Weed's death, Stingo feels a "burdensome shame" over his kinship with the "solidly Anglo-Saxon subhumans who were the torturers," denizens "of that same piney coast near Brunswick where my savior Artiste had toiled and suffered and died" (85).

Nathan, on the other hand, associates what, in his rage, he alleges is Stingo's "refusal to admit responsibility in the death of Bobby Weed" with "that of those Germans who disavowed the Nazi party even as they watched blandly and unprotestingly as the thugs vandalized the synagogues and perpetrated the *Kristallnacht*" (84). Though Nathan is inaccurate in his personalizing of the attack, he is certainly correct in establishing a connection between Southern slavery and Nazi slavery. As Stingo learns more from Sophie about her troubled past, he gains real insight into his own and is able to make parallels between the evils that were committed in both (for example, he connects the Jewish benches in Polish universities and the segregation of Mississippi schoolchildren). And at the end of the novel, as he cries for the earth's lost children, he rightly enjoins them in their tragedies: "Sophie and Nathan, yes, but also Jan and Eva—Eva with her one-eyed *mís* [teddy bear]—and Eddie Farrell, and Bobby Weed, and my young black savior Artiste, and Maria Hunt, and Nat Turner, and Wanda" (625).

When Stingo's stash is stolen from his room at Yetta's, he is relieved to be rid of the "blood money, to get rid of slavery," though on reflection he realizes the impossibility of his words. "How could I *ever* get rid of slavery?" he asks. "And were not all of us, whites and Negro, still enslaved?" (513). (It is significant that, despite his frequent railings at Stingo about the similarities between the South and the Nazis, Nathan, a Jew, replenishes with his generous gift the stash Stingo mistakenly believes Morris Fink, another Jew, had stolen from him.)

When the situation in Brooklyn becomes dangerous, Stingo decides to retreat to the South of his youth. Yet by the time he reaches Virginia, he is aware of the truth of his idol Thomas Wolfe's words about never being able to go home again. The familiar scenes of his childhood, no longer "a chain of bucolic crossroads" but now corrupted ("there was also an extravagant nightmarishness about the passing moonscape . . . . the dreary suburbs, the high-rise penitentiaries, the broad Potomac viscid with sewage" [612]), appear to him as false as the clerical disguise he dons to sign himself and his drunken blonde "wife" into the hotel. Just as Sophie had realized in a moment of epiphany that she could no longer pray, Stingo realizes that he will never live in the South again.

Still dressed as Reverend Entwistle, he makes his solitary journey back to Brooklyn. The Good Book he holds in his hand, he claims, has meaning for him only because of its literary analogues and allusions: he reads from *Job* and thinks of Sophie's trials. Like Sophie, he feels he has lost his faith, which was part of his childlike world, the illusion, the masquerade that he abandons. (In spite of his profession of agnosticism and expressed hate of "the Judeo-Christian God," however, Stingo instinctively turns to religion—as Sophie did—for aid or consolation in times of crisis, such as after Bilbo's death and upon hearing of Weed's lynching.[104])

Near the end of the novel, observes Nagel, Styron very deftly reverses Stingo's false role as minister: "at the funeral Stingo usurps the unctuous Reverend DeWitt and, rejecting the Bible, turns to Emily Dickinson for the benediction over the graves of Sophie and Nathan."[105] Stingo cannot let the Reverend, who pompously blames their deaths on the "failure of the old-fashioned principles of self-reliance" (620), have the last word: Sophie and Nathan had suffered precisely because of what Rhoda Sirlin calls "self-reliance gone mad, individualism turned into totalitarian madness, the blind will to power." DeWitt's religious consolation is thus mere hypocrisy and empty rhetoric, unlike the words of Dickinson, which reveal both her own profound religious doubts and her profound beliefs.[106]

Nor is it religion *per se* that restores Stingo to life after his friends' death. He revisits Coney Island, where he went on his first excursion with Sophie and Nathan; looking at the parachute jump and recalling Sophie's wondrous peals of laughter as she sank earthward with Nathan just a few months before, he reflects on their precipitous decline from grace and is finally able to shed his tears. Stingo himself, as Judith Ruderman notes, has "fallen from innocence into experience, expelled from the amusement park of his youth."[107] Drunk and exhausted, he falls asleep on the beach and dreams "a compendium of all the tales of Edgar Allan Poe," in which he is "being split in twain by monstrous mechanisms, drowned in a whirling vortex of mud, being immured in stone and, most fearsomely, buried alive" (625). The echoes of Poe, whose favorite subject (not coincidentally) was a beautiful woman dying young, help him to reconcile his divided psyche, accept Sophie's loss—and ultimately translate her experience into a modern Gothic tale of horror and madness. The next morning Stingo awakens, in an ample bed of sand which youngsters have protectively heaped on him. "Blessing [his] resurrection," he realizes it is not judgment day, only morning—"Morning: excellent and fair" (626).[108]

Sophie's Choice, like all of Styron's novels, ends with redemption.[109] Nathan, a latter-day prophet made mad by his vision of a mad world, testifying by his own madness to the larger madness around him (and sacrificing himself to it), expiates his personal guilt over the Holocaust by punishing himself and Sophie for their survival; he uses the very chemicals employed by the Nazis to achieve his end. Though potentially a "redemptive knight from the void" (380), Sophie's "savior" in fact becomes her "destroyer" as well as his own; yet Nathan's death serves to remind the world that the great tragedy of the twentieth century claimed more than just its immediate victims.

And Sophie, seeking expiation for her own guilts and for the sins that destroyed her family (beginning with her failure to save her ailing mother; her inability to prevent her husband's and her father's deportation and her ambivalent feelings about their subsequent fate at the hands of the Nazis; her fateful choice that condemns her daughter; her willingness to prostitute herself in an abortive effort to save her son), finds her salvation, ironically, through her damnation. The suffering she tries so hard to internalize not only redeems her self-confessed "badness" (symbolized by the "redemptive" strains of Bach's hymn of hope and of prayer which plays as she lies with Nathan in a final embrace); it also forces her to examine the faith she professes to have lost. And her inevitable death helps Stingo to understand and to deal with his own familial guilts. For while Stingo tried to save Sophie from Nathan as well as from herself, in the end it is Sophie who saves him, not just from his adolescent fantasies but from the inherited genocidal guilt over slavery, which plagues them both. Like Yossarian, Billy Pilgrim, and Chance, who provided meaningful alternatives to the institutions that oppressed their societies, Sophie teaches Stingo his greatest lesson by her example; and, like McMurphy, she dies with the knowledge that her dearest friend will have a better life as a result.

Indeed, Stingo endures and is reborn. Rising from his sandy "grave" with a new, mature sensitivity, he is able at last to create memorable art, "out of his memories of his dramatic friend Nathan and from the tenderness and torment that were inherent in Sophie's choices."[110] And, fittingly, through his book, Stingo manages to resurrect Nathan and Sophie as well, since his art becomes a religious act that offers its own kind of rebirth for the dead.[111] Whereas both Sophie and Nathan, in quest of the grace that would save them, fall prey to the dark gods, Stingo survives the madness (as Styron himself did) to expose it in his fiction: finding, at last, the "darkness visible," Stingo emerges from the "dark woods" of their shared experience into "the shining world,"[112] a world redeemed in part by their sacrificial struggle.

NOTES

Introduction

1. Yalom, *Maternity, Mortality, and the Literature of Madness* 1. The same is true of lesser-known as well as more celebrated sisters like Sylvia Plath, Anne Sexton, Doris Lessing, Margaret Atwood, and Anne Tyler.

2. Feder, *Madness in Literature* 286.

3. Feder 286.

4. Olderman, *Beyond the Waste Land* 95.

5. Styron, *Sophie's Choice* 108, 163, 526, 626.

1. Inmates Running the Asylum: The Individual Versus the Institution

1. Bradbury, *The Modern American Novel* 127.

2. Trachtenberg, "Intellectual Background" 20.

3. Vonnegut, *Wampeters, Foma & Granfalloons* 161.

4. Skinner, *Walden Two* 289.

5. Fiedler, as cited in Bradbury, *The Modern American Novel* 131.

6. Bradbury, *The Modern American Novel* 131.

7. Bradbury, *The Modern American Novel* 132.

8. Ralph Ellison, *Invisible Man* 439.

9. Trachtenberg 5.

10. Trachtenberg 6.

11. John Updike, "When Everyone Was Pregnant," in *Museums and Women, and Other Stories* 92–93.

12. Kiernan, *American Writing Since 1945* 3

13. Trachtenberg 7.

14. David Riesman's *The Lonely Crowd* (1950), written with Nathan Glazer and Reuel Denney. Discussed in Trachtenberg 13–16. See also Kiernan 4–6.

15. Mills, *White Collar* xvi, 353.

16. Quoted in Feder 280–82. Laing also discusses the false self at greater length in chapter 6, "The False-Self System," in *The Divided Self* 100–112.

17. Olderman, *Beyond the Waste Land* 33.

18. Bradbury, *The Modern American Novel* 157.

19. Bradbury, *The Modern American Novel* 157.

20. Kiernan 38.

21. Roth, "Writing American Fiction" 224.

22. Hendin, "Experimental Fiction" 240.

23. Hendin, "Experimental Fiction" 241.

24. Kosinski, *The Painted Bird* 265.

25. Styron, *Sophie's Choice* 603.

26. Lester A. Gelb, "Mental Health in a Corrupt Society" 195.

2. Seeking a Sane Asylum: *Catch-22*

1. Ken Barnard, "Interview with Joseph Heller," rpt. in *A Catch-22 Casebook*, edited by Frederick Kiley and Walter McDonald (hereafter referred to as Kiley and McDonald) 297.

2. Barnard 297.

3. Barnard 297–98.

4. Barnard 298.

5. The term, which appears in other criticism of Heller's work, was first used by Raymond M. Olderman in *Beyond the Waste Land*.

6. Wayne Charles Miller, "*Catch-22:* Joseph Heller's Portrait of American Culture—The Missing Portrait in Mike Nichols' Film," in Kiley and McDonald 384.

7. *Los Angeles Mirror; Chicago Sun-Times; New York Times.* Reviews are cited on the cover of the new paperback edition of *Catch-22* (1961; New York: Dell, 1979). All subsequent references to this edition will be made by page number in the text.

8. Joseph Heller, "*Catch-22* Revisited," in Kiley and McDonald 324.

9. Though, as Robert Merrill is quick to point out, Heller was an innocent twenty-one when he flew his missions ("I was a jackass. I thought it was a lot of fun"); served his tour of duty without protest; and almost certainly did not receive his medals, an Air Medal and a Presidential Unit Citation, for the same reason that the more jaded, disillusioned, twenty-eight-year-old Yossarian was awarded his Distinguished Flying Cross (Robert Merrill, *Joseph Heller* 3–4).

10. "An Impolite Interview with Joseph Heller," in Kiley and McDonald 275, 277.

11. "Some Are More Yossarian than Others," in Kiley and McDonald 335.

12. Barnard 298.

13. Since the publication of *Catch-22*, Heller has periodically returned to teaching, at prestigious institutions such as Yale and the University of Pennsylvania, and has held the position of Distinguished Visiting Writer at the City University of New York.

14. "For two hours almost every night, five nights a week, for seven years,

Heller wrote his novel. Once, for two weeks, he quit in disgust, turned to television and other pastimes, finally bored himself stiff. 'What do people who are not writing novels do with their evenings?' he asked his wife, and then returned to novel-writing." ("The Heller Cult," in Kiley and McDonald 26.)

15. "An Impolite Interview with Joseph Heller" 277.

16. *McHale's Navy*, which ran from 1962 through 1965, was also about American fighting men. In *Halliwell's Television Companion*, Leslie Halliwell and Philip Purser (3rd edition London: Grafton Books, 1986) 494, described the series as follows: "The wacky antics of a PT crew in the World War II Pacific, specifically on the island of Taratupa. Routine goings-on à la Hollywood, and highly popular."

17. Robert Merrill, *Joseph Heller* 10.

18. Barnard 297.

19. Barnard 296.

20. Olderman 95.

21. "An Impolite Interview with Joseph Heller" 288.

22. Solomon, "From Christ in Flanders to *Catch-22:* An Approach to War Fiction," in Kiley and McDonald 94.

23. John Wain, "A New Novel about Old Troubles," in Kiley and McDonald 46.

24. Nelson Algren, "The Catch," in Kiley and McDonald 4–5. But David Seed, in *The Fiction of Joseph Heller,* argues otherwise. Seed writes that "When Nelson Algren stated in his review of Heller's novel that the works of Jones and Mailer were 'lost within' it, he was right to pinpoint the influence but wrong to imply that it is concealed." Seed goes on to demonstrate convincingly how Heller "purged himself of Jones and Mailer, partly by parody and partly by incorporating revised episodes from both novels into his own work" (26).

Shimon Wincelberg, in "A Deadly Serious Lunacy," in Kiley and McDonald 16, concurred with Algren's assessment of *Catch-22.* Wincelberg wrote that "It manages to reduce such fine, naturalistic war novels as those of Norman Mailer, James Jones or Irwin Shaw to mere talented journalism."

It is interesting to note that, in "An Impolite Interview with Joseph Heller" 277, Heller observed that Algren's *The Man With the Golden Arm* became an almost unconscious influence in his "type of the open hero."

25. Robert Protherough, "The Sanity of *Catch-22,*" in Kiley and McDonald 207.

26. Frederick R. Karl notes that Hemingway had similarly used the war as an objective correlative in *A Farewell to Arms.* See Karl, "Joseph Heller's *Catch-22:* Only Fools Walk in Darkness," in Kiley and McDonald 165.

27. Tony Tanner, *City of Words* 72–73.

28. Barnard 296.

29. Heller says, "I wrote it during the Korean War and aimed it for the one after that" (quoted in "Some Are More Yossarian than Others" 336). In an interview with Josh Greenfeld, Heller explained: "Vietnam . . . that was the war I had in mind; a war fought without military provocation, a war in which the enemy is no longer the other side but someone allegedly on your side. The ridiculous war I felt lurking in the future when I wrote the book. So *Catch-22* certainly has more meaning in regard to Vietnam than World War II" (Greenfeld, "22 Was Funnier than 14," in Kiley and McDonald 253).

30. Barnard 296.

31. Sam Merrill, "*Playboy* Interview: Joseph Heller" 61, quoted in Robert Merrill, *Joseph Heller* 12.

32. Hunt, "Comic Escape and Anti-Vision," in Kiley and McDonald 244.

33. Brustein, "The Logic of Survival in a Lunatic World," in Kiley and McDonald 7.

34. Brustein 7.

35. Kennard, "Joseph Heller: At War with Absurdity," in Kiley and McDonald 267.

36. Howard J. Stark, "The Anatomy of *Catch-22*," in Kiley and McDonald 149.

37. Tony Tanner 73.

38. "Some Are More Yossarian than Others" 339.

39. Seed 55.

40. Seed 55–56.

41. Olderman 103.

42. Ramsey, "From Here to Absurdity," in Kiley and McDonald 230.

43. Wain (44) suggests that the structure is not only circular but also spiral, as in *Finnegans Wake*.

44. Ramsey 230.

45. Bass, "Review of *Catch-22*," in Kiley and McDonald 22.

46. Esslin, *The Theatre of the Absurd* 264, as cited in Stark 147.

47. Seed 46. Seed makes reference to Heller, as quoted in C. E. Reilly and Carol Villei, "An Interview with Joseph Heller" 21.

48. "An Impolite Interview with Joseph Heller" 276.

49. James L. McDonald, "I See Everything Twice!: The Structure of Joseph Heller's *Catch-22*," in Kiley and McDonald 103.

50. Stark 150. Such absurd behavior in love is characteristic of other men in the novel (e.g., Nately, Aarfy), not just Yossarian.

51. Barnard 295.

52. Barnard 295.

53. Seed 55.

54. Donald Monk calls Cathcart and Korn the equivalent of the Othello-Iago symbiosis: "distinct but interdependent, the combination of ambition and indecision in the first matches itself to the empirical readiness always

to exploit of the other." ("An Experiment in Therapy: A Study of *Catch-22*," 12–19. Rpt. [with slight revision] in Kiley and McDonald 216.)

55. Seed 55.

56. Wain 45.

57. Solomon 123.

58. McDonald 104.

59. Seed 46.

60. Heller, "On Translating *Catch-22* into a Movie" 359.

61. Seed 46.

62. For a fuller discussion of this technique, see McDonald's "I See Everything Twice!: The Structure of Joseph Heller's *Catch 22*" 102–08.

63. Ramsey 228.

64. G. B. McK. Henry, in "Significant Korn: *Catch-22*," rpt. in Kiley and McDonald 199, writes that the quote from *Lear* lends "an air of tragic authority."

65. Seed 47. Heller also discusses his debt to Faulkner in "On Translating *Catch-22* into a Movie" 359.

66. Stark 154.

67. McDonald 106.

68. Henry 197.

69. McDonald has a slightly different interpretation; he suggests that Mudd's name symbolizes his fate (107).

70. Seed (57) considers the presence of the soldier in white to be "a wry glance at human dispensibility."

71. Ramsey 229–30.

72. Both Robert Merrill, in *Joseph Heller* (23), and Ramsey (230) link this action to *1984* and point out further parallels between the two novels.

73. Seed 36–37.

74. McDonald 108. In his essay "The Literature of Exhaustion," John Barth suggested that the best of contemporary literature also does this.

75. Denniston, "*Catch-22:* A Romance-Parody," in Kiley and McDonald 52–53.

76. Milne, "Heller's 'Bologniad': A Theological Perspective on *Catch-22*," in Kiley and McDonald 59.

77. Robert Merrill, *Joseph Heller* 25. Merrill also links the plum tomato with the Alger Hiss case.

78. Seed 66.

79. Brustein, "The Logic of Survival in a Lunatic World," in Kiley and McDonald 9.

80. In "An Impolite Interview with Joseph Heller" 284, Heller says he *thought* he was making Yossarian an Assyrian; as he later learned, Yossarian is an Armenian name.

81. "An Impolite Interview with Joseph Heller" 285.

82. Karl (162) says that Sweden is like Yeats's Byzantium—"more a state of mind than a real place."

83. Solomon 98.

84. Seed 30. Yossarian's nakedness is both cleansing and subversive of military rank, notes Seed, who also comments on the traditional connotations of disengagement that nakedness has in American literature.

85. Milne 65, quoting Sanford Pinsker, "Heller's *Catch-22:* The Protest of a *Puer Eternis*" 152.

86. James M. Mellard, *"Déjà vu* and the Labyrinth of Memory," in Kiley and McDonald 118.

87. Solomon 98.

88. Karl 163.

89. Karl 162.

90. Stark 156.

91. Solomon 100.

92. Olderman 102.

93. Seed 49.

94. Stark 156.

95. Heller, "On Translating *Catch-22* into a Movie," in Kiley and McDonald 360.

96. Doskow, "The Night Journey in *Catch-22*" in Kiley and McDonald 167. Doskow's is the best discussion of Yossarian's journey through Rome.

97. Doskow 169.

98. Doskow 171.

99. Doskow 172.

100. Denniston 54–55.

101. Milne 67.

102. Robert Merrill 51.

103. Milne 67.

104. Milne 71.

105. Milne 71.

106. John W. Hunt, "Comic Escape and Anti-Vision: Joseph Heller's *Catch-22*," in Kiley and McDonald 243.

107. Karl 162.

108. Milne 67.

109. Hunt 244.

110. Ramsey 233.

111. In "An Impolite Interview with Joseph Heller" (290), Heller notes that as "a consequence of his accepting the compromise that's offered him—the rest of the men will then continue to fly more missions without protesting."

112. Tappman "represents organized religion. He is a good man who is, however, both ineffective and victimized" (Solomon 97).

113. Seed 35.
114. Merrill 51.
115. Denniston 56.

3. Hail to the Chief: *One Flew Over the Cuckoo's Nest*

1. Leeds, *Ken Kesey* 2. Also described in Wolfe, *The Electric Kool-Aid Acid Test.*

2. James E. Miller Jr., "The Humor in the Horror," in Pratt 400.

3. Ken Kesey, "Who Flew Over What?" in *Kesey's Garage Sale* 7.

4. Kesey, "Who Flew Over What?" in *Kesey's Garage Sale* 7.

5. Wolfe 48–49. Also mentioned in Leeds.

6. Kesey, *Kesey's Garage Sale* 14. However, John C. Pratt, in his introduction to *One Flew Over the Cuckoo's Nest: Text and Criticism* xiii, takes issue with Kesey's statement. He writes that "one has only to compare the early and the final versions to see how much change there actually was." And Malcolm Cowley, Kesey's instructor of creative writing at Stanford, observes that "his first drafts must have been written at top speed; they were full of typing errors, as if the words had come piling out of a Greyhound bus too fast to have their clothes brushed. Later Kesey would redo the manuscript and correct most of the misspellings. He had his visions, but he didn't have the fatal notion of some Beat writers, that the first hasty account of a vision was a sacred text not to be tampered with" (Cowley, "Ken Kesey at Stanford" 3).

7. Stephen L. Tanner, in *Ken Kesey* 22, demonstrates that, contrary to what Kesey writes and says about never having met an Indian before, Kesey *was* familiar with Indians. He notes: "Kesey did know a good deal about Indians and had thought and written about them. For an assignment in his radio and television writing class at Oregon he had written 'Sunset at Celilo,' a script about an Indian who returns from the Korean Conflict at a time when the dam was being built at The Dalles and his tribe was being forced to leave their village. An interviewer reports Kesey's telling of 'an Indian in a logger's camp suddenly crazed with the recollection of his blood and racing headlong from the mountain side to attack with his knife the grillwork of a diesel hurtling down the highway paved through his grandfather's land, dying out there bravely and badly, living again in the idea for Chief Broom Bromden, the narrator of *One Flew Over the Cuckoo's Nest.* . . .' On tape he tells about playing football on the same team with a large Indian, about an Indian who worked for them, and about an Indian he had once seen with lipstick all over his face, his cowboy shirt spattered with blood. And mention has already been made of the unpublished story [by Kesey] 'The Avocados,' which sympathetically treats two displaced Indians. It may be that Kesey was looking so anxiously for evidence that drugs could

expand consciousness, partly as a justification of his drug experimenting and proselytizing, that he attributed too much to the peyote." (Tanner quotes in part from an interview with Kesey conducted by Gordon Lish and published in *Genesis West*.)

In *Last Go Round*, his most recent novel (cowritten with Ken Babbs), Kesey recalls his "first time in a teepee. [His] first taste of hot frybread and honey. [His] first glimpse into the dry, ironic world of Indian wit" (xiii). As part of an assignment for his screenwriting class, Kesey, then a junior at the University of Oregon, had traveled to Pendleton, Oregon, site of the famous broncobusting Round-up of 1911. There he met David Sleeping Good, who in exchange for sharing some of Kesey's wine told Kesey "a marvelous yarn" which becomes the core of the novel. Kesey admits that he did not believe the yarn, first told to him by his grandfather, until he heard it repeated by "a teepee full of Indians" (xiii).

8. Kesey, "Who Flew Over What?" in *Kesey's Garage Sale* 14.

9. Kesey, "Who Flew Over What?" in *Kesey's Garage Sale* 7.

10. Leeds 16–17.

11. Kesey, *One Flew Over the Cuckoo's Nest* 178. All subsequent references to the New American Library edition cited in the bibliography will be made by page number in the text.

12. Stephen L. Tanner 27.

13. Stephen L. Tanner 43.

14. Rosenmann, "Kesey's *One Flew Over the Cuckoo's Nest*" 23.

15. Hicks, *In the Singer's Temple* 173.

16. Porter, *The Art of Grit* 20. Also noted in Pratt.

17. Porter 16.

18. Kesey, as several critics have noted, has a real affection for Faulkner. Some of Kesey's early short stories, particularly "Cattail Bog," have the flavor of Faulkner. As evidenced by the story outlines in the Kesey Collection (University of Oregon), occasionally he identifies "a technique or effect as the kind . . . Faulkner uses." In planning his second novel, *Sometimes a Great Notion* (1964), Kesey said in his notes that he wanted "a cross between Faulkner and Burroughs and also me." Faulkner was also a primary source of his experiments with multiple points of view and time, and in "Tools from My Chest" in *Kesey's Garage Sale*, he recommends Faulkner as a useful tool. (Stephen L. Tanner 10, 16, 59–60, 117.)

19. Throughout his story, Bromden uses size as a metaphor for emotional strength, and he equates McMurphy, the mentor he so desperately needs to show him how to beat the system, with his own father, who was destroyed by the Combine. (Stephen L. Tanner 29).

20. Kesey's emphasis on time and his references to clocks (Bancini as a broken clock, Big Nurse's ability to control time, etc.) in *One Flew Over the Cuckoo's Nest* are similar to Vonnegut's treatment of the same themes and

images in *Slaughterhouse-Five* (the radium dial of Billy's father's watch, the clock above the stage in the POW camp, the clock in the Tralfamadorian dome-home, the Tralfamadorians' deemphasizing of clock time, etc.).

21. Porter 23.

22. Wallace, *The Last Laugh* 98.

23. Stephen L. Tanner 29.

24. Porter 25.

25. Fiedler, "The Higher Sentimentality," in Pratt 377. Rpt. from *The Return of the Vanishing American.*

26. Leeds 35.

27. Leeds 43.

28. A comparable scene occurs later in the novel (254), when Sefert turns debility into strength: he goes into an epileptic seizure as he is engaged in sexual intercourse with Sandy, who says with awe afterwards, "I never experienced anything to come even *close* to it" (Wallace 101).

29. Pratt (xiii) writes: "After admitting that the name and character of Billy Bibbit were suggested by Billy Budd, Kesey has denied remembering that the first Billy stuttered in the same fashion as the second."

30. Olderman, *Beyond the Waste Land* 39.

31. Sherwood, "*One Flew Over the Cuckoo's Nest* and the Comic Strip," in Pratt 385.

32. The idea for this may have derived from a tape on the brainwashing of Korean War prisoners which Kesey viewed while working at the Veteran's Hospital. In a letter to Ken Babbs, as cited in Stephen L. Tanner 29, he wrote: "It was most enlightening, especially in terms of the book I am writing. It had a lot to do with the 'Code of Conduct.' Remember it? we used to ridicule it upstairs in the ROTC office at Stanford? Well, I'm becoming very square or something—but I'm beginning to believe the code has a lot to it, a lot about strength. Strength is the key. We need strong men."

33. Sherwood 391.

34. Porter 31–32, 34.

35. Sherwood 387. (Sherwood also notes that she is like "the ratchet wrench, adjusting malfunctioning inmates.") Laszlo K. Géfin, in "The Breasts of Big Nurse: Satire Versus Narrative in Kesey's *One Flew Over the Cuckoo's Nest*" 97, suggests that "Another allusion might point to Orwell's *1984* and the 'rat-sheds' strapped on the face of dissidents, making the connection between Big Brother and Big Nurse."

36. Géfin argues the case a little differently: "Archetypal and psychoanalytic criticism have variously interpreted Big Nurse's big breasts as signs of the Destructive Mother or the Bad Mother; for the former, she is a castrator, while for the latter, as Ruth Sullivan noted [in her article 'Big Mama, Big Papa and Little Sons in Ken Kesey's *One Flew Over the Cuckoo's Nest*'], the inmates 'yearn' that Big Nurse's actions 'should answer the promise of her

anatomy, the promise of softness and abundant giving one can associate with a mother's breast' (39). Such 'straight' readings still support the satirical male-centered concept of power-hungry women becoming the willing instruments of oppression at the cost of their womanhood . . . ." Géfin suggests an analysis based less on satire than on narrative: "As a satirical sign, Miss Ratched's bosom is an undesirable supplement of her machinic 'personality'; but as a narrative sign, it allows for the signification of her thwarted womanhood and humanity" (98).

37. Leeds 27–28.

38. Leeds 26.

39. Stephen L. Tanner 28.

40. Leeds 15.

41. Marcia L. Falk, "Letter to the Editor of the *New York Times*," in Pratt 451–52.

42. Elizabeth McMahon, "The Big Nurse as Ratchet: Sexism in Kesey's *Cuckoo's Nest*" 27, as quoted in Stephen L. Tanner 45.

43. Robert Boyers, "Porno-Politics," in Pratt 436.

44. Olderman 50.

45. Wallace 92.

46. Wallace 92.

47. The relationship between the Indian and the white man is discussed at greater length in the essays by Fiedler (especially 376–81) and Sherwood in Pratt.

48. Leeds 22–23.

49. Wallace 92.

4. Pilgrim's Regress: *Slaughterhouse-Five*

1. Crichton, "Sci-Fi and Vonnegut," 35, as cited in Klinkowitz, *Slaughterhouse-Five* 14–15.

2. Klinkowitz, *Kurt Vonnegut* 20.

3. Giannone, *Vonnegut* 3.

4. Klinkowitz, *Kurt Vonnegut* 21.

5. Joe David Bellamy, "Kurt Vonnegut for President: The Making of an Academic Reputation," in Klinkowitz and Somer 73.

6. Vonnegut, *Mother Night* vi.

7. Klinkowitz, "Kurt Vonnegut, Jr.: The Canary in a Cathouse," in Klinkowitz and Somer 16.

8. Giannone 5.

9. Giannone 6.

10. Somer, "Geodesic Vonnegut: Or, If Buckminster Fuller Wrote Novels," in Klinkowitz and Somer 222.

11. Vonnegut, *Wampeters, Foma & Granfalloons* 161.

12. Giannone (97) notes that Vonnegut wrote some 5,000 pages that he ultimately discarded before settling on the 186 that comprise *Slaughterhouse-Five*.

13. Vonnegut, *Slaughterhouse-Five* 11. All subsequent references to the Dell edition cited in the bibliography will be made by page number in the text.

14. Lundquist, *Kurt Vonnegut* 6.

15. Scholes, "A Talk with Kurt Vonnegut, Jr.," Klinkowitz and Somer 108.

16. Giannone 83.

17. Klinkowitz, *Slaughterhouse-Five* 31.

18. Vonnegut, *Palm Sunday* 296. Also noted in Klinkowitz, *Slaughterhouse-Five* 38. Klinkowitz observes that Vonnegut uses "So it goes" exactly one hundred times in the novel.

19. Lundquist 69.

20. Giannone 84–85.

21. Broer, *Sanity Plea* 92.

22. Giannone 88.

23. Schulz, *Black Humor Fiction of the Sixties* 46.

24. Kurt Vonnegut, *God Bless You, Mr. Rosewater* 13.

25. Somer (Klinkowitz and Somer 245) believes it is precisely this "dynamic tension between his two worlds" that creates the illusion that approximates reality for Billy and that conforms closely enough to the fourth dimension to allow him to experience his beatific vision. ("Dynamic tension," incidentally, is Bokonon's word for the theory of holding equilibrium between good and evil in *Cat's Cradle*.) In terms of Tralfamadore as a waking dream, Broer (87) suggests it may be an ominous one: he reminds the reader that "Tralfamadore" is actually an anagram for "fatal dream."

26. Vonnegut made a similar sad journey home. Before leaving for service in Europe, he received permission to visit his parents at the time of Mother's Day, 1944. However, the day before he arrived, his mother committed suicide by taking an overdose of sleeping pills. (Schatt, *Kurt Vonnegut, Jr.* 15. Also cited in Lundquist 6.) Klinkowitz, in *Slaughterhouse-Five* (ix), notes that "throughout his career Vonnegut will remark upon the dangerous legacy of suicides: that they have left their children with that option themselves."

27. Stanley Schatt (154) suggests a possible relationship between the misguided Weary and the equally misguided former Assistant Secretary of Defense John McNaughton.

28. Broer 93.

29. In the preface to *Welcome to the Monkey House* (x) Vonnegut realizes that the two main themes of his novels—suggested to him by his brother, after the birth of his newborn son, and by his sister, during and after her

dignified death from cancer—are " 'Here I am cleaning shit off of practically everything' and 'No pain.' "

30. Patrick Shaw, "The Excremental Festival: Vonnegut's *Slaughterhouse-Five*" 5, as cited in Broer 94.

31. Another reflexive device is the introduction of the author into his own work, which Vonnegut does indirectly in the person of Kilgore Trout, and directly: "That was I. That was me. That was the writer of this book" (Meeter, "Vonnegut's Formal and Moral Otherworldliness: *Cat's Cradle* and *Slaughterhouse-Five*," in Klinkowitz and Somer 206–07).

32. Greiner, "Vonnegut's *Slaughterhouse-Five* and the Fiction of Atrocity" 43, as cited in Schatt 95.

33. In *Beyond the Waste Land* 217, Olderman notes in particular Vonnegut's "inclusion in *Slaughterhouse-Five* of Harry Truman's announcement that an atom bomb had been dropped on Hiroshima—a document which, despite any truly good arguments for historical necessity, demonstrates a certain pride in man's ability to obliterate anybody who 'deserves' it. The honestly bewildering dilemmas involved in decisions like Truman's and in defending the morality of World War II make Vonnegut's point all the more valid, for these dilemmas" make justification of cataclysms that much easier.

34. Lundquist remarks on the similarity between Billy and Vonnegut in this regard: Vonnegut spends much of his time lecturing. Klinkowitz also comments on it, particularly in *Slaughterhouse-Five: Reforming the Novel and the World*.

35. Broer 88.

36. Tony Tanner, in *City of Words* 198, calls Billy's new vision "the crucial moral issue in the book" because it demonstrates Billy's moral posture.

37. Eliot Rosewater gave similar advice for success. He tells Mary Moody's twins in *God Bless You, Mr. Rosewater:* "Hello, babies. Welcome to Earth. It's hot in the summer and cold in the winter. It's round and wet and crowded. At the outside, babies, you've got about a hundred years here. There's only one rule that I know of, babies—'God damn it, you've got to be kind' " (93).

38. Goldsmith, *Fantasist of Fire and Ice* 28, as cited in Broer 95.

39. Giannone 89.

40. Somer (Klinkowitz and Somer 244) writes that Billy's hallucinations are distinctly different from his time travels. "Billy experiences three hallucinations in his story and the narrator carefully distinguishes them from Billy's time travels. For example, just before Billy is captured by the Germans, he stands on the ice of a frozen creek and dreams that he is ice skating in 'dry, warm, white sweatsocks.' The narrator says, 'Billy Pilgrim was having a delightful hallucination. . . . This wasn't time travel.' "

214

41. Olderman 199.
42. Giannone 94.
43. Klinkowitz, *Slaughterhouse-Five* 98–100.
44. Giannone 92.
45. Giannone 88, 92.
46. Broer 43.
47. Vonnegut, as a character in his own story, feels constraints similar to Billy's. When, as he describes in the first chapter of *Slaughterhouse-Five*, his plane for Dresden leaves without him (inclement weather forces it to reroute, bypassing his airport), he becomes a "non-person" required to spend a "non-night" in a local hotel. "The time would not pass. Somebody was playing with the clocks," he remembers. "The second hand on my watch would twitch once, and a year would pass, and then it would twitch again" (20). An even greater malaise strikes him (and other old soldiers like him) in the late night hours, during which he tries to contact former girlfriends, listens to talk radio, lets the dog out, lets the dog in, and "talk[s] some" with his pet. When he finally goes to bed, though, his wife invariably asks what time it is. "She always has to know the time" (7), he notes. As author, Vonnegut finds time to be a problem in other ways, particularly in terms of establishing the framework for the events he describes in the novel—events that "do not conform to the orderly progression of history." See Klinkowitz, *Slaughterhouse-Five* 29–30 for a fuller discussion, especially of Vonnegut's "time lines."
48. Klinkowitz, *Slaughterhouse-Five* 77.
49. The horse frequently appears as a symbol in contemporary fiction. The cruel and insensitive treatment of the injured horse by the farmer in Jerzy Kosinski's *The Painted Bird*, for example, foreshadows the boy's treatment at the hands of the peasants in the village. In *The Lime Twig*, John Hawkes calls the horse "the flesh of all violent dreams" and uses it to represent certain brute facts about the external world. The horse becomes the materialization of Michael's nightmarish fantasy which leads to violence and death.
50. Vonnegut likens the role of the artist in society to that of the canary in a coal mine. "I sometimes wondered what the use of any of the arts was," wrote Vonnegut. "The best thing I could come up with was what I call the canary in the coal mine theory of the arts. This theory says that artists are useful to society because they are so sensitive. They are super-sensitive. They keel over like canaries in poison coal mines long before most robust types realize that there is any danger whatsoever." (Vonnegut, "Physicist, Purge Thyself," cited by Klinkowitz, in Klinkowitz and Somer 10.)
51. Giannone 84.
52. Olderman 214, 198–99.
53. Somer, in Klinkowitz and Somer 251.

54. Robert Scholes, Rev. of *Slaughterhouse-Five* 23.

55. Kurt Vonnegut, "The Idea Killers" 122, 260, 262.

56. Giannone 83.

57. Several critics have commented on these parallels. For example, see Broer 87; Tony Tanner 199; and Klinkowitz, *Slaughterhouse-Five* 55–56, 105.

58. Leslie A. Fiedler, "The Divine Stupidity of Kurt Vonnegut," as cited in Klinkowitz, *Slaughterhouse-Five* 11–12.

59. Klinkowitz, *Literary Disruptions* 42.

60. Their deaths, so anonymous and unceremonious, mock their heroic military dreams, just as Roland's name, with its allusions to the medieval *Song of Roland,* suggests the haze of romance through which he sees his life (Broer 194).

61. Broer 91.

62. Horton, *The Films of George Roy Hill* 91.

5. Happening by Chance: *Being There*

1. "Insane: Sane" 1381.

2. Sohn, "A Nation of Videots" 52, 26.

3. Aldridge, "The Fabrication of a Culture Hero" 26.

4. Ivan Sanders, "The Gifts of Strangeness: Alienation and Creation in Jerzy Kosinski's Fiction" 174.

5. Klinkowitz, "Jerzy Kosinski: An Interview," quoted in Klinkowitz, *Literary Disruptions* 83.

6. Lavers, *Jerzy Kosinski* 5.

7. Gelb, "Being Jerzy Kosinski" 54.

8. Lavers 6.

9. Jack Hicks, *In the Singer's Temple* 237.

10. Jerzy Kosinski, "The Lone Wolf" 513–14.

11. Hicks 238.

12. Willson Jr., "*Being There* at the End" 60.

13. Delany, "*Being There*" 7.

14. Jerzy Kosinski, *The Art of the Self: Essays à Propos Steps* 34. Reprinted in his *Passing By* 239.

15. Aldridge 27.

16. Sohn 56.

17. Jerzy Kosinski, *Being There* 139. All subsequent references to the Harcourt Brace Jovanovich edition cited in the bibliography will be made by page number in the text.

18. Adrienne Kennedy, letter, *New York Times Magazine* 110.

19. Jerzy Kosinski, "Dead Souls on Campus" 20. Reprinted in his *Passing By* 145.

20. Aldridge 27.

21. Geoffrey Movius, "A Conversation with Jerzy Kosinski" 3.

22. Numerous authors and reporters have commented on Reagan's tendency to confuse fact and film. For instance, in *The Acting President*, Bob Schieffer and Gary Paul Gates characterize the former President as an actor surrounded by aides who wrote the script, helped him memorize his lines, and set the scenes. Schieffer and Gates discuss the influence of television on political campaigns and examine in particular the packaging of Reagan for television. "Television," they note, "gives voters the opportunity to make instant judgments about whether they 'like' or 'dislike' someone, and . . . the vast majority of Americans liked Reagan." They saw him as authoritative and grandfatherly and forgave him for things that other politicians simply could not get away with. Everybody's "favorite relative," Reagan remained serene while others snickered over his gaffes; and his campaigns, full of "imagery and generalities," were only enhanced by "the nature of television" (189).

23. McAleer, "*Being There*" 173.

24. Kosinski and Jones, screenplay of *Being There* 103.

25. See Edith Hamilton, *Mythology* 87–88.

26. Tucker, "*Being There*" 222.

27. Kosinski, "The Lone Wolf" 517.

28. Klinkowitz, *Literary Disruptions* 97.

29. For a full discussion of the Narcissus myth, see Marcuse, *Eros and Civilization* 165–67.

30. Plimpton and Landesman, "The Art of Fiction: Jerzy Kosinski" 200.

31. For a full discussion of the Narcissus myth in Barth's work, see Schulz, *Black Humor Fiction in the Sixties*.

32. Hicks 235.

33. Lewis, *The American Adam* 5. See also Noble, *The Eternal Adam and the New World Garden*.

34. Sanders 179.

35. References to Chance appear everywhere, from national and international magazines and papers to, perhaps fittingly, *TV Guide*. Even *Chronicle of Higher Education*, in a story about the educational system in the United Kingdom, struck a remarkably Chance-like note. A British educator justified fiscal restraint by arguing that "Like the good gardener . . . we know that pruning is necessary if the strongest shoots are to grow to the full potential." ("British Government's Plan for Centers of Excellence Spurs Serious Debate over Quality of Universities" A-43.)

36. Arlen, "From the TV Viewer's Perspective" 54–55.

37. Arlen 57.

38. Jerzy Kosinski, "TV as Babysitter," in his *Passing By* 138. The essay as it appears in this volume was revised in November 1989 from one originally written for NBC-TV Comment, 3 September 1972.

39. Sohn 52.
40. Sohn 25.
41. Sohn 25.
42. Sohn 25.
43. Arlen 56. Also mentioned in Sohn 30.
44. Sohn 26.
45. Sohn 26.
46. Arlen 56.
47. Sohn 25.
48. Kosinski, "TV as Babysitter," in his *Passing By* 136.
49. Sohn 56.
50. The term "plug-in drug" was popularized by author Marie Winn.

6. When Dark Gods Prey: *Sophie's Choice*

1. William Styron, *Darkness Visible* 78–79.
2. *Sophie's Choice* (1979) was Styron's fifth book but his fourth novel. *Lie Down in Darkness* (1951) was followed by a novella, *The Long March* (1956), *Set This House on Fire* (1960), *The Confessions of Nat Turner* (1967), and *A Tidewater Morning: Three Tales from Youth* (1993). Styron's play, *In the Clap Shack*, was published in 1973. *This Quiet Dust and Other Writings*, a collection of nonfiction, appeared in 1982, and *Darkness Visible*, another nonfiction work, appeared in 1990.
3. Reviews as cited in the Bantam paperback edition of *Sophie's Choice*.
4. John Gardner, "A Novel of Evil" 16.
5. Steinem, "Night Thoughts of a Media Watcher," as cited in Rhoda Sirlin, *William Styron's Sophie's Choice* 27–28.
6. Durham, "William Styron's *Sophie's Choice:* The Structure of Oppression" 449.
7. James Ellison, "William Styron: A Conversation" 27.
8. Wiesel, "Art and the Holocaust: Trivializing Memory" 1, cited in Sirlin 9, and by other critics. Wiesel does not name Styron but refers to him only as "an American novelist."
9. Rosenfeld, *A Double Dying*, cited by Sirlin and other critics.
10. Berger, *Crisis and Covenant* 33, cited in Sirlin 12–13.
11. Cynthia Ozick, "A Liberal's Auschwitz" 152, cited in Sirlin 13.
12. Styron, *Sophie's Choice* 37. All subsequent references to the Bantam edition cited in the bibliography will be made by page number in the text.
13. Styron, foreword, Sirlin ix–x.
14. "A Conversation with William Styron," in Sirlin 103.
15. Styron says the book was "suggested by a mere germ of experience. I had been living in a boarding house in Brooklyn one summer after the war and such a girl lived on the floor above me; she was beautiful, but ravaged.

I never got to know her very well, but I was moved by her plight. Then, about five years ago, I awoke one morning with a remembrance of this girl; a vivid dream haunted my mind. I suddenly sensed that I had been given a mandate to abandon the novel I had been at work on and write her story" ("About the Author," opposite p. 626 in Bantam's 1980 paperback edition).

16. Styron, foreword, Sirlin x. In "Interviews with William Styron," in Morris 62, Morris discusses with Styron the actual Sophie; Styron says, "The girl I knew in the rooming house—the original Sophie—did not have the experience of having to choose between her children. I linked her with another woman who *did* have to choose. As you say, Sophie is a composite." And Lang, in "God's Averted Face: Styron's *Sophie's Choice*" 215, cites Styron's comments from his essay, "Auschwitz's Message." There, Styron speaks of "the once devoutly Catholic Polish girl I knew many years ago, the memory of whom impelled my visit to Auschwitz. It was she, who, having lost father, husband, and two children to the gas chambers, paid no longer any attention to religion since she was certain, she told me, that Christ had turned His face away from her, as He had done from all mankind."

17. "Conversation," in Sirlin 102.

18. Leon, "Styron's Fiction: Narrative as Idea," in Morris 145.

19. "Conversation," in Sirlin 104.

20. Styron told interviewer Morris (Morris 59) that he prefers the term "Auschwitz experience" to "Holocaust" because "I find the latter too parochial for what I was attempting."

21. "Conversation," in Sirlin 105.

22. Pearce, "Sophie's Choices," in Morris 285.

23. After quoting descriptions of the brutal deaths of two Jews at the Treblinka extermination camp, Steiner observed that precisely at the same hour, "the overwhelming plurality of human beings, two miles away on Polish farms, five thousand miles away in New York, were sleeping or eating or going to a film or making love or worrying about the dentist. This," he admitted, "is where my imagination balks. The two orders of simultaneous experience are so different, so irreconcilable to any common norm of human values, their coexistence is so hideous a paradox—Treblinka *is* both because some men built it and almost all other men let it be—that I puzzle over time." Stingo, as narrator, cites Steiner's observations in *Sophie's Choice* 262–63.

24. Pearce 286.

25. Sirlin (121) suggests war does not seem to be just a temporary madness, as Melville put it, but the human condition in the twentieth century.

26. Ruderman, *William Styron* 95–96, describes the two "orders" that exist—Höss, the "higher" order, in his heavenly, well-lit sanctuary; Sophie, the "lower" order, in her hellish, dark cellar. Ruderman also discusses the use of religious language to contrast the two orders.

27. Durham uses this approach (of Sophie's identity being "relational") to define her relationships.

28. Styron, *Darkness Visible* 5.

29. James Ellison 27.

30. Sylvia's helplessness is noted by several critics, including Sirlin and Durham.

31. Durham 451.

32. Sirlin 33.

33. "Conversation," in Sirlin 111.

34. Durham 457.

35. Sirlin 49.

36. Durham 458.

37. Lang 229. Rosenfeld, in *A Double Dying: Reflections on Holocaust Literature*, translates Jemand von Niemand as "Nobody."

38. "Conversation," in Sirlin 110. A possible parallel might be Daisy's reaction to the announcement of her daughter's birth in *The Great Gatsby*.

39. Durham 455.

40. Ruderman 98.

41. Durham 450.

42. Styron, foreword, Sirlin xi.

43. Coincidentally, this is also an important date for Stingo, since it is the birthday of his father, of his literary mentor Thomas Wolfe, and of Nat Turner, a slave who served a master as brutal as Sophie's.

44. Lang 224.

45. Richard L. Rubenstein, "The South Encounters the Holocaust: William Styron's *Sophie's Choice*" 427.

46. Sirlin 50.

47. The lost child motif is prevalent throughout the novel. In addition to the children lost in the camps or in the other Nazi-condoned programs, Eddie Farrell, son of Stingo's senior editor at McGraw-Hill, was killed in fighting in the Pacific; Frank Jr., son of Stingo's father's friend, Frank Hobbs, drowned; Maria Hunt threw herself from a Manhattan window. Even Sophie (in a classic example of transference) tells Höss an unconvincing and untrue tale about a younger sister who was sexually assaulted—by a Jew—and who later committed suicide. Much later, the insipid clergyman presiding over the double funeral arranged by Larry Landau calls the doomed lovers "lost children" (620). And the novel ends with Stingo's tears for Sophie, Nathan, Jan, Eva, Bobby Weed, Artiste, Nat Turner, and Wanda, "who were but a few of the beaten and butchered and betrayed and martyred children of the earth" (625).

48. Ruderman 99.

49. Pearce 284.

50. Sirlin 41.

51. In addition to the numerous Grail images, there is a suggestion of the King Arthur-Guinevere-Lancelot love triangle in the relationship of Nathan, Sophie, and Stingo.

52. Emmi's care, writes Styron in the novel, leaves Sophie feeling "simultaneously ministered to and victimized" (486). Similarly, Nathan's loving treatment of Sophie ultimately turns into a kind of terrorism.

53. Ruderman 101.

54. Dreams also play an important role in *Catch-22, One Flew Over the Cuckoo's Nest,* and *Slaughterhouse-Five.* And Chance's world in *Being There* has similarly dreamlike aspects.

55. Durham 457.

56. Durham 454–55.

57. In "Conversation," in Sirlin 113, Styron makes reference to "some critic [who] rather poignantly or graphically pointed out in his review that when Sophie died, Stingo's sperm was inside of her."

58. Stingo and Sophie also make love in front of the mirror of their Washington hotel (viewing, "as on a pornographic screen, our pale white entwined bodies splashing back from the lusterless mirror on the bathroom door" [604]).

59. Sirlin 24.

60. Lang 217.

61. Nagel 503.

62. Pearce 291.

63. "Conversation," in Sirlin 110.

64. The Oedipal fixations are discussed in "Dreams and the Two Plots in Styron's *Sophie's Choice,*" an unpublished paper by Daniel W. Ross, as cited by Coale in "Styron's Choice: Hawthorne's Guilt in Poe's Palaces" 520.

65. Durham 454.

66. Ruderman 119.

67. Styron, *Darkness Visible* 84.

68. As Lang (225) writes, "This displacement of God by the state is further emphasized elsewhere in the novel when Sophie finds herself in the room of Höss's daughter, Emmi. There Sophie sees on the wall a sampler whose embroidered legend reads: 'Just as the Heavenly Father saved people from sin and from Hell, Hitler saves the German Volk from destruction.' "

69. Nagel 503–04.

70. Lang 221.

71. Morris, "Interviews with William Styron," in Morris 59.

72. Smith, "Bach *vs* Brooklyn's Clamorous Yawp: Sound in *Sophie's Choice*" 527. Smith (525) also makes a connection between musical imagery and voices in *Sophie's Choice:* "These metaphors go well beyond the clichés of our language, such as 'Sophie chimed in,' or 'I sensed a note of pleading in my voice.' Styron speaks of tones of voices as 'falsetto,' 'for-

tissimo,' 'mezza voce,' 'loutish vibrato,' 'sotto voce,' and refers to certain talk as like an 'aria.' Moreover, on occasion these descriptions get extremely delicate, as Styron utilizes music to help him catch the tone and rhythm of speech. 'There was something plaintive, childlike in her voice, which was light in timbre, almost fragile, breaking a little in the upper register and of a faint huskiness lower down.'"

73. Ruderman (2) notes that Styron's mother was an accomplished musician who studied voice and piano and later worked as a music instructor. Especially after the onset of the cancer that eventually took her life, she instilled in her only son a love of music and books.

74. Durham 456.

75. Conversely, recalls Styron in *Darkness Visible*, it was the sound of a passage from the Brahms "Alto Rhapsody" that his mother used to sing that saved him from suicide and thus restored him to life. The music, which "pierced my heart like a dagger," forced him to remember all the happy sounds of his own life (66).

76. Ruderman 104.

77. Durham 460.

78. Durham 460.

79. Nagel observes that "It is no accident that the guilt-ridden Stingo reads 'The Bear,' nor, for that matter, that he gives it to Sophie to read. As does Faulkner's Southern initiate, Ike McCaslin, Stingo feels sullied by his inheritance, as Sophie does by hers. Both read the Faulkner story, and both, like Ike McCaslin, must deal with something from their pasts: for Stingo, slave money, and, for Sophie, being 'both victim and accomplice, accessory' in the holocaust" (510).

80. Durham (460–61) notes that "the one linguistic skill for which we hear Sophie consistently praised is her perfect command of German, an ambivalent accomplishment at best given the historical setting of the novel."

81. Durham 462–63.

82. Nagel 504.

83. "Conversation," in Sirlin 114. John Lang (223) views the relationship between Nathan's violence and the Nazi brutality a little differently. He writes: "Through the character of Nathan, Styron underscores the contrast between irrational violence and the cool, methodical violence perpetrated by the Nazis in the concentration camps. Nathan's violence can be attributed to insanity. No such cause, however, can explain the violence of those who ran the slave labor and death camps. Those men and women, the vast majority of them civilians, were eminently rational, their work that of the dispassionate bureaucrat whose only aim is efficiency."

84. Nagel 505.

85. Shepherd "The Psychopath as Moral Agent in William Styron's *Sophie's Choice*" 608.

86. Shepherd 608.

87. Nagel 506.

88. Pearce 290–91.

89. Pearce 290.

90. Sirlin 23.

91. Ruderman 95. Though her name rhymes with "Ah, feed us," she denies Stingo precisely the sexual nourishment he craves and drives him "to the brink of madness" (213) by her refusal to perform those sexual acts of which she so cavalierly speaks.

92. Ruderman (107) points out: "Stingo had fantasized about his marriage bed with Sophie, wondering whether it would be large enough to accommodate their lovemaking. At the end he stands over Sophie's real marriage bed, the one in Yetta's boarding house on which she and Nathan now lie intertwined in death. . . . [this] leads him to read over their common grave the poem by Emily Dickinson."

93. Ironically, this is precisely Sophie's position: she is secretary to three different men (Bieganski, Höss, Blackstock) but never realizes her desire to write about her own experiences. Stingo, for instance, who does write about his experiences, endures and is saved, whereas Sophie is destroyed.

94. Nagel notes that Stingo's rejection of the prescribed dress parallels Sophie and Nathan's preference for wearing costumes. His rebellious outfit, however, represents "the exuberant rebellion of youth" and does "not conceal pathology" (509).

95. Styron's "Call me Stingo" echoes Melville's "Call me Ishmael." Styron has commented: "I realized that this was very important in order to make this story as seductive as I could make it, as dramatically compelling. I had to back off and give the reader—from the very first page—a sense of who was talking, which is a very good dramatic device and an old-fashioned one, but one that if done properly almost never fails. It's at the heart of storytelling and is the art of the novel—to establish oneself with a great authority as the narrator who's going to tell you a very interesting story, but who has not gotten around to telling you the story yet. A good example of this device is in *Moby-Dick*, where Ishmael goes through a long, wonderfully comic episode in New Bedford right before he gets you on the ship. He establishes the right to dominate your attention. I didn't do this with anything so obvious as *Moby-Dick* for a model, but just used a device that has been used many, many times" (West, *Conversations with William Styron* 236). Rhoda Sirlin devotes a long chapter of her book to establishing interesting parallels between *Sophie's Choice* and *Moby-Dick*.

Jules Chametzky, in his article "Styron's *Sophie's Choice*, Jews and Other

Marginals, and the Mainstream" (cited in Nagel 508), adds that "Like Ishmael in *Moby Dick* . . . Styron's fictionalized and mythicized self is the only one left alive at the end of the novel to tell its story." Yet Ruderman (93) notes that Stingo's enjoinder to the reader, while lending an element of grandeur to the story by recalling the opening of *Moby Dick*, also "quietly mocks the heroic aspirations of the narrator, whose name, unlike Ishmael's, is not one that any grown-up person would feel comfortable in uttering."

96. Styron writes that since Stingo "had no experience whatever to draw upon . . . the novel is in part the story of a young man in quest of experience" (Atlas, "A Talk with William Styron" 18).

97. Durham 460.

98. Judith Ruderman points out that such strong brotherly male bonding is typical of Styron's novels and occurs also between Harry Miller and Lennie, Nat Turner and Hark, Tom Culver and Al Mannix, Peter Leverett and Cass Kinsolving. (123–24).

99. Nagel 510.

100. Durham (459) notes that Stingo "consistently finds himself a sexual eavesdropper, a sort of oral voyeur, for whom knowledge of the act of love is limited to the words other people pronounce during sex." He hears Sophie and Nathan's "raging lovewords showering down" (91) from the room above his; and at the Hotel McAlpin, he overhears "each nuance of that bliss" (362) of the amorous couple in the next room.

101. Sirlin (47) says that "Styron seems to be suggesting that the sexual act is both physical and spiritual, is as close to salvation as we humans are likely ever to get."

102. Halio, in "Fiction about Fiction" 226 (cited by Shepherd 606), observes that Stingo's long-delayed moment of sexual ecstasy "coincides with his fullest glimpse into the horrors that Sophie has endured in the death camps."

103. Nagel 510.

104. Lang 226–27.

105. Nagel 512.

106. Sirlin 79.

107. Ruderman 108.

108. *The Confessions of Nat Turner* begins with "Judgment Day," during which Nat Turner dreams about redemption. In some ways it is as if *Sophie's Choice* ends where the earlier novel begins.

109. Pearce (295–96) writes: "*Lie Down in Darkness* ends, after the suicide of Peyton Loftis, with a baptism presided over by Daddy Faith. *The Long March* ends, after the defeat of Captain Mannix, in a comic recognition scene that affirms Mannix as 'Christ on a crutch.' The apocalyptic *Set This House on Fire* ends with Cass Kinsolving being redeemed by the innocent Francesca. Nat Turner is redeemed by the voice of the murdered Margaret

Whitehead speaking words of love from the New Testament. And now Sophie, who went through hell in Auschwitz and then again in Brooklyn, and whose nightmares of submission have been cruelly revived by Nathan's mad jealousy, ends her life on an apricot bedspread in the tender embrace of her lover—while Stingo, who has come not only to love but identify with her, is, like Ishmael, who identified with Ahab, reborn from the vortex."

It is also fitting that Nathan and Sophie serve as agents of Stingo's redemption, since his initial encounter with them begins with his crucifixion: their humping, he complained, was "another nail [to] amplify my crucifixion" [53].

110. Nagel 513.
111. Ruderman 108.
112. Styron, *Darkness Visible* 83–84.

SELECTED BIBLIOGRAPHY

Aldridge, John W. "The Fabrication of a Culture Hero." *Saturday Review* 24 April 1971: 25–27.

Algren, Nelson. "The Catch." *The Nation* 4 November 1961: 358. Rpt. in Kiley and McDonald 3–5.

Arlen, Gary H. "From the TV Viewer's Perspective." *WATCH Magazine* March 1980: 54–57.

Atlas, James. "A Talk with William Styron." *New York Times* 27 May 1979: 1, 18.

Barnard, Ken. "Interview with Joseph Heller." *Detroit News* 13 September 1970: 19, 24, 27–28, 30. Rpt. in Kiley and McDonald 294–301.

Bass, Milton R. "Review of *Catch-22*." *Berkshire* (Mass.) *Eagle* 31 October 1961: 6. Rpt. in Kiley and McDonald 21–23.

Bellamy, Joe David. "Kurt Vonnegut for President: The Making of an Academic Reputation." Klinkowitz and Somer 71–89.

Berger, Alan L. *Crisis and Covenant: The Holocaust in American Jewish Fiction.* Albany: SUNY Press, 1985.

Boyers, Robert. "Porno-Politics." Rpt. from "Attitudes toward Sex in American 'High Culture.'" *Annals of the American Academy of Political and Social Sciences* 376 (March 1968): 36–52. Rpt. in Pratt 435–41.

Boyum, Joy Gould. *Double Exposure: Fiction into Film.* New York: Universe Books, 1985.

Brackman, Jacob. "Review of *Catch-22*." *Esquire* September 1970: 12, 14. Rpt. in Kiley and McDonald 363–66.

Bradbury, Malcolm. *The Modern American Novel.* New York: Oxford University Press, 1983.

Bradbury, Malcolm, and Sigmund Ro, eds. *Contemporary American Fiction.* London: Edward Arnold, 1987.

Braudeau, Michel. "Why I Wrote *Sophie's Choice*." *L'Express* 28 February 1981: 76. Rpt. in West 243–55.

"British Government's Plan for Centers of Excellence Spurs Serious Debate over Quality of Universities." *Chronicle of Higher Education* 18 November 1987: A43.

Broer, Lawrence R. *Sanity Plea: Schizophrenia in the Novels of Kurt Vonnegut.* Ann Arbor: UMI Research Press, 1989.

Brustein, Robert. "The Logic of Survival in a Lunatic World." *The New Republic* 13 November 1961: 11–13. Rpt. in Kiley and McDonald 6–12.

Caramello, Charles. *Silverless Mirrors: Book, Self, & Postmodern American Fiction.* Tallahassee: Florida State University Press, 1983.

Casciato, Arthur D., and James L. W. West III. *Critical Essays on William Styron.* Boston: G. K. Hall, 1982.

Chametzky, Jules. "Styron's *Sophie's Choice,* Jews and Other Marginals, and the Mainstream." *Prospects* 9 (1984): 433–40.

Coale, Samuel. "Styron's Choice: Hawthorne's Guilt in Poe's Palaces." *Papers on Language and Literature* 23.4 (Fall 1987): 514–22.

Cowley, Malcolm. "Ken Kesey at Stanford." *Kesey.* Ed. Michael Strelow and the staff of the *Northwest Review.* Eugene, Oreg.: Northwest Review Books, 1972. 1–4.

Crichton, J. Michael. "Sci-Fi and Vonnegut." *New Republic* 26 April 1969: 33–35.

Delany, Paul. "*Being There.*" *New York Times Book Review* 25 April 1971: 7, 58.

Denniston, Constance. "*Catch-22:* A Romance-Parody." Kiley and McDonald 51–57.

Doskow, Minna. "The Night Journey in *Catch-22.*" *Twentieth Century Literature* 12.4 (January 1967): 186–93. Rpt. in Kiley and McDonald 166–74.

Durham, Carolyn A. "William Styron's *Sophie's Choice:* The Structure of Oppression." *Twentieth Century Literature* 30.4 (Winter 1984): 448–64.

Ellison, James. "William Styron: A Conversation." *Psychology Today* January 1983: 27.

Ellison, Ralph. *Invisible Man.* New York: Random House, 1952.

Esslin, Martin. *The Theatre of the Absurd.* Garden City, N.Y.: Doubleday, 1961.

Eubanks, Georgann. "William Styron: The Confessions of a Southern Writer." *Duke Magazine* 71 (September–October 1984): 2–7. Rpt. in West 265–75.

Falk, Marcia L. "Letter to the Editor of *The New York Times*" 1971. Rpt. in Pratt 450–53.

Feder, Lillian. *Madness in Literature.* Princeton: Princeton University Press, 1980.

Federman, Raymond, ed. *Surfiction: Fiction Now and Tomorrow.* 2nd ed., enl. Chicago: Swallow Press, 1981.

Fiedler, Leslie A. "The Divine Stupidity of Kurt Vonnegut." *Esquire* September 1970: 195–97, 199–200, 202–04.

———. "The Higher Sentimentality." *The Return of the Vanishing American.* New York: Stein and Day, 1968. Rpt. in Pratt 372–81.

228

Gardner, John. "A Novel of Evil." *New York Times Book Review* 27 May 1979: 1, 16–17.

Géfin, Laszlo K. "The Breasts of Big Nurse: Satire Versus Narrative in Kesey's *One Flew Over the Cuckoo's Nest*." *Modern Language Studies* 22.1 (Winter 1992): 96–101.

Gelb, Barbara. "Being Jerzy Kosinski." *New York Times Magazine* 21 February 1982: 42–46, 49, 52–54, 58.

Gelb, Lester A. "Mental Health in a Corrupt Society." *Going Crazy: The Radical Therapy of R. D. Laing and Others*. Ed. Hendrik M. Ruitenbeek. New York: Bantam, 1972. 191–207.

Giannone, Richard. *Vonnegut: A Preface to His Novels*. Port Washington, N.Y.: Kennikat, 1977.

Goldsmith, David. *Fantasist of Fire and Ice*. Popular Writers Series, pamphlet no. 2. Bowling Green, Ohio: Bowling Green University Popular Press, 1972.

Greenfeld, Josh. "22 Was Funnier than 14." *New York Times Book Review* 3 March 1968: 1, 49–51, 53. Rpt. in Kiley and McDonald 250–55.

Greiner, Donald J. "Vonnegut's *Slaughterhouse-Five* and the Fiction of Atrocity." *Critique* 14 (1973): 38–51.

Halio, Jay. "Fiction about Fiction." *Southern Review* 17.1 (Winter 1981): 225–34.

Halliwell, Leslie, with Philip Purser. *Halliwell's Television Companion*. 3rd ed. London: Grafton Books, 1986.

Hamilton, Edith. *Mythology*. New York: New American Library, 1942.

Hassan, Ihab. *Radical Innocence: The Contemporary American Novel*. Princeton: Princeton University Press, 1961.

Hawkes, John. *The Lime Twig*. Norfolk, Conn.: New Directions, 1961.

"The Heller Cult," *Newsweek* 1 October 1962: 82–83. Rpt. in Kiley and McDonald 24–26.

Heller, Joseph. *Catch-22*. 1961. New York: Dell, 1979.

———. *Catch-22: A Dramatization*. New York: Delacorte, 1973.

———. "*Catch-22* Revisited." *Holiday* April 1967: 45–60, 120, 141–42, 145. Rpt. in Kiley and McDonald 316–32.

———. "On Translating *Catch-22* into a Movie." Kiley and McDonald 346–62.

———. *Something Happened*. New York: Knopf, 1974.

Hendin, Josephine. "Experimental Fiction." Hoffman 240–286.

———. *Vulnerable People: A View of American Fiction Since 1945*. New York: Oxford University Press, 1978.

Henry, G. B. McK. "Significant Korn: *Catch-22*." *Critical Review* 9 (1966): 133–44. Rpt. in Kiley and McDonald 187–201.

Hicks, Jack. *In the Singer's Temple: Prose Fictions of Barthelme, Gaines,*

Brautigan, Piercy, Kesey, and Kosinski. Chapel Hill: University of North Carolina Press, 1981.

Hoffman, Daniel, ed. *Harvard Guide to Contemporary American Writing.* Cambridge: Belknap Press of Harvard University Press, 1979.

Horton, Andrew. *The Films of George Roy Hill.* New York: Columbia University Press, 1984.

Hunt, John W. "Comic Escape and Anti-Vision: Joseph Heller's *Catch-22.*" *Adversity and Grace: Studies in Recent American Literature.* Ed. Nathan A. Scott, Jr. Chicago: University of Chicago Press, 1968. 91–98. Rpt. in Kiley and McDonald 242–47.

"An Impolite Interview with Joseph Heller." *The Realist* November 1962: 18–31. Rpt. in Kiley and McDonald 273–93.

"Insane: Sane." Editorial. *Journal of the American Medical Association* 19 March 1973: 1381.

Jones, Peter G. *War and the Novelist: Appraising the American War Novel.* Columbia: University of Missouri Press, 1976.

Karl, Frederick R. *American Fictions, 1940–1980: A Comprehensive History and Critical Evaluation.* New York: Harper and Row, 1983.

———. "Joseph Heller's *Catch-22:* Only Fools Walk in Darkness." *Contemporary American Novelists.* Ed. Harry T. Moore. Carbondale: Southern Illinois University Press, 1965. 134–42. Rpt. in Kiley and McDonald 159–65.

Kennard, Jean E. "Joseph Heller: At War with Absurdity." *Mosaic* 4.3 (Spring 1971): 75–87. Rpt. in Kiley and McDonald 255–69.

———. *Number and Nightmare: Forms of Fantasy in Contemporary Fiction.* Hamden, Conn.: Archon Books, 1975.

Kennedy, Adrienne. Letter. *New York Times Magazine* 28 March 1982: 110.

Kennedy, William. "Who Here Doesn't Know How Good Kosinski Is?" *Look* 20 April 1971: 12.

Kesey, Ken. *The Further Inquiry.* New York: Viking, 1990.

———. *Kesey's Garage Sale.* New York: Viking, 1973.

———. *One Flew Over the Cuckoo's Nest.* New York: New American Library, 1962.

———. *Sometimes a Great Notion.* New York: Viking, 1964.

———, with Ken Babbs. *Last Go Round: A Dime Western.* New York: Viking, 1994.

Kiernan, Robert F. *American Writing Since 1945: A Critical Survey.* New York: Frederick Ungar, 1983.

Kiley, Frederick, and Walter McDonald, eds. *A Catch-22 Casebook.* New York: Thomas Y. Crowell, 1973.

Klein, Marcus. *After Alienation: American Novels in Mid-Century.* Cleveland: World Publishing Co., 1964.

Klein, Marcus, ed. *The American Novel Since World War II.* Greenwich, Conn.: Fawcett, 1969.

Klinkowitz, Jerome. "Jerzy Kosinski: An Interview." *Fiction International* 1 (Fall 1973): 31–48.

———. *Kurt Vonnegut.* London: Methuen, 1982.

———. "Kurt Vonnegut, Jr.: The Canary in a Cathouse." Klinkowitz and Somer 7–17.

———. *Literary Disruptions: The Making of a Post-Contemporary American Fiction.* Urbana: University of Illinois Press, 1975.

———. *Slaughterhouse-Five: Reforming the Novel and the World.* Boston: Twayne, 1990.

———. "Why They Read Vonnegut." Klinkowitz and Somer 18–30.

Klinkowitz, Jerome, and John Somer, eds. *The Vonnegut Statement.* New York: Delacorte/Seymour Lawrence, 1973.

Kosinski, Jerzy. *The Art of the Self: Essays à Propos Steps.* New York: Scientia-Factum, 1968.

———. *Being There.* New York: Harcourt Brace Jovanovich, 1970.

———. *Blind Date.* Boston: Houghton Mifflin, 1977.

———. "Dead Souls on Campus." *New York Times* 13 October 1970: 45.

———. "The Lone Wolf." *American Scholar* 41.4 (Autumn 1972): 513–14, 516–19.

———. *The Painted Bird.* Boston: Houghton Mifflin, 1965.

———. *Passing By: Selected Essays 1962–1991.* New York: Random House, 1992.

———. *Pinball.* New York: Bantam, 1982.

———. *Steps.* New York: Random House, 1968.

Kosinski, Jerzy, and Robert C. Jones, screenwriters. *Being There.* Dir. Hal Ashby. Lorimar, 1979.

Laing, R. D. *The Divided Self.* 1960; rpt. New York: Pantheon Books, 1969.

———. *The Politics of Experience.* New York: Pantheon Books, 1967.

Lang, John. "God's Averted Face: Styron's *Sophie's Choice.*" *American Literature* 55.2 (May 1983): 215–32.

Lavers, Norman. *Jerzy Kosinski.* Boston: Twayne, 1982.

Leaming, Barbara. "Jerzy Kosinski: *Penthouse* Interview." *Penthouse* July 1982: 129–30, 167–71.

Leeds, Barry H. *Ken Kesey.* New York: Frederick Ungar, 1981.

Leon, Philip W. "Styron's Fiction: Narrative as Idea." Morris 124–46.

Lewis, R. W. B. *The American Adam: Innocence, Tragedy, and Tradition in the Nineteenth Century.* 1955. Chicago: University of Chicago Press, 1967.

Lish, Gordon. "What the Hell You Looking in Here for, Daisy Mae? An Interview with Kesey." *Genesis West* 2.5 (1963): 17–29.

Lundquist, James. *Kurt Vonnegut.* New York: Frederick Ungar, 1977.

Marcuse, Herbert. *Eros and Civilization: A Philosophical Inquiry into Freud.* 1955. Boston: Beacon, 1966.

McAleer, John J. *"Being There." Best Sellers* 1 July 1971: 173.

McDonald, James L. "I See Everything Twice!: The Structure of Joseph Heller's *Catch-22." University Review* 34 (Spring 1968): 175–80. Rpt. in Kiley and McDonald 102–09.

McMahon, Elizabeth. "The Big Nurse as Ratchet: Sexism in Kesey's *Cuckoo's Nest." CEA Critic* 37.4 (1975): 25–27.

Meeter, Glenn. "Vonnegut's Formal and Moral Otherworldliness: *Cat's Cradle* and *Slaughterhouse-Five."* Klinkowitz and Somer 204–20.

Mellard, James M. *"Déjà vu* and the Labyrinth of Memory." *Bucknell Review* 16.2 (1966): 29–44. Rpt. in Kiley and McDonald 109–21.

———. *The Exploded Form: The Modernist Novel in America.* Urbana: University of Illinois Press, 1980.

Merrill, Robert. *Critical Essays on Kurt Vonnegut.* Boston: G. K. Hall, 1990.

———. *Joseph Heller.* Boston: Twayne, 1987.

Merrill, Robert, and John L. Simons. "Snowden's Ghost: The Waking Nightmare of Mike Nichols' *Catch-22." New Orleans Review* 15.2 (Summer 1988): 96–104.

Merrill, Sam. *"Playboy* Interview: Joseph Heller." *Playboy* (June 1965): 59–61, 64–66, 68, 70, 72–74, 76.

Miller, James E. Jr. "The Humor in the Horror." Pratt 397–400.

———. *Quests Surd and Absurd.* Chicago: University of Chicago Press, 1968.

Miller, Wayne Charles. *"Catch-22:* Joseph Heller's Portrait of American Culture—The Missing Portrait in Mike Nichols's Movie." Kiley and McDonald 383–90.

Milne, Victor J. "Heller's 'Bologniad': A Theological Perspective on *Catch-22." Critique* 12.2 (1970): 50–69. Rpt. in Kiley and McDonald 58–73.

Mills, C. Wright. *White Collar.* New York: Oxford University Press, 1951.

Monk, Donald. "An Experiment in Therapy: A Study of *Catch-22." London Review* 2 (Autumn 1967): 12–19. Rpt. in Kiley and McDonald 212–20.

Moore, Harry T., ed. *Contemporary American Novelists.* Carbondale: Southern Illinois University Press, 1965.

Morris, Robert K., and Irving Malin, eds. *The Achievement of William Styron.* Rev. ed. Athens: University of Georgia Press, 1981.

Movius, Geoffrey. "A Conversation with Jerzy Kosinski." *New Boston Review* 1.3 (Winter 1975): 3–6.

Mustazza, Leonard. *Forever Pursuing Genesis: The Myth of Eden in the Novels of Kurt Vonnegut.* Lewisburg: Bucknell University Press, 1990.

Nagel, Gwen L. "Illusion and Identity in *Sophie's Choice." Papers on Language & Literature* 23.4 (Fall 1987): 498–513.

Nelson, Joyce. "*Slaughterhouse-Five:* Novel into Film." *Literature/Film Quarterly* 1.2 (1973): 149–53.

Noble, David W. *The Eternal Adam and the New World Garden: The Central Myth in the American Novel Since 1836.* New York: Grosset and Dunlap, 1968.

Olderman, Raymond M. *Beyond the Waste Land: The American Novel in the Nineteen-Sixties.* New Haven: Yale University Press, 1972.

Ozick, Cynthia. "A Liberal's Auschwitz." *The Pushcart Prize: Best of the Small Presses.* Ed. Bill Henderson. New York: Pushcart Book Press, 1976. 149–53.

Pearce, Richard. "Sophie's Choices." Morris 284–97.

Pinsker, Sanford. "Heller's *Catch-22:* The Protest of a *Puer Eternis.*" *Critique* 7.2 (Winter 1964–65): 150–62.

Plimpton, George, and Rocco Landesman. "The Art of Fiction: Jerzy Kosinski." *Paris Review* 54 (Summer 1972): 183–207.

Porter, M. Gilbert. *The Art of Grit: Ken Kesey's Fiction.* Columbia: University of Missouri Press, 1982.

Pratt, John C., ed. *One Flew Over the Cuckoo's Nest: Text and Criticism.* New York: Viking, 1983.

Protherough, Robert. "The Sanity of *Catch-22.*" *The Human World* 3 (May 1971): 59–70. Rpt. in Kiley and McDonald 201–12.

Ramsey, Vance. "From Here to Absurdity: Heller's *Catch-22.*" *Seven Contemporary Authors: Essays on Cozzens, Miller, West, Golding, Heller, Albee, and Powers.* Ed. Thomas B. Whitbread. Austin: University of Texas Press, 1968. 99–118. Rpt. in Kiley and McDonald 221–36.

Reilly, C. E., and Carol Villei. "An Interview with Joseph Heller." *Delaware Literary Review* (Spring 1975): 19–21.

Riesman, David, with Reuel Denney and Nathan Glazer. *The Lonely Crowd: A Study of the Changing American Character.* New Haven: Yale University Press, 1950.

Rosenfeld, Alvin H. *A Double Dying: Reflections on Holocaust Literature.* Bloomington: Indiana University Press, 1980.

Rosenmann, John B. "Kesey's *One Flew Over the Cuckoo's Nest.*" *The Explicator* 36.1 (Fall 1977): 23.

Ross, Daniel W. "Dreams and the Two Plots in Styron's *Sophie's Choice.*" Unpublished paper, cited in Coale.

Roth, Philip. "Writing American Fiction." *Commentary* 31.3 (March 1961): 223–33.

Rothman, David J. *The Discovery of the Asylum: Social Order and Disorder in the New Republic.* Boston: Little, Brown, 1971.

Rubenstein, Richard L. "The South Encounters the Holocaust: William Styron's *Sophie's Choice.*" *Michigan Quarterly Review* 20.4 (Fall 1981): 425–42.

Ruderman, Judith. *William Styron*. New York: Ungar, 1987.

Sanders, Ivan. "The Gifts of Strangeness: Alienation and Creation in Jerzy Kosinski's Fiction." *Polish Review* 19.3–4 (Autumn-Winter 1974): 171–89.

Schatt, Stanley. *Kurt Vonnegut, Jr.* Boston: Twayne, 1976.

Scheff, Thomas J., ed. *Labeling Madness*. Englewood Cliffs, N.J.: Prentice-Hall, 1975.

Schieffer, Bob, and Gary Paul Gates. *The Acting President*. New York: Dutton, 1989.

Schiff, Stephen. "The Kosinski Conundrum." *Vanity Fair* June 1988: 114–19, 166–70.

Scholes, Robert. "A Talk with Kurt Vonnegut, Jr." Klinkowitz and Somer 90–118.

———. Rev. of *Slaughterhouse-Five*. *New York Times Book Review* 6 April 1969: 1, 23.

Schulz, Max F. *Black Humor Fiction of the Sixties*. Athens: Ohio University Press, 1973.

Scott, Nathan A., ed. *Adversity and Grace: Studies in Recent American Literature*. Chicago: University of Chicago Press, 1968.

Scotto, Robert M., ed. *Joseph Heller's* Catch-22: *A Critical Edition*. New York: Dell Publishing, 1973.

Seed, David. *The Fiction of Joseph Heller*. New York: St. Martin's Press, 1989.

Shaw, Patrick. "The Excremental Festival: Vonnegut's *Slaughterhouse-Five*." *Scholia Satyrica* 2.3 (1976): 3–11.

Sheehy, Gail. "The Psychological Novelist as Portable Man." *Psychology Today* December 1977: 54–56, 126, 128, 130.

Shepherd, Allen. "The Psychopath as Moral Agent in William Styron's *Sophie's Choice*." *Modern Fiction Studies* 28.4 (Winter 1982–83): 604–11.

Sherwood, Terry G. "*One Flew Over the Cuckoo's Nest* and the Comic Strip." *Critique* 13.1 (1971): 96–109. Rpt. in Pratt 382–96.

Sirlin, Rhoda. *William Styron's Sophie's Choice: Crime and Self-Punishment*. Ann Arbor: UMI Research Press, 1990.

Skinner, B. F. *Walden Two*. 1948. New York: Macmillan, 1976.

Smith, Frederik N. "Bach vs Brooklyn's Clamorous Yawp: Sound in *Sophie's Choice*." *Papers on Language and Literature* 23.4 (Fall 1987): 523–30.

Sohn, David. "A Nation of Videots." *Media and Methods* April 1975: 24–26, 28, 30–31, 52, 56–57.

Solomon, Eric. "From Christ in Flanders to *Catch-22:* An Approach to War Fiction." *Texas Studies in Literature and Language* 11.1 (Spring 1969): 851–66. Rpt. in Kiley and McDonald 94–101.

"Some Are More Yossarian Than Others." *Time* 15 June 1970: 66–74. Rpt. in Kiley and McDonald 335–45.

Somer, John. "Geodesic Vonnegut; Or, If Buckminster Fuller Wrote Novels." Klinkowitz and Somer 221–54.

Stark, Howard J. "The Anatomy of *Catch-22.*" Kiley and McDonald 145–58.

Steinem, Gloria. "Night Thoughts of a Media Watcher." *Ms.* November 1981.

Styron, William. "Auschwitz's Message." *New York Times* 25 June 1974: 37.

———. *The Confessions of Nat Turner.* New York: Random House, 1967.

———. "A Conversation with William Styron." Appendix to Sirlin. *William Styron's Sophie's Choice.* Ann Arbor: UMI Research Press, 1990. 101–22.

———. *Darkness Visible: A Memoir of Madness.* New York: Random House, 1990.

———. Foreword. *William Styron's Sophie's Choice: Crime and Self-Punishment.* By Rhoda Sirlin. Ann Arbor: UMI Research Press, 1990. ix–xii.

———. Interview. By Stephen Lewis. Canadian Broadcasting Corp. 1983. Published in *Art out of Agony: The Holocaust Theme in Literature, Sculpture and Film.* Toronto: CBC Enterprises, 1984. 171–90. Rpt. in West 256–64.

———. *In the Clap Shack.* New York: Random House, 1973.

———. *Lie Down in Darkness.* Indianapolis: Bobbs-Merrill, 1951.

———. *The Long March.* New York: Random House, 1956.

———. *Set This House on Fire.* New York: Random House, 1960.

———. *Sophie's Choice.* 1979. New York: Bantam Books, 1980.

———. *This Quiet Dust and Other Writings.* New York: Random House, 1982.

———. *A Tidewater Morning: Three Tales from Youth.* New York: Random House, 1993.

Sullivan, Ruth. "Big Mama, Big Papa and Little Sons in Ken Kesey's *One Flew Over the Cuckoo's Nest.*" *Literature and Psychology* 25 (1974): 34–44.

Tanner, Stephen L. *Ken Kesey.* Boston: Twayne, 1983.

Tanner, Tony. *City of Words: American Fiction 1950–1970.* London: Jonathan Cape, 1971.

Trachtenberg, Alan. "Intellectual Background." Hoffman 1–50.

Tucker, Martin. "Being There." *Commonweal* 7 May 1971: 221–23.

Updike, John. *Museums and Women, and Other Stories.* New York: Knopf, 1972.

Vernon, John. *The Garden and the Map: Schizophrenia in Twentieth-Century Literature and Culture.* Urbana: University of Illinois Press, 1973.

Vonnegut, Kurt. *Breakfast of Champions, or, Goodbye Blue Monday.* New York: Delacorte/Seymour Lawrence, 1973.

———. *Cat's Cradle*. New York: Delacorte, 1963.

———. *God Bless You, Mr. Rosewater*. 1965. New York: Dell, 1973.

———. "The Idea Killers." *Playboy* January 1984: 122, 260, 262.

———. *Mother Night*. New York: Delacorte, 1966.

———. *Palm Sunday: An Autobiographical Collage*. 1981. New York: Laurel, 1984.

———. "Physicist, Purge Thyself." *Chicago Tribune Magazine* 22 June 1969: 44, 48–50, 52, 56.

———. *Player Piano*. New York: Charles Scribner's Sons, 1952.

———. *The Sirens of Titan*. 1959. New York: Dell, 1977.

———. *Slaughterhouse-Five; or, The Children's Crusade, a Duty-Dance with Death*. New York: Dell, 1969.

———. *Wampeters, Foma & Granfalloons (Opinions)*. 1974. New York: Dell, 1976.

———. *Welcome to the Monkey House*. New York: Delacorte, 1968.

Wain, John. "A New Novel about Old Troubles." *Critical Quarterly* 5 (Summer 1963): 168–73. Rpt. in Kiley and McDonald 43–49.

Wallace, Ronald. *The Last Laugh: Form and Affirmation in the Contemporary American Comic Novel*. Columbia: University of Missouri Press, 1979.

Wasserman, Dale. *One Flew Over the Cuckoo's Nest*. New York: Samuel French, 1974.

West, James L. W., III, ed. *Conversations with William Styron*. Jackson: University Press of Mississippi, 1985.

Whitbread, Thomas B., ed. *Seven Contemporary Authors: Essays on Cozzens, Miller, West, Golding, Heller, Albee, and Powers*. Austin: University of Texas Press, 1968.

Wiesel, Elie. "Art and the Holocaust: Trivializing Memory." *New York Times* 11 June 1989, Sect. 2: 1.

Willson, Robert F., Jr. "*Being There* at the End." *Literature/Film Quarterly* 9.1 (1981): 59–62.

Wincelberg, Shimon. "A Deadly Serious Lunacy." *New Leader* 14 May 1962: 26–27. Rpt. in Kiley and McDonald 16–18.

Winn, Marie. *The Plug-in Drug*. New York: Viking, 1977.

Wolfe, Tom. *The Electric Kool-Aid Acid Test*. New York: Farrar, Straus and Giroux, 1968.

Yalom, Marilyn. *Maternity, Mortality, and the Literature of Madness*. University Park: Pennsylvania State University Press, 1985.

INDEX

Absalom, Absalom!, 44
Achilles, 54
Adamic characters, 4, 53, 118, 132, 147–48, 149
Aeschylus, 1
Ahab, 225n.109
Algren, Nelson, 23, 205n.24
All the King's Men, 195
American dream, 3, 50, 108, 138
American Dream, An, 17
Animal Farm, 23
Antiwar (Vietnam) demonstrations, 12
Aristophanes, 97
Artaud, Antonin, 1
Art of the Self, The, 140–41
Assistant, The, 17
Auschwitz, 4, 104, 156, 158, 160, 161, 163, 165–73, 176, 177, 178, 180–85, 187, 189, 190, 192, 196, 219nn.16, 20, 225n.109
"Avocados, The," 209n.7
Awakenings, 150

Babbs, Ken, 64, 210n.7, 211n.32
Baldwin, James, 9
Barth, John, 1, 14, 16–17, 23, 39, 147, 207n.74
Barthelme, Donald, 16
Battle of the Bulge, 101, 109
"Bear, The," 222n.79
Beatles, 12
Being There (film): screenplay for, 144–45, 148
Being There (novel), 133, 136–53 passim; biblical dimension of, 147; gar-
den in, 4, 16, 140, 142, 146, 148; Kosinski's experiences as basis for, 21, 136, 138–39, 142, 150–53; mirror imagery in, 143–45; Narcissus myth in, 145–47; TV in, 116, 134, 136, 141, 142–44, 145–46, 149, 217n.35; "videocy," 136; wasteland in, 4
—Chance, 2, 3–4, 5, 16, 17, 42, 134, 139, 140–53, 202, 217n.35, 221n.54; as Adamic figure, 4, 53, 118, 146–48, 149; as Chauncey Gardiner, 4, 140, 152; idiot savant prototypes for, 149–50; as minority, 3; as new Narcissus, 145–47; as outsider, 138–39, 149; as redeemer, 148, 153; as type of his creator, 147–48
—Louise (the maid), 148
—Old Man, The, 14, 16, 140, 143–44
—Rand, Benjamin (Ben), 139–40
—Rand, EE (Elizabeth Eve), 17, 140, 144, 145, 148, 149; as biblical Eve, 147
—Skrapinov, 149
Bellow, Saul, 9
Belsen (Bergen-Belsen), 106
Bettelheim, Bruno, 160
Bible, 1, 130, 200
Big, 150
Big Brother, 143, 211n.35
Birdy, 1
Black humor, 14
Blind Date, 138
Borowski, Tadeusz, 160
Brothers Karamazov, The, 128
Budd, Billy, 84, 134, 211n.29

Burroughs, William, 210n.18
Bush, George, 29, 143

Campbell, Joseph, 1, 118
Camus, Albert, 27
Candide, 140, 149
Catch-22, 1, 2, 14, 16, 20–61 passim,
68, 69, 133, 136, 153, 195, 204n.13,
205n.24, 206n.29, 208n.111,
221n.54; anachronisms in, 25;
Catch-18 as original title of, 35, 47;
cross as symbol in, 49–50, 52, 59;
déjà vu in, 33, 36; disappearance of
characters in, 48; doublespeak in,
39–41, 60; Heller's experiences as
basis for, 20–22; interchangeability
of characters in, 45–46; Jew as prototype of victim in, 38; as morality
play, 49; "Night of Horrors" as original chapter title in, 55; paradox in,
25, 26, 30, 59; as parody of American dream, 50; recurring images in,
33–34; repetitive actions in, 34; reviews of, 21, 23; structure of, 32–37,
42–45; title of, 35; time in, 41–42;
as war fiction, 22–25, 26; wasteland
in, 4, 55
—Aarfy, 56, 206n.50; name symbolism of, 56
—Appleby, 26
—Cathcart, Colonel, 2, 25, 37, 38,
57–58, 60, 206n.54; as avaricious
administrator, 26, 28, 43, 45, 50; as
capitalist, 24, 49, 52; doublespeak
of, 39–40; and "odious deal" with
Yossarian, 54, 56–57, 59; quest of,
for *Post* cover, 34, 49; sympathy
letter from, 46, 47
—Chief White Halfoat, 37, 48, 68; as
dispossessed Native American, 33
—Clevinger, 57; ill-fated mission of,
44, 47, 48; trial of, 37–38
—Daneeka, Doc, 26–27, 44; as living
dead man, 46–47
—Daneeka, Mrs., 47, 48
—Dunbar, 33–34, 41, 45, 57; disappears, 48; spurned, 47

—Glorious Loyalty Oath Crusade,
25, 29
—Hungry Joe in, 36–37
—Korn, Colonel, 24, 38, 39, 45, 49,
54, 60, 206n.54; gag rule of, 40,
42
—Major Major, 28, 29, 33, 34, 48–49,
54; father of, 24; as "Washington
Irving," 48
—Minderbinder, Milo, 3, 29–30, 41,
55, 59; as biblical serpent, 53–54; as
double-dealer, 36, 51–52; as false
god, 50
—Mudd, 46, 51–52, 207n.69
—Nately, 44, 57, 59, 206n.50; discussion of age of, 42; name symbolism
of, 54
—Nately's whore, 34, 43; as symbol
of guilt, 31, 57
—Orr, 26; encounter of, with prostitute, 44; escape of, as resurrection,
58, 60; name symbolism of, 59;
nonappearance of, in novel, 53
—Peckem, General P. P., 24, 33, 34,
38, 39, 40; "prolixity," 31
—Scheisskopf, General, 40, 59, 60;
love of parades, 34, 37–38; name
symbolism of, 34
—Scheisskopf's wife, 17
—Snowden episode, 41, 42–44, 51, 53,
56, 57–58
—Soldier in white, 47–48, 51, 207n.70
—Tappman, Chaplain, 4, 28, 45,
208n.112; defies authority, 60; has
feeling of déjà vu, 35–36, 44; trial of,
37–39
—Wintergreen, 26, 30–31; as clerk
who runs war, 27, 31
—Yossarian, 2, 17, 24–38, 41–46, 49–
61, 78, 92, 114, 116, 151, 153, 202,
204n.9, 206n.50, 207n.80, 208n.96;
as Adamic figure, 4, 53; based on
Heller, 21; as Christ figure, 59; descent of, to the underworld, 55;
double vision of, 35; as hero, 59;
insubordination of, 28–29; journey
of, to Rome, 54–56; as mythic fig-

ure, 54, 59; nudity of, 43, 53, 76, 208n.84; as outsider, 3, 52; rebirth of, 4; redemptive mission of, 59; retreat of, to hospital, 27–29, 41, 58; as savior, 61; as symbol, 53; as "Washington Irving," 28

Catch-22: concept of, 2, 3, 25–32, 45, 53, 57, 58; mutability of, 23, 32

Catcher in the Rye: Holden Caulfield in, 13, 17

Cat's Cradle, 102, 127, 213n.25

"Cattail Bog," 210n.18

Céline, Louis-Ferdinand, 106, 122

Children's Crusade, 104, 105–06, 109

Civil Rights Movement, 11–12, 25

Cold War, 10, 11, 25

Confederacy of Dunces, A: Ignatius J. Reilly in, 17

Confessions of Nat Turner, The, 157, 159, 218n.2, 224n.108

Coolidge, Calvin, 51

Cowley, Malcolm, 73, 209n.6

Crichton, J. Michael, 100

Darkness Visible, 156, 183, 218n.2, 222n.75

David Sleeping Good, 210n.7

Deer Park, The, 17

Denney, Reuel, 12

Depression, Great, 100

Destruction of Dresden, 114

Dickinson, Emily, 98, 194–95, 200, 223n.92; as "Emil Dickens," 175

Divided Self, The, 13

Dołęga-Mostowicz, Tadeusz, 150

Dominick and Eugene, 150

Dostoevsky, Fyodor Mikhailovich, 1

Dresden, 42, 102–06, 107, 110–11, 113, 116–17, 119, 121, 123, 124, 126, 127, 128, 215n.47; revisionist history of, 114–15; as symbol of artistic ideal, 54; as symbol of technological evil, 4, 14, 101, 104, 108, 120; Vonnegut's 1967 visit to, 102–03

Dulles, John Foster, 25

Dyzma, Nikodem, 150

Eacker, Lieutenant General, 114

Echo, 145

Echolalia, 33, 114

Ego psychology, 15

Electric Kool-Aid Acid Test, 64, 66

Eliot, T. S., 114; as false identity in *Catch-22,* 34

Ellison, Ralph, 9, 16

Epic: conventions, 71, 81; tradition, 54

Experimental novel of '60s and '70s, 14, 15–18

Fall of man, 54, 146–47

Farewell to Arms, A, 205n.26

Faulkner, William, 44, 179, 188, 207n.65, 210n.18, 222n.79

Finnegans Wake, 206n.43

Fitzgerald, F. Scott, 64

Ford, Gerald, 11

Ford Foundation, 138

Forman, Milos, 53

Franklin, Benjamin, 51

Freudian symbolism, 17, 54, 111

Friedman, Bruce Jay, 14

From Here to Eternity, 23

Further Inquiry, The, 64

Future Is Ours, Comrade, The, 138

Gender stereotyping, 4; in *One Flew Over the Cuckoo's Nest,* 94–97; in *Sophie's Choice,* 157–58, 162, 165, 168, 177, 182, 189–90

Giles Goat-Boy, 1, 14

Glazer, Nathan, 12

God Bless You, Mr. Rosewater, 127; Eliot Rosewater in, 108, 114, 128, 214n.37

Good Soldier Schweik, The, 23

Graduate, The, 107

Grass, Günter, 13

Great Gatsby, The: Daisy in, 220n.38; Nick Carraway in, 74

Greek tragedy, 1

Gulliver, 140, 149

Harte, Bret, 85
Hawkes, John, 215n.49
Heller, Joseph, 1, 9, 14, 23, 24, 25, 32,
  37, 41, 42, 44, 47, 52, 53, 55, 59, 61,
  68, 108, 153, 204nn.9, 13,
  205nn.14, 24, 29, 206n.29,
  207nn.65, 80, 208n.111; autobio-
  graphical basis for fiction of, 20–22;
  and fear of flying, 22; influences on,
  48; military experience of, 20–22;
  similarities of, to Yossarian, 21–22;
  and writing of *Catch 22*, 21–22
Hemingway, Ernest, 22, 64, 205n.26
Hera, 145
Herzog: Moses Herzog in, 41
Hirohito, emperor of Japan, 8
Hiroshima, 8, 9, 101, 102, 104, 109,
  214n.33
Hiss, Alger, 207n.77
Hitchcock, Alfred, 128
Hitler, Adolf, 8, 10, 24, 25, 131, 143,
  165
Hoffman, Ernst Theodor Amadeus, 1
Holocaust, 5, 158–59, 161, 179, 193,
  201, 219n.20
Homer, 1
Hoover, J. Edgar, 10
Horton, Willie, 143

Iliad, 54
Inmates running the asylum, 5, 18,
  67, 96
Institution as oppressive force, 1–5,
  12; in *Being There*, 136–37, 141,
  152–53; in *Catch-22*, 28, 48, 49,
  52–54, 60–61; in *One Flew Over the
  Cuckoo's Nest*, 66–69, 88–89, 94,
  98; in *Slaughterhouse-Five*, 102,
  133–34; in *Sophie's Choice*, 156,
  162, 189, 195
In the Clap Shack, 218n.2
Invisible Man, 9
Invisible Man (character), 16

John Paul II (Pope), 11
Johnson, Lyndon Baines, 12
Jones, James, 205n.24

Jong, Erica, 97
Joyce, James, 31, 42

Kafka, Franz, 1
Kariera Nikodema Dyzma, 150
Kennedy, Adrienne (student of Kosinski), 142
Kennedy, John F., 11, 143
Kennedy, Robert, 11, 115–16, 119
Kesey, Faye, 64
Kesey, Ken, 14, 21, 23, 42, 89, 104,
  108, 112, 153, 161, 209n.7,
  210nn.7, 18, 211n.29; accusations
  of sexism and racism against, 94–
  97; autobiographical basis for fiction of, 64–66; concern of, for Indians' plight, 67–68; and electroshock
  therapy, 66; at Menlo Park (psychiatric ward), 64–66; with Merry
  Pranksters, 64; poetic quality of
  prose of, 71–73; at Stanford, 64,
  73, 209n.6, 211n.32; themes of, 94–
  95
Kesey's Garage Sale, 65, 210n.18
King, Martin Luther, Jr., 11, 115,
  119
Kinsolving, Cass, 16, 182, 224nn.98,
  109
Kogon, Eugen, 160
Korean War, 4, 11, 25, 206n.29,
  209n.7, 211n.32
Kosinski, Jerzy, 5, 9, 12, 14, 16, 64,
  108, 134, 146–48, 215n.49; autobiographical basis for fiction of, 21,
  136, 138–39, 142, 150–53; concerned about power of media, 143,
  153; personal success of, 137–39;
  and Polish literary contexts, 149–
  50; response of, to Polish totalitarianism, 137–38; as screenwriter,
  144–45; and TV, 136, 143, 150–53;
  at Yale, 142
Krushchev, Nikita, 11

Laing, R. D., 13, 15–16
Lancelot, 1, 14; Anna in, 69
Last Gentleman, The, 150

Last Go Round, 210n.7
Lautréamont, Le Comte de (Isidore Lucien Ducasse), 1
Leary, Timothy, 64
Lengyel, Olga, 160
Lennon, John, 11
Lie Down in Darkness, 158, 218n.2, 224n.109
Lime Twig, The, 215n.49
"Literature of Exhaustion, The," 207n.74
Loftis, Milton, 182
Loftis, Peyton, 182
Lonely Crowd, The, 12
"Lone Wolf, The," 139, 146
Long March, The, 218n.2, 224n.109
Lord Jim, 185
Lost in the Funhouse, 39, 147
Lovell, Vik, 64–65
LSD, 64, 65

MacArthur, General Douglas, 25
McCarthy, Senator Joseph, 10, 25
McCaslin, Ike, 222n.79
McHale's Navy, 22, 205n.16
McLuhan, Marshall, 141
McNaughton, John, assistant secretary of defense, 213n.27
Madness as symbol, 1; in *Being There*, 153; in *Catch-22*, 28–29, 44, 59–61; in *One Flew Over the Cuckoo's Nest*, 84, 94, 98; in *Slaughterhouse-Five*, 116–19, 134; in *Sophie's Choice*, 156, 193, 202
Mailer, Norman, 17, 132, 205n.24
Malamud, Bernard, 17
Malcolm, 150
Malcolm X, 11
Malraux, André, 161
Man with the Golden Arm, The, 205n.24
Melville, Herman, 85, 219n.25, 223n.95
Merry Pranksters, 64
Meursault, 149
Michałko, 149
Mila-18, 35

Military-economic complex, 21, 164, 204n.5
Mills, C. Wright, 13
Mitty, Walter, 118, 126
Moby-Dick, 85; Ishmael in, 74, 223–24n.95, 225n.109
Mother Night, 101
Mountain Girl, 64
"Much Madness Is Divinest Sense," 98
Müller, Gerhard, 105–06, 110, 119
Mussolini, Benito, 143
Muteness, 68–69, 76, 80

Nagasaki, 8
Naked and the Dead, The, 23
Name symbolism, 34, 54, 56, 59, 67–68, 84, 86–87, 118, 197, 207n.69, 211n.35, 220n.37, 223n.91
Narcissus, 145–47
Nemesis, 145
Nerval, Gérard de, 1
New Life, A, 17
Nichols, Mike, 107
Nietzsche, Friedrich Wilhelm, 1
Niewiadomski, Piotr, 150
1984, 48, 207n.72, 211n.35
Nixon, Richard, 12, 25
No Third Path, 138

Oakhurst, John, 85
O'Hare, Bernard, 104–05
O'Hare, Mary, 104–06, 132
One Flew Over the Cuckoo's Nest (film): Big Nurse's name in, 53
One Flew Over the Cuckoo's Nest (novel), 2, 14, 21, 33, 58, 60, 64–98, 195, 209nn.6, 7, 221n.54; animal imagery in, 82–83, 92–94, 125; attitudes toward Blacks in, 94–97; attitude toward women in, 94–97; the Combine in, 67, 69, 74, 81, 88, 95, 96, 136, 153, 164, 210n.19; comic role reversals in, 95–96; cross images in, 86; electroshock therapy (EST) in, 66, 67, 69, 73, 78, 86, 104, 134, 136; fishing trip as Pentecost

One Flew Over the Cuckoo's Nest (continued)
in, 79; "fog" in, 42, 69–70, 82; hand symbolism in, 77–79, 83, 91, 92; Kesey's experiences as basis for, 64–66; and laughter, recuperative power of, 74–76; machine vs. nature in, 67, 69–70, 79–80, 81; messianic symbolism in, 81–82; nurses' station as symbol in, 92; restoration of potency as central theme of, 78–80, 83, 89–90, 92–93, 94; slaughterhouse imagery in, 104; symbolic castration in, 80, 88, 92, 211n.36; time in, 210n.20; wasteland in, 4
—Bancini, Pete, 78, 210n.20
—Bibbit, Billy, 17, 83, 112, 211n.29; and assertion of masculinity, 84; name symbolism of, 84; as perpetual child, 90, 134; sexual initiation of, 90–91; speech defect of, 90; suicide of, 91
—Bibbit, Mrs. (Billy's mother), 88, 90–91
—Big George, 77, 85
—Bromden, Chief, 4, 16, 33, 42, 67–82, 86, 88, 91–94, 96–98, 151, 161, 210n.19; called Chief Broom, 67, 209n.7; creation of, inspired by peyote, 66; dog as totem of, 93–94; escape of, 2, 82; and EST, 67, 69, 73; as "half-breed," 3, 82; Indian father of, 67–68, 74; as McMurphy's second self, 82; muteness of, 68–69, 80; name symbolism of, 67–68; as narrator, 66, 70–74; potency of, restored, 80; and suffocation of McMurphy, 80–81; as symbol for disenfranchised, 3; vote of, on World Series, 70; white mother of, 67–68, 70
—Candy, 17, 72, 79, 83, 85–86, 90; as threat to Ratched, 89
—Cheswick, 85
—Ellis, 77–78, 84
—Harding, Dale, 77, 85–86, 89, 92–93; emasculation of, 82–83, 93; restoration of potency of, 83
—Harding, Vera, 83–84, 90; and emasculation of husband, 89
—McMurphy, Randall Patrick (Mack), 2, 17, 58, 60, 70–98, 114, 116, 134, 153, 202, 210n.19; as Adamic figure, 4; cap of, as symbol, 81; confrontations of, with Ratched, 71, 75–76, 91–92; as "dedicated lover," 71–72; feminine qualities of, 97; foreshadowing of death of, 78; as Grail Knight, 4, 75; and hand symbolism, 77, 78, 91, 92; healing laughter of, 75–76; as hero, 85; name symbolism of, 84; relationship of, with Bromden, 70–74, 76–82, 94, 96–97; as savior, 81, 86; unusual underwear of, 76, 85; as war veteran, 84; as Western hero, 74, 82, 84–85
—Ratched, Nurse (Big Nurse), 4, 17, 67–70, 74–98, 133, 153, 210n.20; attitude of, toward women, 88–89; breasts of, 88, 91, 211–12n.36; as machine, 75, 86–88, 91, 95, 212n.36; name symbolism of, 86–87, 211n.35; sublimation of passion of, 87–89; as tyrannical mother, 3, 68, 77, 79, 90, 91–92; uniform of, 87–88, 91; violation of station of, 91–92
—Sefert, 17, 211n.28
—Spivey, Dr., 79
On the Bus, 64
Orwell, George, 211n.35
Ovid, 147
Ozick, Cynthia, 159

Painted Bird, The, 136, 137, 215n.49; child narrator (nameless Boy) in, 16, 69, 148
Palm Sunday, 106
Pearl Harbor, 8, 22
Percy, Walker, 1, 14, 150
Perot, Ross, 143

Index

Peyote, 64, 66, 210n.7
Picasso, Pablo, 128
Pinball, 148
Player Piano, 103
Poe, Edgar Allan, 4, 201
Politics of Experience, The, 13
Prague Spring, 12
Presley, Elvis, 12
Prus, Bolesław, 149
Purdy, James, 150
Pynchon, Thomas, 16, 119

Rabbit Run: Sister Mim in, 17
Rain Man, 150
Raskolnikov, 54
Reagan, Ronald, 11, 143, 217n.22
Riesman, David, 12
Rimbaud, Arthur, 1
Roethke, Theodore, 1
"Rose for Emily, A," 74; Emily Grierson in, 179; Homer Barron in, 179
Rosenham, D. L., 136
Roth, Philip, 9, 14–15

Salinger, J. D., 1, 13
Scholes, Robert, 14
Schwarz-Bart, André, 160
Set This House on Fire, 218n.2, 224n.109
Sex in the contemporary American novel, 17; in *Being There*, 145, 149; in *Catch-22*, 34, 36, 44, 56; in *One Flew Over the Cuckoo's Nest*, 71–72, 81, 84, 85, 87–91, 92, 94; in *Slaughterhouse-Five* 108, 113, 126, 129, 132; in *Sophie's Choice*, 157, 164, 168–70, 171–74, 178, 181, 186, 190, 193–95, 197–98
Shakespeare, William, 1
Shaw, Irwin, 205n.24
Sinatra, Frank, 12, 105
Sirens of Titan, The, 103, 119
Skinner, B. F., 9
Slaughterhouse-Five, 1, 2, 14, 42, 54, 69, 100–134, 140, 213n.12,

214nn.31, 33, 221n.54; animal imagery, 122, 125–27, 215n.47; biblical resonance of, 107, 118; and Cinderella, 122, 134; clock imagery in, 121–22, 125, 210–11n.20, 215n.47; color imagery in, 123; echolalia in, 114; "mustard gas and roses," 123, 129; patterns of imagery in, 116–18, 123–27; reviews of, 132; scatological imagery in, 110; *schlachthof-fünf*, 104, 116; similarities of, to *Being There*, 150, 153; "so it goes" as theme in, 104, 106, 111, 119, 123, 213n.18; time in, 41, 121–23, 174, 210–11n.20, 215n.47; title and subtitles of, 103–106; vision imagery in, 116–18, 121–22; Vonnegut's experiences as basis for, 21, 101–6, 112–16, 119, 123, 125, 132, 213n.26; wasteland in, 4, 126
—Campbell, Howard, 128, 133
—Derby, Edgar, 106–08, 115, 121, 130; as human extension of Dresden, 107–08, 109; as surrogate father to Billy, 116, 134
—Ilium, 108, 113, 116, 118, 125; as unheroic city, 102, 111
—Lazzaro, Paul, 115, 122
—Merble, Lionel, 107, 116
—Merble, Valencia, 107–08, 112–113, 122, 124–25, 132; death of, 116; as symptom of Billy's disease, 112
—Pilgrim, Billy, 16, 84, 107–34, 151, 153, 161, 174, 202, 211n.20, 213n.25, 214nn.34, 36, 40; as Adamic figure, 4, 118, 132; as chaplain's assistant, 108–09, 116; coat of, 112, 125; as "dumper," 110, 116; as embodiment of American dream, 3, 108; as mate to Montana, 4, 17, 113, 117, 118, 119, 127, 129, 132; name symbolism of, 118; Oedipal fantasies of, 113; as optometrist, 116; as perpetual child, 90; as prisoner of war, 42, 116; shoes of, 109; as survivor, 2, 109, 110–11, 127

243

—Pilgrim family, 107, 109, 111–13, 115, 116, 119, 124, 129
—Rosewater, Eliot, 128, 132
—Rumfoord, Bertram Copeland, 114–15, 128, 133
—Spot, 107, 116, 125
—Tralfamadore/Tralfamadorians, 4, 17, 110, 125, 129–32, 140, 153, 211n.20, 213n.25; as alternative reality, 2, 108; limitations of vision, 117–20; sense of time in, 115, 120–23, 130, 174
—Trout, Kilgore, 127–31, 132, 134, 214n.31; as persona for Vonnegut, 128
—Weary, Roland, 116, 119, 126–27, 133, 213n.27, 216n.60; fascination of, with torture, 111, 122; as one of Three Musketeers, 109, 112
—Wild Bob, Colonel, 116, 133
—Wildhack, Montana, 17, 113, 117, 127, 129; as new Eve, 4, 118, 132
Slovik, Eddie, Private, 109, 119
Sól ziemi, 150
Sometimes a Great Notion, 210n.18
Song of Roland, 216n.60
Sophie's Choice, 2, 4, 14, 15, 16, 21, 42, 69, 74, 114, 153, 156–202 passim, 218nn.2, 15, 219n.23, 220n.47, 223–34n.95, 224n.108; accusations of and defense against charges of sexism in, 157–58; Arthurian motif in, 221n.51; Auschwitz in, 156, 158, 160, 161, 163, 165–73, 176, 177, 178, 180–85, 187, 189, 190, 192, 196, 219nn.16, 20, 225n.109; and Catholicism, 160; Grail images in, 221n.51; language in, 188–90, 219n.26, 222n.80; Lebensborn program in, 170, 172; music in, 165, 171, 184, 185–88, 221–22n.72, 222n.73; narrator of, 160, 189, 223–24n.95; Oedipal fixations in, 180, 221n.64; redemption in, 171, 174, 181, 183–84, 185, 201–02; reviews of, 156–57, 218n.3; slavery in, 156,

161, 180, 198–99, 222n.79; Sophie's choice in, 167–68; Styron's experiences as basis for, 21, 159–60, 195, 218–19nn.15, 16
—Artiste, 198–99, 220n.47
—Bieganski, Prof., 168, 177, 183, 188, 189, 196, 223n.93; anti-Semitism of, 168, 186; attitude of, toward Sophie, 163–66, 187
—Blackstock, Dr., 173, 178, 188, 191, 223n.93
—Blackstock, Sylvia, 162–63, 173, 220n.30
—Dürrfeld, Dr. Walter, 164, 170–72, 175, 180, 184, 186; as Sophie's demon lover, 170–72, 177
—Eva (Sophie's daughter), 167, 176, 189, 199, 201, 220n.47; beloved flute of, 187–88
—Grimball, Mary Alice, 193, 197
—Höss, Emmi, 175, 221nn.52, 68
—Höss, Frau, 171, 185, 188
—Höss, Rudolf, 15, 114, 162, 175, 188, 196, 219n.26, 220n.47, 223n.93; as assailer of Sophie's identity, 168–71, 176; as betrayer of Sophie and Jan, 172, 173, 189; as failed believer, 183–84
—Jan (Sophie's son), 167, 169, 170, 172, 176, 185, 189, 191, 192, 199, 220n.47
—Jozef, 166, 175
—Kazik, 165–66, 169, 175, 177, 188
—Landau, Larry, 184, 190–91, 197, 220n.47
—Landau, Nathan, 2, 3, 4, 5, 14, 140, 153, 156, 164, 186, 187, 188, 195, 196, 220n.47, 221nn.51, 52, 222n.83, 223n.92, 224n.100, 225n.109; biblical aspect of, 193; as cinematic character, 176; expression of Jewish identity of, 192; and love of costuming, 191–92, 223n.94; as mentor to Stingo, 197, 199, power of, over Sophie, 173–79, 181–84, 190, 194; as redemptive

knight, 174, 201; relationship of, with brother, 190–91; sadism, of 171, 177, 189; as St. Nathan le Bon, 190; suicide of, 200–202
—Lapidus, Leslie, 17, 189, 193, 194, 196, 197, 223n.91
—Sophie (Zawistowska), 2, 3, 4, 5, 14, 15, 16, 17, 42, 140, 148, 151, 156–202 passim, 219nn.16, 26, 220nn.27, 43, 47, 221nn.51, 52, 57, 58, 68, 72, 222nn.79, 80, 223nn.92, 93, 94, 224nn.100, 102, 225n.109; as Mrs. Entwistle, 182, 200; as "Irma Griese," 176–77; and love of costuming, 176, 179; and love of music, 165, 171, 185–88, 201; maternal identity of, 166–70, 172, 176; as Medea, 167; mistreatment of, by men, 162–66, 168–72, 173–74, 178, 181; "rebirth" of, in Brooklyn, 4, 173; relational identity of, 162, 164–65, 166, 170, 175, 177, 181, 220n.27; suicide attempts of, 172, 184–85
—Stingo, 2, 3, 17, 74, 156, 157, 159–62, 167, 177–202, 219n.23, 220nn.43, 47, 221nn.51, 57, 58, 222n.79, 223nn.91, 92, 94, 223–24n.95, 224nn.96, 100, 102, 225n.109; as Reverend Entwistle, 182, 200; guilt of, over mother, 180; identity of, as writer, 195–96, 197; reenacting sexist behavior, 168, 176, 181; relationship of, with father, 165, 196; relationships of, with other women, 193–94, 197–98; as Sophie's confessor, 179–80; Southern heritage of, 198–200
—von Niemand, Fritz Jemand, 164, 167–68, 177, 184, 189, 220n.37
—Wanda (Muck-Horch von Kretschmann), 171, 185, 186, 189, 199; as lesbian, 166; as victim, 163, 220n.47
Sophocles, 1
Sot-Weed Factor, The, 17

Sound and the Fury, The, 44
Stalin, Josef, 10, 12
Steinem, Gloria, 157
Steiner, George, 161, 196, 219n.23
Steiner, Jean-François, 160
Steps, 140
Styron, William, 14, 15, 16, 42, 108, 132, 148, 153, 156–61, 162, 182, 201, 218n.8, 219nn.16, 20, 221nn.52, 57, 221–22n.72, 223nn.73, 75, 83, 223n.95, 224nn.96, 98, 101; autobiographical basis for fiction of, 21, 159–60, 195, 218–19nn.15, 16; mother's love of music, 222nn.73, 75; near-madness of, 156, 183, 202; suicidal thoughts of, 156, 222n.75
Sunshine (Kesey's fourth child), 64

Technological evil, 8, 66, 94, 100, 102, 120, 121, 129
Theater of the Absurd, 32
This Quiet Dust and Other Writings, 218n.2
Thurber, James, 126
Tidewater Morning: Three Tales from Youth, A, 218n.2
Tin Drum, The, 13; Oskar Matzerath in, 69
Toole, John Kennedy, 23
Trakl, Georg, 1
Treblinka, 219n.23
Truman, Harry, 214n.33
Turner, Nat, 193, 199, 220nn.43, 47, 224nn.98, 109
Twain, Mark, 84

Ulysses, 42; Leopold Bloom in, 31, 41
Updike, John, 10
Uris, Leon, 35

V., 16
Vietnam War, 11, 98, 103, 107, 115, 119, 206n.29
Vonnegut, Bernard, 102

Vonnegut, Kurt, 1, 14, 42, 90, 100–107, 110, 117, 119, 124, 133–34, 150, 153, 161, 210n.20, 213n.12, 214nn.31, 34, 215nn.47, 50; autobiographical basis for fiction of, 21, 101–06, 112–16, 119, 123, 125, 132, 213n.26; education of, 101–02; Guggenheim fellowship of, 103; main themes of novels of, 108, 213–14n.29; parents of, 103, 213n.26; sister of, 100, 213–14n.29; Trout as persona for, 127–31; warnings about technology, 8–9, 66, 100–103, 120–21; work of, at General Electric, 102, 103

Walden Two, 9
War as symbol, 4
War fiction, 22–25
Warren, Robert Penn, 195
Wasteland, 4, 55, 75, 84, 88, 114, 126
"Waste Land, The," 86, 88
Watergate scandal, 12
Weed, Bobby, 199, 200, 220n.47

Weir, Ernest T., 138, 139
Weir, Mary Hayward, 138, 139
Welcome to the Monkey House, 213n.29
Wharton, William, 1
"When Everyone Was Pregnant," 10–11
White Collar, 13
"Who Flew Over What?," 65
Wiesel, Elie, 158, 160, 218n.8
Wilson, Charles E. ("Engine Charlie"), secretary of defense, 51
Winn, Marie, 218n.50
Wittlin, Jozef, 150
Wolfe, Thomas, 194, 200, 220n.43
Wolfe, Tom, 64, 66
World War I, 8, 122
World War II, 5, 8, 11, 14, 25, 69, 100, 124, 126, 206n.29, 214n.33
Wright, Richard, 9
"Writing American Fiction," 15

Yeats, William Butler, 208n.82

Zoo, 64